AsEverWas
memoirs of a beat survivor

Hammond Guthrie

AsEverWas
memoirs of a beat survivor

Hammond Guthrie

saf publishing

First published in 2002
by SAF Publishing under the Poptomes imprint

SAF Publishing Ltd.
149 Wakeman Road,
London.
NW10 5BH
ENGLAND

email: info@safpublishing.com

www.safpublishing.com

ISBN 0 946719 54 3

Cover and book design: David @ The Unit

Printed in England by the Cromwell Press, Trowbridge, Wiltshire.

Appreciation

My heartfelt thanks to the following individuals for their friendship, therapeutic encouragement, and astute editorial counsel: my wife Margaret, Peggy Luke Sava, Tsambla, Liam O'Gallagher and Robert Rheem, Peter Stansill, (Barry) Miles, John 'Hoppy' Hopkins, Richard Aaron of AMHERE Books, Denise Enck of Empty Mirror Books, Dan O'Neill (Odd Bodkins), Bruce Mackey, Herb Gold, Lawrence Ferlinghetti, Max Crosley, and His Holiness – The Dalai Lama.

CATHARSIS

"HERE DOWN ON DARK EARTH, before we all go to Heaven."

Jack Kerouac: *Piers of the Homeless Night.*

To the many who have passed, and the few who remain,
steadfast to the end.

Some names have been changed to protect the misunderstood.

CONTENTS

7

PART FOUR – Amsterdam

PART FIVE – Tangier

PART SIX – Asilah

PART SIX – Amsterdam (Reprise)

Foreword

John "Hoppy" Hopkins

Estranged from his parents at an early age, Hammond made up for the loss by exerting his sense of adventure, coupled with an uncanny ability to socialize positively with just about everyone he met. Consequently, where others might have faltered, he moved from scene to scene – first on the West Coast, later in Europe and Morocco – almost magically protected by his innate bonhomie and easy going lifestyle, while having extraordinary and often hilarious adventures.

We first met in San Francisco in the late 1960s when the Haight-Ashbury was at the height of the sixties American youth diaspora; draft dodgers were leaving for Europe, and particularly England. Although Hammond was clever enough to dodge the draft without having to emigrate, the cost of freedom had become too expensive and he split the US with his wife Wendy, and headed east. As Hammond and Wendy passed thru London we met again, this time in the squats of Prince of Wales, a half derelict inner city zone where you all you needed to steal a house was a jemmy and a lookout.

All sorts of happenings and counter culture events, were flowing in a continuous stream. The underground press, arts labs, psychedelic night clubs and sheer exuberant street life, coupled with the international exchange of ideas and experiences, made the cities of Western Europe a cultural melting pot. For a life-artist like Hammond this was evidently more than just fun.

Adept at writing, staging spontaneous events and ingesting neuro-active substances, Hammond swam thru the culture like a salmon in familiar ocean currents. He could have become a well-known poet or a masterly oil painter, a film maker or a travel guide. But the thing about generalists is you never know where they are going to pop up next. And through the whole of *AsEverWas*, runs his laid back delivery – serious yet very funny, and with an old-world politeness reminiscent of Alistair Cooke's *Letters from America* (and unlike Mr. Cooke, Hammond doesn't suffer from the impediment of a hungry ego).

The dramatis personae of *AsEverWas* include many figures both well known and little known, too numerous to name. But to pick a few at random from a cast of hundreds, look out for poets Allen Ginsberg, author William Burroughs, singers Nico & Carmen McRae, streetwise Hube the Cube, musician Pete Townshend, Digger Emmett Grogan, and TV presenter Kenneth Allsop. Or the cameos of actor Del Close, an unreformed happenings artist (who later wrecked my own piano in a Notting Hill church hall – but that's for another time). Then there are the funny episodes. I can't ever remember laughing so much as I did at the surreal absurdity and nail-biting suspense of Hammond's Moroccan adventure.

One other thing. This is a true story, all of it. And the fact that it stops at 1976 can mean only one thing: watch out for the sequel, folks. Hammond has returned to his artistic roots and he's riding high.

John "Hoppy" Hopkins
London, 2002

Preface

When seriously acute anxiety and chronic fear of abandonment, merge with a long-term displacement from a well-received art world career in Amsterdam and painful divorce from my cherished first wife, an ill-fated second marriage to someone I didn't love, and a somewhat regrettable series of liaisons – carried out with the stunningly beautiful spouse to the then sitting president of a certain big city's Ironworkers Union – and who would most probably like to have my knees nailed to a concrete floor – when these life complications become terminally locked within a deeply seeded bed of bad-son-syndrome – inconveniently distempered by swarms of hallucinatory castigations regarding the ill-fated decisions of my quasi-illustrious past, and most importantly, my utter lack of vision for a future self – when these and the unexaggerated more reach beyond the Personus Mentis, and begin boring a parasitic hole into one's Golgi Complex – it's time to find an appropriate pain killer.

At the time, I was a licensed, though thankfully unemployed, emergency room triage nurse with a significant pharmacopoeia at hand, so, I prescribed for myself: thirty 100mg. methadone and twenty quarter-grain Phenobarbital tablets, to be mixed with an early loading dose of liquid Dramamine to keep the pre-dissolved powders of doom in my stomach. Following this, and after leaving my 1989 bullet-grey Camry station wagon in the far-away lot of an all night market – I checked into a desperate motel room near the beach in Oxnard, California under an assumed name (one I fully expected would soon be exchanged for "John Doe") – and, just to be on the safer side of my rapidly disintegrating horizon, I had prepared a syringe full of Seconal sleep juice,

11

which I planned to inject into my anticubital space immediately after drinking the melange of previously listed end-of-the-line narcosia.

As odd as this seems in retrospect (though I have learned that it isn't uncommon), I felt perfectly relieved and at peace with myself for the first time in so many, years – after all, I was finally going to take care of the problem – right? Well, that all depends on your point of view – but in next-to-the-last-moments such as this one, it is said that one's life passes before one's eyes, and apparently I was not to become the exception to the overly referred to adage.

PART ONE – CALIFORNIA

Growing Up

Post World War II life in Dinuba, California, the San Joaquin Valley's self-proclaimed "Raisin Capitol of the World," was not going well for my parents, C. Robert and Sonya. Between one of my father's debilitating migraine headaches, and mother's Zen and other non-Dinubian readings at the public library, they agreed to a divorce due to the "cruel and unusual punishment" that was happening around the four-year-old me.

As soon as the ink on their paperwork was dry, my father, unable to weather his divorced status in our rural hometown, moved to Los Angeles to study criminology. My mother, who was in no way prepared for maternal reality or the rural multi-generational lifestyle, surrendered to my father's post-nuptial demand and agreed to never see me again. While my parents quietly disappeared into their respective ionospheres, I settled into the large farm house built by my great-grandfather, Epamanonadous Hawkins, a tent revivalist, and his wife Mary Coombs, a full blooded Cherokee Indian. There I would be raised, like my father and his sister, "Catherine with a C," by my paternal grandparents, Ruby and Charlie. Following a month or two of motherless country life I began to whine and pout, missing the comfort and security of her maternal presence. Though my grandfather was usually silent about the issue, my grandmother was quite vocal when it came to putting my mother down, and finally, perhaps out of frustration, told me that she was dead. I was under the distinct impression that my mother would eventually return, and this abandoned son-shattering news sent me into panic, causing me to begin potentially chronic stuttering. Horrified by the results of her untruthful and plainly cruel outburst, my Grandmother bustled me off to Vic the family doctor and notified my father.

All I c-ccould s-sstutter w-wwas "d-ddead?"

My mother suddenly resurfaced to prove that she wasn't in fact dead, but did inform me that she would be "going away," and would "not be coming back." I remember the red nightgown she wore and cherished the set of silver spurs she brought to me from Mexico. The visit was brief, and after her departure I stopped the stuttering, but not the apprehension and anger I immediately began to repress. Dad remained in Los Angeles studying criminal behavior, Mom dove back into her own private ionosphere, and I nervously continued with parentless child life – an alienating and relatively self-contained experience rather like learning to play catch with yourself.

Over the next ten years of frequently confusing rural life, I would on rare occasion spend part of the summer with my tall and mysterious horn-rimmed father. He took me on unexpectedly exciting and rather weird vacations such as the drive we took across America visiting inner city police departments and the FBI Headquarters in Washington DC. He took me along when he addressed the British Parliament, and again when he spoke to the delegates of the United Nations in the Netherlands, but the oddest of these sporadic vacations had to be the six weeks I spent living on the grounds of San Quentin Prison when my upwardly mobile father was a member the parole board. He watched Caryl Chessman, the Mulholland Drive "Red Light Bandit" suffocate on cyanide fumes in the prison's well-painted gas chamber. I rarely saw my father while I was there, and spent the better part of the days wandering the rocky shore surrounding the intimidating block of concrete, watching the sea gulls poop, while hard-looking inmates made my bed and prepared my institutional meals. Otherwise, my secretive and stoic father would send me typed postcards and make the occasional hometown visit, ostensibly to catch up on my growth process, but mostly we hung out with his friend Bud, who owned and operated the local crop-dusting outfit in nearby Orosi, a country-bumpkin town about as thrilling as your fingernail.

Life on a horse ranch as an only child can be more adventurous and is certainly less competitive than living in town with on-site parents and possible siblings. I wanted to believe, living as I did in our multi-generational home, that my life would have a degree of consistency. This comforting illusion stayed with me until I was old enough to realize that the people who cared for me were distorting the truth about my life and the known whereabouts of my not-to-be-mentioned mother, whom I grew to feel must be the worst woman in the world, though a woman I unconditionally loved nonetheless. This storm of abandonment and ill-defined loss only caused me to become more withdrawn than ever. My grandmother even went to the extreme of burning all the family photographs that contained my mother – leaving me to visit and quietly weep with my only salvaged photograph of her, crouched behind the water heater, where I covertly hid the framed studio portrait.

Before I endured the two sets of braces, supplementary headbands, early peer intimidation and numerous family disorders, I was a quietly insecure, gawky-looking, buck-toothed country boy, who rode horses and pigs, grew up quickly, tried to keep his inner wits about him, and according to some became a rather handsome young man. By the time I turned fourteen I was mannered, well traveled, six feet tall, strong, though non-athletic, and well on my way to becoming a terminally secretive, overly sensitive and parent-less teenager about to enter high school. Then, my off-site father, who had gone on to become a well known criminologist at the University of Southern California and who occasionally served as an unidentified advisor to sitting Presidents, the FBI and to the anonymous Directors of Central Intelligence, decided to remarry.

My step-mother, Arlene was and still is an intelligent, blonde, and quite attractive MD, several years younger than my father. When I first met her she lived in a fantastic beach house in Manhattan Beach, California, drove a white Corvette convertible, and laughed infectiously. After the wedding, however, (a secluded ritual to which I was not invited,) her beach-front home became an anonymous stucco duplex near the Pasadena freeway and the Corvette was inexplicably transformed into a duplicate of my father's robin's egg blue Volkswagen Beetle. Unfortunately, Arlene's initially bright and interesting personality began to take on my father's noncommittal and perfectly distant persona. His natural inclination toward secrecy (he was an Office of Strategic Services alumnus), coupled with his years of studying crime while working with the nation's police force, had turned my father into an eternally suspicious, six foot four, unforthcoming, horn-rimmed version of TV's emotionless Perry Mason. He was a complete mystery to me and an intellectual void, yet he could speak volumes with his nearly silent vocabulary.

I had been geographically and psychologically estranged from him for the better part of eleven years, and though my grandparents loved me dearly and treated me like a prince, my only real desire in all that time was to have a set of on-site parents and a dog – much like Andy Hardy or The Beaver. So it was with the uncertain tears that only previously parentless children can shed that I left my grandparents on the ranch in Dinuba, to be reunited in South Pasadena with my father, stepmother Arlene and the general concept of parents. Something I knew little about. As we headed home from the Los Angeles airport in one of the blue bugs, I momentarily backseat-basked in my imagined portents for a normal life. My naive reverie came to an abrupt halt as I was just four steps inside the front door of our gray stucco duplex. Before I had even seen the bath tub, the kitchen, or my own room, Dad unrolled a set of blueprints for the enormous sailboat they planned to build and live aboard the following year. My fourteen-year-old heart sank as my father with uncharacteristic enthusiasm pointed out a tiny slice of a cabin, situated next to the chain locker in the boat's fore peak. My adolescent brain simply wouldn't or couldn't translate "room of my own" into "cabin by the chain locker of my own," and my prayers for the utopian life began to feel a little misplaced. I was informed shortly thereafter that we weren't allowed to have pets of any species in our duplex-complex. It was a disappointing start to be sure, and I felt like heading back to the ranch and the security of my grandparent's arms, but I managed to settle in well enough, and enrolled as the new guy in school.

South Pasadena was then a small town on its own, filled with white, upper-middle-class families who seemed to take great pride in their segregation, divided as they were both physically and racially from the mix in Pasadena proper (actually a separate city) by the old ivy-clad Pasadena freeway – one of LA's prettiest thoroughfares. The well-manicured town was touched on its southern border by the ultra-conservative guardians of an older, inherited wealth, living in small mansions in the elite enclave of San Marino – home to the Huntington Hartford Library which houses Gainsborough's portraits of "Blue Boy" and "Pinky."

These were the early days of what would become Surfin' USA, and like any kid fresh off the ranch I wanted to blend in with my new surroundings. At school, I made friends with the fledgling surf set, and saved my weekly allowance to buy a seven foot Wardy brand surf board (they had such a cool logo!) with an aqua blue, single-skeg fin. Unfortunately, my instrument of sand and surf went largely unused because my father didn't approve of my new friends and proclaimed that I was "consorting with a bad element." I just wanted to fit in, make new friends, learn to surf, and be exactly like all the other seemingly everyday teenagers. Things at home began to truly go awry one weekend when my on-site parents were away at the boat building yard in Huntington Beach, and I was (by choice) home alone.

A toddler I recognized from the neighborhood was outside on our lawn crying because she had wet herself, and as I helped her out of her soggy yellow diapers, the old hag who lived in the gray duplex next door yelled at me from her kitchen window with the "Nixon for Governor" sticker plastered on it.

"Stop messing with that little girl right now!"

Her unwelcome screech frightened the little girl, who ran away in tears. Naive to such recriminations, I didn't know what the old woman was talking about. I threw the diaper away and forgot about the incident, but later that night, after Dad and Arlene had returned home, the little girl's parents showed up on our doorstep with the old hag and a child protective services detective. They and my parents were interrogative and stone silent as I uneasily explained the situation, and from their facial expressions, I could sense there was doubt in the house as to the credibility of my statement. To mollify the little girl's parents and the armed detective, my father said he would send me to see a child psychiatrist. It hurt my feelings deeply that my parents seemed to be somewhere in the middle, rather than being protectively on my side of the issue, but as directed I went to see the bespectacled doctor in his dark leather room.

For his benefit, I again repeated what had happened and expressed my confusion over the matter. After reassuring me that I was fine, the doctor asked me what I thought of my father. I told him the truth, which in retrospect was probably a big mistake. Though I was found to be innocent of toddler molestation, it was deemed by my inscrutable father, after speaking privately with the psychiatrist, that I needed more adult supervision, and from then on my weekends were spent "not working on the boat" in Huntington Beach. The boat designer and his yard were located near the shore, behind a smoke spewing oil refinery. And though the piles of rusting sheet metal didn't resemble much in the beginning, the steel would form the sleek hull to the sister ship of "The Yankee," a well known ketch, famed for sailing around the world in the 1950s with a documentary film crew following in its wake.

I just wanted to be land-locked alone at home or on the waves, learning how to surf, but I was forced to stay at the boat yard, and over time I grew to really detest that boat. In so many ways it came to represent the loss of everything I had hoped for while growing up on the ranch in Dinuba, and I openly displayed my complete lack of interest in their project. I was strictly along for the ride, stubbornly refused to help, and spent the boring hours drawing crazy patterns in the scrap-infested sand dunes with a stick and watched the wretched thing grow. A few weekends of this routine and my parents couldn't stand the situation any longer, so they offered to send me to summer camp in Carlsbad, California. The colorful brochure for the place indicated white cottage accommodations and a private beach where I could finally learn to surf, but to be honest, any place that separated me from my parents and their quasi-nautical life sounded great to me, so I jumped ship at the offer.

Growing Out

As it turned out, Camp Pacific was the 'nom du summer' for the Army Navy Academy Military School. As we pulled to the curb in front of the white-washed campus my father suggested I "really check the place out," adding that I "might want to go to school there in the Fall." So it was with a refreshing, yet at the same time foreboding perspective that I waved good-bye, as I stood under the central archway where the academy motto, "Pro Deo Et Pro Patria" (For God and For Country) was boldly written. Feeling a little trepidacious, I walked up the palm-lined pathway leading to the administration building with a youthful angst, thinking that nothing would ever be the same.

Camp Pacific indeed had a pristine beach front supported by terrific waves, a recreation hall, a gymnasium and a secluded lagoon for canoe paddling. The older, more established campers lived in the advertised cottages, but the rest of us lived in pairs in one of the many quadrangled dorms surrounding the campus. Some of the campers, my room-mate Steve included, were in truth military school cadets who lived on campus and away from their families for most of the year. To a man they didn't recommend the school as a place for higher learning and Steve suggested that I run away from home when I told him of my father's parting words.

Nonetheless, six weeks later when my parents inquired, "Well, what did you think of the academy?"

I told them I thought it seemed like a great place to go to school – "Where do I sign up?"

My surprising attitude might seem strange, but the daunting prospect of spending my high school years away from my on-site family, ensnared in a military school, seemed to me the best available option. Running away was out of the question – Dad wouldn't let me return to the ranch in Dinuba – and I wasn't about to live on their claustrophobic boat. So, by default, I packed my duffel bag and opted for the cadet corps.

My first term at the academy was spent in abject terror of the hazing-crazed section commanders and unrepentant brigades of sadistic upper-classmen. Ornamental sword-strapping "officers of the day" and their "sergeants of the guard" were especially vicious, using their brass-riveted, web pistol belts to frequently issue rations of completely unmerited discipline. Everything and anything was preceded by a sharp salute followed by a resounding "sir!" Smoking was allowed only if you had an authorized permit to do so, and as I had neglected to tell my parents about my freshly acquired addiction, I was at the mercy of my section commander, Senior Cadet Izbecki, who forced me to supply him with a weekly carton of flip-top boxes in order to freely indulge myself. All under-class men were fair game for senior noncoms at any hour of the day or night for the unexpected snap-to. These were intimidating sessions involving endless domestic drills where the officers would drop a twenty-five cent piece on your bed and if the coin didn't bounce high enough, they would flip the mattress. Serial terrorists all, they would repeat the drill until our square cornered linens produced the desired effect.

The academy dress code was particularly itchy, and with the exception of gray twills worn for rifle cleaning and drill practice, our daily everything: pants, long sleeved shirt, and tie, was made of thick gun-blue wool. We wore grommet-lined, wool caps with patent leather-brims, our shoes were spit-shined to a near mirror finish, and the heavy brass buckle on our belts had to be laboriously shined with evil smelling polish. For weekends and informal occasions we had our semi-dress blues: wool pants, starched long-sleeved white shirts and a wool tie worn under a heavy wool blouse with brass insignia buttons. For parades and formal events we wore our full dress uniforms: corset tight wool and brass-buttoned waistcoats with tails, two bands of heavily starched webbing strapped the chest and held in place by a breastplate. This uncomfortable ensemble was completed by a pair of board-starched white pants, cotton gloves, and a chin-strangling shako top hat with a bottle-brush pompom. On parade Sundays, and in appearance only, we represented the possibly elite corps of the military future, but the US Marines at nearby Camp Pendelton sarcastically referred to us as "The Bell Hops."

During the off hours (about three hours a day) we were allowed to wear bathing trunks or boxer shorts with a T-shirt. No other civilian clothing was allowed on campus, though we all had our hidden stashes. We purchased our uniforms and other mandatory cadet supplies at the N&C Company run by Nate and Carl, a pair of comical and strangely foreign dirty old men. They were the school's only non-military personnel and the back room of their store often provided an out-of-quarters smoke house and safe-haven for favored cadets. Over time, I became quite friendly with Nate and Carl and would eventually become a member of their much coveted G Club, but I was never, much to my delight, looked upon by anyone with authority as being "a favored cadet." The school year passed and I was relatively unscathed by the experience, but in lieu of a second trip to Camp Pacific, I opted to spend the summer months on the ranch in Dinuba.

My friend Dennis and some other hometown buddies of mine put together a band called the Delmonics or something equally Peppermint Lounge-sounding, and secured a summer job playing rock'n'roll for the sons and daughters of Bass Lake vacationers. Bass Lake is a summer/winter resort nestled into the high peaks of the Sierra Nevada mountain range near Yosemite National Park, then comprised of a family market, postal annex, gas pump and coffee shop. Nearer to the water's edge, there was a rustic lodge where Dennis and the Delmonics played Thursday through Sunday, for a pittance wage and their cabin accommodations. I was at the end of my summer leave away from the academy and decided to hang out with my friends for a last-minute week of freedom, and settled in with my sleeping bag, anticipating rock'n'roll, underage beer drinking and vacationing daughter thrills.

A Business Card from the Edge

I woke up one morning just before Labor Day weekend to what sounded like an endangered airplane strafing the cabin. I stumbled out to the porch to see what was making the infernal racket but there were no aircraft in sight. Down in the village however, hundreds of leather-clad outlaw bikers were growling into Bass Lake on vicious looking motorcycles. The rest of the Delmonics were finally roused from their stupors by the beastly roar. "What's going on out there?" they demanded. "Mayhem and perhaps the slaughtering of innocents," I shouted back. Like a sluggish school of lemmings they came to the porch in awe of the warrior-like procession through town, and heading, we all jested, "for their lake-side camp ground somewhere near an inlet to the river Styx."

When the army of bikers finished purchasing all the alcohol in the general store, leaving the village peacefully unoccupied, I walked down to the cafe for my cup of morning coffee while the rest of the Delmonics fought over being first in the cabin's cold spring shower. As I neared the small cafe, I noticed the three Harley-Davidson motorcycles parked outside. They were the most fantastic machines I had ever seen, but knowing better than to linger, I entered the cafe, where a lone waitress stood behind the empty counter with a concerned look on her face. As I sat down to order she said the cafe was going to close soon and that perhaps I should come back later in the day. I said that was ridiculous, it was just 9:30 a.m. All I wanted was a cup of fresh coffee and I'd be out of there. She started to protest, when a smooth voice, with what I thought was a Latin accent said, "Why don't you just give the kid what he wants and put it on our tab."

The waitress retreated into the kitchen and I turned around to thank my new friend. Staring in my direction were three of the most ominous-looking human beings I had ever laid eyes on. My ruggedly-handsome, neatly trimmed and leather-vested, though questionably Latin benefactor motioned me over to their table, and one of the other bikers, who wore a pair of impenetrable sunglasses slid over, and gestured for me to sit down with them.

I really didn't know much if anything truthful about the Hell's Angels, but I knew enough to be very polite, and thanked them for intervening on my behalf, adding that I hoped I hadn't interrupted anything. They assured me that all was well and asked if I was enjoying the Lake. I told them I was having a fine time with my friends the Delmonics, and innocently invited them to stop by the Lodge later that night for a little Delphonia. They thanked me for the open invitation, but declined, saying they were going to be pretty busy with their own little party. The third biker, a tough-looking, scar-pocked man with longish hair and extremely piercing eyes, asked me if I "drank beer or smoked dope." I told him I certainly drank beer and had "tripped out on LSD once," but hadn't smoked any dope, which was the truth. (Never tell an Angel anything but the truth.) My outlaw companions cracked up at this as the waitress brought my coffee to our table. "Cream and sugar?" she asked.

Not wanting to appear wimpy in any way, I declined my usual additives and tried to down the mountain sludge without seeming to be in a hurry (another good rule of thumb around Angels). It didn't take much reflection on my part to see that these seemingly light-hearted bikers were three very serious and most probably dangerous characters. We bantered back and forth as I drained my cup, and the waitress didn't ask me if I wanted a refill. I thanked them again for the coffee, saying I should get back and see what Dennis and the Delmonics were doing, and as I got up to leave, my benefactor pulled a small card from his vest pocket and handed it to me.

"Here, take this," he said, "it might come in handy some day."

I accepted his gift without looking at it and wished them all well.

When I got back to the cabin, I refrained from telling my friends that I had just invited three warriors from Hades to the dance, and in private I fished out the card, reading it for the first time. Neatly emblazoned at the top was the foreboding image of the motorcycle club's winged skull logo and the words: *You have just been assisted by a senior member of the Hell's Angels Motorcycle Club*, neatly printed underneath. In the bottom right corner of the card was the handwritten name of my coffee-clatch benefactor, Zorro.

A few years later I stumbled across a newspaper article about the Oakland Chapter of the Hell's Angels, with a photograph of five or six of the modern day gladiators, and three of them looked very familiar to my Delmonic memory bank. Two were identified in the caption and described briefly as, "Zorro, Sergeant at Arms, and Sonny Barger, President of the Oakland Hells

Angels." (He was the one who asked me if I smoked dope back at the cafe.) The other biker, "Terry the Tramp," who still had on his impenetrable sunglasses, was, according to the caption, "from another Bay Area Chapter." I felt truly honored and saved Zorro's business card from the edge, until finally using it one rainy methamphetamine-soaked night outside the sand-blown city of Barstow, California.

A desperately poor excuse for a desert out-post, Barstow is just six-tenths of a mile beyond the middle of nowhere and about a hundred and sixty miles from where I wanted to be – it's where tumbleweeds go to die. I was also flat broke, having left the change from my only twenty on the counter at a grimy service station somewhere out in the Mojave desert – I was having some personal problems.

Nearly defeated by my circumstance, and as I was attempting to hitch-hike in the general direction of home, an enormous, and I mean E-Norm-Us biker wearing Angel colors with a Nomads bottom rocker roared up to the fading store front across the road. My speed-drenched brain suddenly remembered Zorro's wallet-worn card, and looking much like a decommissioned extra from a Desert Zombie flick, I stumbled up beside the hairy behemoth, presented him with Zorro's card, and haltingly uttered with all due respect, "I think I could use a little more assistance please." The wildly intimidating biker took one quick look at the card and stuffed it into his sizeable vest pocket. He sized me up for a just a second, smiled as only an Angel from Hell can, and said, "Hop on little buddy and I'll take you anywhere in the country you want to go."

It was perfectly obvious that I was coming down without a parachute, so the benevolent biker laid a hit of Angel crank on me, and with record-breaking speed I was standing on my doorstep in Costa Mesa.

Never Got To Visit Venus

Following my revelry at Bass Lake, I returned to the academy for my second and less terrifying year as a cadet, while my parents' boat, freshly painted black and newly christened the EPOCA, was in the water and two-thirds of the way towards completion when they moved aboard. The slip for our aquatic mobile home was on Terminal Island, a greasy little spit of land in-between the desolate oil-slick city of Wilmington and skid row San Pedro. It was also the setting for the Terminal Island Federal Prison, the future home of one "No-Name Maddox", aka Charles Manson.

The EPOCA was moored near one of Bethlehem Steel's massive storage depots, and just next to an odoriferous vegetable oil factory. I couldn't wait to get home on leave and sleep next to the chain locker! Actually, I tried to avoid going back to the boat altogether by staying at the academy or visiting the land-locked homes of my fellow cadets on the infrequent leave. But every few months we were actually required to go home for three days, and I developed a covert routine for these decidedly non-festive occasions. Like many cadets, I kept a set of street clothes hidden in my room at school and when I would arrive at the Long Beach bus station I would change into my civvies in the bathroom. I would have already informed my father that I was arriving on another bus much later in the day, and after folding my uniform into a station locker I would spend time at The Pike.

An ages-old amusement park, The Pike was located on the beach next to a seedy area known locally as The Jungle, which consisted of countless lost souls, crumbling tenement buildings and alcoholic dives. The Pike however, had everything an adventurous cadet could want. There was an amazing wooden double roller coaster called The Zipper that towered above the more cheesy carnival rides, Freak Shows, Age Guessing Booths, and Penny Arcades that dotted the park. Its environs teemed with tattoo parlors, drunken sailors, Military Police, prostitutes, transvestites and groups of cigar-smoking hucksters shouting their come-a-longs amid a dizzying array of greasy cafes, games of chance and Palm Readers. Among the many oddities worthy of Ripley's *Believe It Or Not*, was a life-sized mummy wrapped in mock Egyptian tape that hung above a passageway near one of The Pike's exits. It hung there until the failing amusement park was demolished in the late sixties, and when it was taken down, "The Mummy" turned out to be the all-too-real corpse of an American Indian reported missing in action fourteen years earlier.

After amusing myself at the amusement park, I would go back to the Greyhound station, and change into my uniform before my father would arrive to fetch me, unaware of my pre-visit doings. The rest of the weekend would be spent with him and step-mother Arlene, not-working on the EPOCA, listening to the harbor waves slap against the steel hull, and sneaking in and out of the stinking vegetable oil factory, until Sunday, when I would be dropped off at the bus station for the trip back to Carlsbad. I would of course repeat my quick-change and run around The Pike again before catching the late evening bus back to the academy.

One morning, as the Commandant's Victrola spewed Reveille, I got out of bed and seriously dislocated my right knee-cap. This spontaneous injury put me on crutches for six weeks of physical therapy with an official excuse from any number of mandatory activities. I had to spend the absentee time in my room, supposedly studying, and while the rest of the corps marched around

23

in circles over on the parade grounds, I got to know Morey, the assistant groundskeeper. Nobody talked to Morey. In fact, nobody even talked *about* Morey. He was a harmless but very suspicious-looking scarecrow of man in his mid-fifties with a long pointed nose. Morey uniformly wore a sweat-stained fedora, a rumpled long-sleeved white dress shirt buttoned up to the Adam's apple, an old pair of khaki pants held in place by a purple belt, and a pair of constantly purple socks. To further his colorful mystique, he drove a purple 1962 Studebaker to work everyday. Morey kept mostly to himself, but during my convalescence he would stop by my room to chat and try out his "psychic healing business" on my injured patella.

I liked Morey, and as I got to know him better, he confided to me that he lived in a purple house behind the Bank of America building in nearby Oceanside where he was a well-tenured member of a religious group he called "The I-AM," who believed in "reincarnation, psychic healing and astral travel to Venus." Morey believed himself to be "the return-bodiment of George Washington." He told me that in his "present bodiment" he "traveled to Venus all the time," and in between hand passes over my dysfunctional knee-cap, Morey would describe Venus to me. He said, "Everything on Venus exists in the ultraviolet spectrum," and that the Venusians traveled about "on beams of ultraviolet light instead of using roads or sidewalks." He went on to say that "language doesn't exist on Venus," and when I asked him to explain this, he said, "Venusians just think to each other." Morey said that he and his I-AM cohorts were especially good at psychic healing because of their "frequent trips through the vaporous clouds of ultra-violet gas surrounding Venus." I asked Morey if I could go to Venus with him. He said that I could, but that first I had to get permission from my own "God Presence." I found his prerequisite particularly difficult because at the time I felt I was the unbaptized son of the worst woman in the world and a spiritually absent father. I didn't have a "God Presence!" and as a result, I regrettably didn't get to go to Venus. My therapeutic conversations with Morey did however help my knee and to spark what has become a life long interest in religious and philosophic exploration. Up to that point in my life the only religion I had encountered was in Dinuba when I was five years old.

My Grandmother and her bevy of sisters were all members of the flock in the local Church of Christ, and they started taking me along to the services on Sunday. The church had full immersion baptisms administered by the church minister Jondee Banks, and behind the altar was Jondee's Jerusalem Pool, where the dunkees wore an extra large white dress shirt and Jondee donned black-rubber bib and hip boots to keep dry during the sacred near-drownings.

One Sunday a silver-plated serving tray of broken saltine crackers and little paper cups of grape juice was passed to me. As I perused the potential snacks my grandmother whispered in my ear that this was "the blood and the bones of our Christ savior," adding that as soon as I was "baptized" in Jondee's Jerusalem Pool, I would be able "to eat and drink his host," whatever that was. I loudly protested that I wasn't about to eat bones or drink blood, even if it did look like crackers and smelled like Welch's grape juice – I wasn't having any of it! My Grandmother tried to calm me down by taking me outside to explain. It was "all make believe," she said, "that's not really blood and bones." Why I would want to pretend to eat bones and drink blood, especially in church didn't make any sense to me and I started to cry, because I was convinced that my life was about to be forever altered in Reverend Jondee's Jerusalem Pool.

As a result of my innocent protests, I didn't have to go into a church again until it became mandatory for me to attend "the service of my choice" at the academy. I joined forces with the Episcopalians because their service was within easy walking distance from the academy, and I didn't have to march in formation across town like the Protestants and Catholics did. Following my faith-healing sessions and listening to Morey talk about his I-AM crowd, I started watching the Neo-Catholic rituals with an expanding curiosity.

Single sex boarding schools have been the subject or setting for numerous films, such as Harold Becker's *Taps* and Lindsay Anderson's *If*, where the writers try to satirically express the frustrations and rebellious angst felt by teenage conscripts everywhere. Some of these portrayals give a pretty accurate picture of the pranksterite mentality of America's juvenile soldiers, such as taking over the armory, putting dozens of live grunion into a heavily chlorinated swimming pool, or burning down the academy. But these fanciful tales usually fail at their conclusion, when the exhausted and seemingly grateful cadets return happily into the loving arms of their parents. Things were a little different at the Army Navy Academy.

I went to school with the potentially rich and semi-famous sons of some of America's elite. Among the core was the son of TV's Edgar 'Judge Roy Bean' Buchanan; Tony Miller, scion to the bawdy scribe Henry Miller; and Pete Levy, child to one of the famous Andrews Sisters, who sang at one Academy function on the same bill with Les Brown and his Band of Renown. Pete graduated the year before me, along with actor Leif Erickson's son. For the most part we were spoiled, semi-abandoned, non-conformist misfits who were rather obnoxious to our teachers and openly hostile toward the academy and the military in general, but none of us were prepared for the drastic actions of our classmates Lawless and Clarke. They didn't appear to socialize with one another during the school year, but during a vacation the two seemingly dissimilar cadets (Lawless was a complete idiot and Clarke was a second lieutenant), drove to Corpus Christi, Texas in a stolen Ford Thunderbird. Here one of the two misfit cadets murdered three innocent fishermen with a scope enhanced deer rifle. The disenchanted duo reportedly planned to steal the fishermen's boat and head for Venezuela, where they hoped to instigate revolutionary frenzy using the large cache of weapons they had stolen from Mr. Clarke's private collection. They were eventually sentenced to lengthy prison terms.

On the whole, we were a creative and diverse crew of near-genius IQ level malcontents, class-agitators, unqualified nerds, and in many cases, the less than wanted first children of the "We made it back from World War II" generation. Though our fathers were unquestionable patriots, many of us didn't appreciate the glories of War and abhorred field-stripping, cleaning and reassembling our standard US caliber-thirty gas-operated M-1 semi-automatic rifles. We detested the mandatory marching around the campus, and did everything we could to get out of drill practice. I eventually joined the color guard, carried the State flag, and avoided the laborious practice altogether.

Some of us didn't take well to staying in our rooms at night and on occasion we (I) would roll over the walls and take the bus into near-by Oceanside to see skin-flicks and search for cadet-friendlly girls. We (I) put the "five-gallon buckets of live grunion into the heavily chlorinated swimming pool." (You can easily imagine the ensuing grunion cemetery.) We (I) couldn't stand the "S.O.S." (Shit On A Shingle) meals and would heap three or four servings of the shredded meat and glue cuisine onto a single plate before tossing the gloppy mess up in the air, where it would stick to the ceiling for days.

We were extremely horny teenagers, and repeatedly jacked ourselves (and each other) off in the concrete shower stalls of our homoerotic captivity. The exploration of physio-psychic danger, if not outright mental-escape was paramount to many of us, and for some, drinking bottles of cough syrup or sniffing model airplane glue from brown paper sacks took the edge off of things. Others of us found the portals of discovery associated with altered brain-blood chemistry quite by accident – such as the time I went home on weekend pass with my roommate Chip.

The Acid Test

Chip lived in the town of Huntington Beach, and his parents had thoughtfully flown off to Palm Springs for the weekend, leaving Chip and me with their wheels – a pearl white 1964 Chevrolet Impala two-door with red leather interior and wire-rimmed white-wall tires – talk about styling! Cruising Hollywood Boulevard in the sixties was every out-of-town teenagers' dream, and we were no exception. Hair clipped for active duty, and dressed for non-military school action in our stay-pressed slacks, button-down collars and Brogue shoes hardly worn from sitting in our closets at home, Chip and I thought we were ready for just about everything. What little we knew as we approached Sunset Boulevard and pulled along side a miasma of color that quickly transformed itself into a unusual looking school bus with a Plexiglas bubble on its roof. The destination plaque on the front of the bus read: "FURTHUR."

Traffic began to move at a snail's pace when Chip asked me if I had ever heard of writer Ken Kesey. I responded sharply with, "Big Nurse is probably watching us!" "Well," Chip proclaimed, "I think that bizarre bus we just passed is his." Chip then asked if I had ever heard of LSD. I thought it must be the acronym for Kesey's Alma Mater! Chip cracked up as he futilely tried to explain the chemical's unusual properties, and enthusiastically turned the Impala into a side street to park. Back on Sunset we found the colorful bus and a young man dressed in an orange day-glow jumpsuit dancing in the warm Santa Ana wind, arms akimbo and moving like an engrossed Dervish in slow motion. As we approached the oblivious character, Chip pointed to a scroll of butcher's paper over the front door of a building that read: "Can You Pass The Acid Test?" Chip asked the jumpsuit guy if there was any LSD inside. "Inside what?" he responded.

Beyond the door separating us from the outside world was a long white corridor, at the end of which was a desk, where an attractive young woman asked us if we wanted to "take the Acid Test?" We each gave her three dollars admission and received our membership cards (yes, I still have mine) for an Incorporated entity called "Intrepid Trips." She pointed to a door on her left and said, "It's in there." Behind the door was a large room augmented by a pounding version of Wilson Pickett's r&b hit, "In the Midnight Hour." As we walked on down the hall we found that we were soon standing in the middle of a frenetic rock band! Chip and I were feeling a little out of our element – one of the guitar players looked at us like we were from another realm altogether – yet his guitar and exaggerated expression screamed at us to move within, where unfamiliar colors and indeterminate sounds came at us from everywhere and nowhere. I remember looking at my wrist watch – it was 7 p.m.

Forty or fifty brightly dressed people wandered or clawed their way around the room's liquid-like lighting, scaffolding was everywhere and an unused set of trap drums sat silently in the shadows without its skins. I walked through a blinding wall of nearly aluminum light and came to a green door marked: "Quiet, Baby Sleeping!" and on the other side several people were gleefully bending over a wash tub dipping sugar cubes and little paper cups. Beside them was a card table with a large supply of cups and cubes next a colorful little sign that read: "Take One or Too Many!" Erring on this side of safety, I went back into the arena, where Chip was nowhere to be seen. Decades later I found him curled up under a card table peering through a piece of green glass.

Intrepid Trips indeed!

When I again looked at my watch, it was 10 p.m. Chip and I had been inside for three hours and the band was still playing "In The Midnight Hour!" The strobe-lit distractions of Lady Godiva's silken hair passed in front of my face forever as I merged atop some of the scaffolding. There I found the overhead projectors, and joined the finger painters, smearing oil and colored goo onto pieces of convex glass which threw a prismatic liquid light across the room's ceilings and floors – while down scaffolding, film loops roamed ill-defined space like cinematic-flies soaring through an ageless atmosphere. The band finally stopped playing but the soundtrack continued with a reverberating voice;

"The Police Are Coming In The Door and There Is No Paranoia!"

(And then faster) -

"ThePoliceAreComingInTheDoorandThereIsNoParanoia!"

(And then much slower) -

"T.h.e..P.o.l.i.c.e..A.r.e..C.o.m.i.n.g..I.n..T.h.e..D.o.o.r..a.n.d..T.h.e.r.e..I.s.. N.o..P.a.r.a.n.o.i.a!"

I have no idea if "The Police" ever came in the door but there certainly wasn't any "Paranoia!"

There was a most frenetic man in what I imagined to be his late thirties, dressed in neon-horizontal orange and yellow stripes, with flaming red hair, a pointed red mustache and an equally stunning Vandyke beard. He was dervishing uninhibitedly away with an extremely beautiful woman, who wore an elegant floor-length mink coat with nothing but lace pantied bare skin under her expensive pelts. Oblivious to the astounding atmosphere surrounding them, they disappeared – replaced by the rapid-fire voice of a handsome man wearing the torn remains of a white T-shirt who sat on the floor rhythmically beating a bottle – taunting and challenging the air with the refrain: "Indecipherables Everywhere!" The ever-present band, loop lights, liquid flesh-cameras and poly-echoic tapes played in sync as I enthusiastically sat in with the band by air-drumming Gene Kruppa/Sandy Nelson on trap set without skins. My button-down collar long gone I played the night away and when next I looked for my watch it was 7 a.m.! People were leaving, packing Test equipment or, like Chip, staring at bare light bulbs through pieces of broken glass.

After we were finally kicked out of the Test Space, Chip and I headed for a nearby Denny's restaurant to consume expanding plates of scrambled eggs before cautiously driving into sleepy Beverly Hills. Cruising the Sunday morning streets of the rich and famous in our pearl white Impala, we shouted at the world to: "Wake up! and smell the roses."

Chip and I dutifully returned to military school with our secret intact. Then one day we picked up a copy of *Life* Magazine. The front page article, written by a journalist named Larry Schiller was about LSD, and inside the cover was a full page photo of my Lady Godiva swirling about in a sea of repeated light, along with the mink-pelted woman and her Vandyked Dervish partner. The photo's caption identified the stunningly memorable woman as Rory Flynn, daughter of the late swashbuckling actor Errol Flynn. Other captions, other photos passed as Chip and I flipped the pages in fear that our farcical cadet-mugs would be shown drooling liquid light, as both of our parents subscribed to the magazine. No photos revealed our recent whereabouts, and the article went on to describe the FURTHUR crew as Ken Kesey, (who wasn't there), Neal Cassady, hero of Jack Kerouac's novel *On The Road* (who was), assorted Merry Pranksters and a musical group (formerly known as The Warlocks) now called the Grateful Dead.

Did Chip and I pass the Acid Test? In retrospect I'm not really sure, but the Army Navy Academy was most certainly never the same.

Post Dosium

During my senior year, the bizarre extra-curricular activities of certain cadets, such as my chlorinated grunion run and the hazing of vulnerable under class men into pairs of liniment soaked underwear only increased. Another favorite prank was sending new recruits one by one down to the armory to be measured for their rifles. My next door neighbors, cadets Cockwell and Splott, were particularly surreal. For example, every year the Pentagon would send a General to the academy for a white-gloved Federal Inspection of the campus and its spotless cadet corps. Two weeks prior to the distasteful two day encounter, we had to laboriously, and on a daily basis until inspection, field strip our rooms and spend the days polishing them to a ridiculous sheen. To amuse themselves, Cockwell and Splott stuffed up the cracks to their room, and after running in any number of garden hoses, they filled their home away from home to the window sills with water. Donning swim fins, snorkels and goggles, we used their room as a swimming pool until the linoleum tiles floated to the surface. The water completely destroyed the room which became so mildewed that Cockwell and Splott had to be temporarily relocated to other quarters, and their previous abode was turned into a paint storage closet during the formal inspection.

Darryl Barnforth was another inventive cadet who had a wonderfully explosive night-time hobby. He loved to fill large, clear plastic laundry bags with natural gas taken from his room heater, and then attach a lit fuse to the rising balloon's alcohol-soaked tail. Darryl's pyrotechnics became more and more spectacular until one of his fiery play-things caused the thick, upper tier windows of the academy's gymnasium to shatter, prompting Darryl to move along to other, equally nefarious though less destructive, hobbies.

Major Brooks, the Commandant of Cadets (commonly known as "Zipper Lip" because of a hairline deformity), finally went over his edge one day, and during a general assembly the Dean of Students had to lead him off stage, muttering incoherently to himself. This was a milito-schizoid episode brought on by the outstanding all-to-true rumor that his wife was having it off with any number of cadets. In his unintelligible yet memorable wake, the Pentagon put the iron-jawed Commander Bruce in charge, and things started to go down hill fast.

Following a brawl and near fire-fight between a number of armed cadets (Chip and myself included), with an equally prepared gang of Samoans from Oceanside, Major Bruce rounded up the troublemakers among us, took away our senior privileges and moved us locks, stocks and barrels into the worst dorms on campus – the micro-cubic Anderson Hall. Bruce himself became our Section Commander and force fed us a steady diet of white glove inspections, unexpected snap-to's, and tedious military propaganda. Thinking on our feet, we drew lots based on our Anderson cubicle numbers to see which set of roommates might escape this purgatorial imposition, and Chip's and my room number was drawn. The rest of our "Way After Taps Club" buddies went to the new Commandant to plead our case. They all lied on the Academy's age old Code of Honor that Chip and I were "completely innocent bystanders" and that we should be "released forthwith," with full restoration of our senior privileges. To our surprise and great relief the 'old school' Commandant agreed, and Chip and I were quickly transplanted into a lovely cottage with a view of the Pacific Ocean, where we could again listen to our stereos and continue to cause trouble without the official scrutiny of Major Bruce.

We were a randy bunch of punsters and had plainly cruel monikers for just about everyone on staff, such as the science teacher who had a metal plate inserted under his scalp – we called him "Clank". Then there was "Snowball" the academy's white-haired and periodically confused honcho – the self-promoted Colonel (actually corporal) Atkinson. "Bozo" was the dim-witted night tactical officer, driven into early retirement by our irritating pranks like frequently removing the pins from the hinges on our doors, which without warning would fall out on to the unwitting clown during his late night rounds.

For injuries and illness we went to the infirmary to be tampered with by 60-year-old nurse "Wacky," who regardless of the severity of the cadet's condition routinely accused them of "gold-bricking" – and "Shaky," the academy doctor who waved his thermometer around in circles not unlike comic Art Carney mime-directing an orchestra. Prior to the auto accident and subsequent head injuries that rendered him less than capable with a thermometer, Shaky had been a prominent brain surgeon. "Jumpy" the History teacher came back from Korea with a severe case of shell shock, and in his honor, we would often toss our history books to the floor, sending Jumpy in search of cover under his desk.

Most of my classmates didn't like much, if anything, about the academy, the military or their parents. We believed almost nothing the government said and secretly vowed to bring it down. The gregarious and at times illegal antics of my graduating class was responsible for the enforced removal of the academy's 2"x2" advertisement in *National Geographic* Magazine, and we were proud of it. After our graduation ceremony was over the Pentagon actually sent reinforcements to the Army Navy Academy, and significant changes were made. The only good thing about the academy was that it provided me with a better than average education, while keeping me away from my parents and their dreaded boat. On graduation day, my father wanted to know my plans for the future and asked me what I thought about West Point, the Naval Academy or Officer's Candidate School. I told him that I would never serve a day in the Armed Forces, as I was decidedly against conscription and thought that the U.S. military presence in Southeast Asia was undeniably criminal. I then boldly suggested that my time spent in military school had been in many ways for his benefit, and that the rest of my life frankly belonged to me.

To say the least, he was very disappointed, and most of all with my total contempt for the Selective Service System. When he finally calmed down I told him that I planned to move to Costa Mesa in Orange County with Chip, where I would continue my education in deferment from the military. With some reservation, he offered me a two hundred and twenty-five dollar a month stipend to get me on my feet. Quite a gesture towards continuing education from someone who had just invested close to $50,000 sending me to high school. I took the money and ran.

To Tijuana and Back

Chip and I rented an inexpensive bungalow in Costa Mesa, then an anonymous lower-middle class community on the inland outskirts of coastal haven Newport Beach. Once we settled in, our first domestic problem was how to circumvent the laws surrounding the underage purchasing of alcohol. Ever the industrious ex-cadets, we decided to become United States Marines, and to achieve our illegal status as drinking age adults, we hopped into Chip's souped-up tabernacle blue VW bug with gray tinted windows and headed for the False Identification Center in Tijuana, Mexico.

Rolling purposefully under moon-lit sky, we had just passed Dana Point's infamous Dead Man's Curve when we began to feel nauseous and faint. Chip pulled over to the shoulder and we fell out of the customized bug literally gasping for breath. Thick smoke began to pour from the tinted windows and after checking the engine compartment, we discovered a disconnected hose spewing exhaust fumes directly into the cab!

Once recovered from our near carbon monoxide poisoning we carried on, and finally crossed into Mexico at the San Ysidro border. Until the mid-1970s, and following a significant change in Mexico's ruling government, Tijuana's historic Revolution Boulevard was a combination dirt and soft tar road with an overly elevated curbside, running from the blood-tinged sand of the municipal bullring in the north, to the Copacabana-like jai alai arena in the south. During daylight hours, the busy ten to fifteen block city-center portion of the boulevard was a donkey cart and taxi congested disorganization of serape and piñata filled curio shops, bug infested hotels, off-site betting parlors, pass-port photo/money exchanges, and some fairly decent restaurant bars such as The Long Bar Cantina. But once the sun went down, most of these businesses closed up for the night to accommodate the quickly drunk, internationally salacious hustling trade and red neon lights illuminated the dusty strip until dawn.

It was a thriving arena of iniquity with an ungodly number of raunchy sex bars nestled against the unpredictable cities garbage and carrion strewn side streets – infamous home and harbor to some of the sleaziest vice and official corruption this side of Manila. Just the thing for two would-be Marines, and as no potential Marines in their right minds would enlist sober, we made our way to the Hampton Hotel, where we had been told the piano bar offered cheap mixed drinks without the distraction of indigenous hustlers. We tossed back a couple of stiff ones and I went to relieve myself in the men's room (one of the cleanest in town), and as I stood at the pristine row of urinals, a Henry Miller at sixty look-alike stumbled up next to me. As we pissed in concert he reached over and gently squeezed me!

"Nice cock," he slurred. "Howse-ya like tah cum-back to my room en snuff your salami up my gasket?"

Ever the gentleman, I replied, "Not tonight, thank you," and rejoined Chip at the bar.

Once we were sufficiently juiced, we left the Hampton and set out into the muggy air to find our fresh set of papers. Within minutes we were quite literally pulled into an atrocious dive called The TNT Club by a gang of Mexican hookers, who right away began hot-handedly groping us front and back for the money we had thoughtfully stuffed into our socks. We managed to pull ourselves away and hesitantly moved into the sordid darkness of the club. In the back of the place we found a small stage in the round, or in this case, in the square, where six or seven drunken businessmen were laid out on their polyester backs. As Chip and I sat down at one of the filthy tables, a middle-aged woman got on stage, hiked her skirt up to her waist, and bare pussy-exposed, she proceeded to squat down onto the first supplicant face. The equally inebriated crowd went wild with enthusiasm. Warm Mexican mini-bottles in hand, Chip and I soaked up the progressive scene with fascination as, one after another, the men received their hairy facials. One overly enthusiastic guy paid the rather good-looking slut an extra twenty bucks to let him yank out a sizeable clump of her pubic hair with his teeth! Abstaining from the main attraction, Chip and I drank more mini-beers and paid a couple of butt-ugly whores two bucks to jack us off under the table.

Back on the street again, we were assailed by the insistent cacophony of taxi-blare and cat-calling busk from all the street vending serape salesmen, disco-sex club barkers, police sirens, fairly obvious just-about-anything dealers and Polaroid photo-op hucksters with their braying fly-encrusted donkeys, absurdly painted to resemble dwarf zebras.

"Hay Meesters, you want pussy photos?"

"Hay Meesters, you want Spanish Fly?"

"Hay Meesters, you want fuck my seester?"

We bought switchblades instead, and jumped into a taxi. After bracing our cab driver with poly-gutteral inquiries, he assured us that our "new Marine identification cards" could be purchased for "tweenty dolares each at the Chicago Club," adding that for a nominal fee he would "put the wheel into the action" – and off we went to yet another whore-filled club. Chip and I settled in at one of the tables onto some decrepit folding chairs while our taxi driver and our forty dollars conferred with a scar-faced mobster type at the bar. On the club's stage, four bare naked women leisurely strutted around squeezing their engorged Mexican nipples, their poorly shaved labial lips and splaying open their brown anal maximus. As the patently ugly sluts paraded themselves about the slightly elevated stage, they would more than occasionally pick up a long-neck mini-beer bottle from a customer's stage-apron table. The presumed whores would first take a long swig of the cheap-tasting beer and then insert the bottle stem deep into one of their dripping cavities, and with ultimate slut-gusto the unrestrained women would vigorously masturbate themselves with the bottle necks before returning the mini-beers to their proper owners. The house point of honor seemed to be for the uninhibited customer to then finish the mini-beer while the women on stage gleefully and unabashedly played with their beer-infused and thoroughly unappetizing whatever on stage while the house band, a Yardbird clone group who couldn't understand a word of what they were singing in rote English, played as back-up for the pathetic routines happening on stage.

Chip and I quickly switched to drinking cheap shots of whiskey along with our well-guarded mini-beers because aside from wanting to become fictitious Marines, we really did need to be earnestly drunk in order to put up with this type of grossly demeaning floor show. Our driver soon returned and led Chip and me through a series of back rooms to be photographed for our ID's. Once captured for inactive duty, the photographer invited us to "watch a film on the house," while he and our driver went to on the printers. Readily agreeing to the free diversion, Chip and I entered a tiny smoke-filled viewing room, where a pre-World War projector was being run by an even older projectionist. The archaic contraption's sprocket keys rattled away as two projected women endeavored, with some success, to fellate a drowsy dapple horse on a filthy bed sheet screen hung on the wall. Ten minutes into the scenario I was ready for less equine diversions, so I left Chip on the whiskey-nod and wandered down a hallway, where I was lured into a latrine-green stall containing an old army cot, by one of the most pitiful looking whores of all time.

"Pleeze Meester," she seductively coughed, "Me sucky cinco dolores okay?"

It seemed like a deal at the time so I whipped it out for the poor toothless thing to gobble. Zipping things up, she now wanted ten bucks for the blowjob instead of five.

"Hell No!" I said, and handed her four ones.

She started screaming at the top of her lungs: "Peenchie Pindehoe! – Chinga tu Madre, Cabron! – Ramon! Ramon!"

"Ramon" appeared out of nowhere and grabbed me by the throat, lifting me off the floor and up against the seedy back-room wall. He called for his two buddies, who began chattering in Mexican with the toothless whore. I heard one of them say in pigeon-English, "Teek-heme-een-the-alley!" My young non-Marine life began to flake before my eyes, when in walked the cab driver and Chip holding up our Service identity cards. Surveying the scene in front of them with open mouths agape our astonished driver screamed at Ramon to release me, which he did. The cabbie chattered back and forth with my assailants while the whore continued bellowing: "Teen Dolores! Teen Dolores!" The cab driver started laughing hysterically and said, "Fucking Puto! Look at you. Nobody's gonna geeve you teen bucks for a stinking blow job!" As a group we stared at the pathetic woman who was now on the verge of tears. Ramon, and my other would-be assailants, having somehow saved face, laughed and began slapping me on the back for being such a good sport! After declining a third round of watered down drinks, Chip and I managed to get out of the place essentially unscathed.

Thinking we were now in the relative safety of the street, we were immediately set upon by two decidedly menacing Mexican Policia. They demanded to see our papers, so Chip and I presented them with our hot off the press military laminations. Then they searched us spread-eagled against a crumbling brick wall, and confiscated our new switchblades, but because we were Marines, they said, they were going to let us go if we gave them money.

Knifeless and another forty dollars poorer, filled with mobster-whiskey infused adrenaline, Chip and I jumped into the first decrepit taxi cab that came along and told the driver to take us to the Blue Fox Club, a notorious back alley den of iniquitous perversion, where once upon a time the "donkey act" was supposed to have been the main attraction. The sub-equine frolics were on an off-night, and with a row of fresh drinks in front of us, Chip and I had to settle for a pair of obese, truly revolting hookers who looked more like Sumo wrestlers, and whose unrefined act consisted of sucking numbered billiard balls up off the stage using the well-trained muscles of their cavernous vaginas, leaving pink snail trails in place of the billiard balls. Quite an unusual sight to be sure, but drunk or not, enough was quite enough. Chip and I decided it was time to cut our losses and head back to Costa Mesa.

We stumbled outside the bar and into a group of equally drunk suit-and-tie guys from San Diego. Within seconds we were all high fiving each other in the alley when a taxi pulls up and all six of us piled in. The young suits seemed to know where we were headed, but Chip and I were clueless. The cab swerved around the back streets and finally came to halt in the recess of a pitchblack alleyway. After he got his money, the mute driver sped off into the Mexican night as quickly as he had arrived. From the poorly-lit doorway of a crumbling tenement our bleary little group was greeted by the Mexican version of boxer Sonny Liston, who politely escorted us into the building and up three flights of filthy stairs. On the landing of each latrine-green floor there was a large, quad-rangled balcony, filled with a wide variety of whores and their International blend of customers – groveling, drinking, snorking, and staring vacant-eyed and dazed over the balcony rails into the trash strewn rat-infested patio below. Everything smelled like industrial strength disinfectant. When we got to the third floor the suits seemed to vanish into the maze of pea green stalls, and then our host, 'El Liston', looked at Chip and me as if we were prey frozen in his truck headlights.

"Let's see your god damn money!" He growled

Well, by this time we didn't actually have any money, having spent nearly all our resources on false identification, switchblades, whiskey and mini-bears, police extortion, under the table hand/blow jobs and cab fares. So, like a couple of startled rabbits, we turned on our ex-cadet heels and ran down the three flights of stairs, out the front door, up the dark alleyway, down around the back street, until lo and behold, there it was – Chip's car!

The next day, safely behind the walls of our bungalow redoubt in Costa Mesa, Chip and I proudly sipped our gin and tonics, and pondered how grati-fying it was to finally be Marines.

Very Selective Services

Following my eighteenth birthday I was hereby ordered to "report forthwith" to the nearest Selective Service Board to received my military classification for conscription. I knew beforehand that being a soon-to-be ex-cadet and the only son of a former O.S.S. operative and Criminologist turned Political Scientist would not increase my chances for simple deferment. The officer in charge looked over my Academy records which indicated that I could salute, march in formation and disassemble, clean and then reassemble a "U.S. caliber 30, M-1, gas-operated, air-cooled, semi-automatic weapon, weighing nine and one half pounds with a maximum effective range of five hundred yards sir!" He sug-gested that I might want to consider Officer's Candidate School as the next step in my "military career," ending I was sure, in a leech-infested rice paddy somewhere in Southeast Asia as a second lieutenant. I left without offering him much except my name, rank and social security number.

Now that Chip and I were living in Costa Mesa and fresh bait for the draft board we enrolled in the freshly constructed Golden West University in nearby Garden Grove. I signed up for a full fifteen unit load of classes in subjects such as Political Science, Psychology, History of Western Civilization, English Literature, Biology and Theater Arts. I then informed the Board of my position as a full-time student and received my student deferment "forthwith." At school however, I completely ignored all of my classes, and when the last day for dropping classes arrived, I dropped them all but Theater Arts and enrolled in a handful of new subjects like Beginning Physics and the Principles of Logic. Two-thirds of the way through the school year, I applied for a transfer to Orange Coast College in Costa Mesa. Once this was accomplished I had to again enroll in new classes, and thus continued my deferred status as a full-time student who studiously never went to class. With lots of free time and curiosity on my hands, I began hanging out with operatives from SDS (Students for a Democratic Society) at the University of California Irvine Campus. My activist friends advised that my days of freedom were numbered and that I should cultivate a back-up plan.

Shortly thereafter I attended a workshop with activist and then husband of folk singer Joan Baez, David Harris. At the break, he and a few others (myself included) went out on the balcony overlooking the campus. David asked if anyone wanted to burn their draft card. So, I pulled mine out and perused the official fine print, which read that I was "required by law to have this notice in (my) personal possession at all times," and that I was to "surrender it upon entering active duty in the Armed Forces."

It concluded by stating that failure to do so would result in "a fine and possible imprisonment of up to five years or both." Knowing that I would never consent to conscription of any sort, I held out my card and asked for a match. I was proud that David Harris himself lit the phosphorous for my SSS card (I still am), and together we watched it turn to ashes, joyfully celebrating my commitment to resist.

While I was attending Orange Coast College I helped form an organization we called Students For Intellectual Participation (SIP). The school's tragically hip psychology teacher acted as SIP's faculty advisor, giving us official sanction on campus, and we held lots of secret meetings.

All was well and anonymous at SIP headquarters until we decided to host an unsanctioned outdoor conference on the conservative-minded campus. We made colorful fliers, littered the campus and surrounding area with wet Gestetner paper, and invited our friends from SDS to help us denounce mandatory conscription in general and America's illegal presence in Southeast Asia in particular. The school's administration responded by yanking our faculty advisor, and declared us a rogue group without campus sponsorship. We ignored the administration's proclamation and finished our "conference." Next, and covertly dressed in conservative drag, the members of SIP attended a political rally being held in a refurbished Costa Mesa blimp hanger, for then Governor of Alabama, George C. Wallace.

Governor Wallace and his immediate family (including his mother on tambourine) sang a riotous chorus of "Dixie" to a full house of Orange County right-wing conservatives and John Birch Society members. During the Governor's opening address, our anti-Wallace fan club stood up in unison on the folding chairs, issued straight arm salutes and repeatedly shouted "Sieg Heil!" One of the faithful in the neighboring white Christian majority jumped across the aisle with a de-boning knife and slashed one of our members in the upper arm, and we were immediately surrounded by off duty Orange County Sheriff's Deputies who quickly escorted us out of the blimp hanger to our cars. As the Deputies recorded our names and license plate numbers into their black leather books, we politely informed them that we were simply exercising our right to free speech. They let us go with stern warnings not to come back.

"We've got your numbers!" they ominously added.

A week later, I received notice from the school board stating that I had "completed less than five scholastic credits in over a year of study at two campus locations," and due to my conduct regarding the now forbidden SIP organization, I would not be tolerated. Therefore, I was summarily dismissed from the student body and barred from campus. The letter went on to add that the Selective Service System would be immediately notified of my new status as a non-student. Shortly thereafter I received the dreaded brown envelope with the slick green embossed paper inside, informing me that I was ordered to "report forthwith" for an appointment date at the induction center in Los Angeles for my pre-induction physical.

Mine was a war against my government's policy of mandatory conscription, and the years spent at the Army Navy Academy was all the time I was going to waste toward accepting the military's "List of General Orders." In lieu of pretending to be a Jesuit wanna-be or Amish pacifist, and with some creative SDS subterfuge, I was able to delay my physical exam for about eight months. Time enough to plan my counter attack and locate a sympathetic orthopaedist, who kindly wrote a letter to the draft board stating that I had a "chronic case of water on the knees" and that, I wasn't to "run, jump or lift anything heavy." Then I lopped off my near shoulder-length hair into a pseudo-military cut, purchased a pair of clear glass spectacles along with a few psychology books, and settled in for some serious anti-conscription benzedrine therapy.

Following a day or two of continuous Research and Development, I diagnosed myself as being a "borderline sociopath with episodic depression, suffering from severe claustrophobia, frequent migraine headaches – with a superficially repressed hostility regarding his immediate family." Books in hand, I began studying for the part symptom by symptom, scrying into the bathroom mirror, until I was a reasonable facsimile of a rather normal looking draftee with glasses – who upon further examination would prove to be quite unacceptable for military service.

The Doors of Induction

I got up on the appointed morning to an extra large breakfast, six mega-vitamins and a dozen 100 mg. benzedrine tablets. I didn't want to be late for the charter bus to the Induction Center; an ominous, six story building that looked right out of George Orwell's novel *1984*. I remember getting my shoes shined outside a little cafe next door – I wanted to look my best. At exactly 8 a.m. the steel plated Doors of Induction opened, sucking nearly three hundred of us inside like a Hoover vacuum. As a group we were herded into a large classroom with standard wooden school desks and told to take seats. Once we settled down, forms and freshly sharpened #2 pencils were handed out by an amorphic sergeant, who spent the next twenty minutes explaining how to fill the things out. Then without asking if we had any questions, he left the room.

Aside from our names, current classifications and social security numbers, the intake form consisted of questions such as:

Did I ever "wet the bed as a child?" ("Yes")

Was I "comfortable with enclosed spaces?" ("No!")

Was I a "homosexual?" (I left it blank)

Did I get "headaches or have vision trouble?" ("Yes").

"Was I now a member or had I ever been a member of the Communist Party?" ("No," but added the clarifying words: "not currently registered to vote.")

I made sure to misspell my last name at every opportunity, using the dyslexic "Guthrei." I answered simple questions and then crossed out my answer, only to write the same answer in underneath the scratched entry, and tore the corners from the page. Every action, subtle or not, was grist for a mill-run that I prayed would eventually lead me to the Army psychiatrist's office.

After the form fillings-in we were ordered upstairs single file into a dressing room with wire baskets on the walls, and given a small draw-string bag with a number corresponding to our individual wire baskets. A sergeant ordered us to strip down to our shorts, undershirts, shoes and socks, and further instructed us to put our valuables into the little bags – everything else went into the like numbered basket. So, along with my watch, wallet and comb, I tucked my considerable stash of benzedrine tablets into the bag and, as directed followed the blue line painted on the floor down a pale green corridor to the first station, where another amorphic sergeant blindly handed me my "Document File." He ordered me to carry the file in my "right hand," and to keep my draw-string bag in my "left," and to again "follow the painted blue line on to the next station," where I was to have my blood pressure checked. As soon as I turned away from his desk I switched my order of carry – valuables to the right and the document file gripped tightly in my left hand, hoping that by the end of the day it would no longer resemble a neat manila folder.

At the blood pressure station, an induction person reached out and took hold of my valuables bag by mistake. He told me I had it "all wrong," repeating the directive that I was to carry my document file in my right hand. My blood pressure must have been hard-wired to my hypothalamus due to all the speed I had been ingesting, but the medic just jotted down some numbers and passed me on to toe the painted yellow line.

Along the way I ducked into a latrine stall to gobble more pills, before moving briskly along to have my vision checked. After correcting my document grip, the one stripe orderly asked me how long I had been wearing glasses – "Five years," I lied. Then he asked me read the eye chart with one eye closed, which I did with much difficulty without my fake glasses, and then perfectly with them on. He asked if I was "myopic or hyperopic," and I answered that I really didn't know, but suggested that I could be both. The orderly flinched and after checking the lenses of my optics he said he thought that my glasses weren't prescription issue. I said I didn't know about that, but that my doctor told me to wear them all the time, so I did. The bespectacled Private First Class just filled in the blank and sent me down another pale green hallway, this time following a black line on the floor to have my hearing checked.

Admonished yet again about my order of document and bag carry, the hearing technician locked me into a gray soundproof testing booth. I immediately began screaming to be let out because I couldn't breathe. Trying to reassure me, he said that the test would only take a few minutes. I said okay, but after three failed attempts to check my hearing, the frustrated orderly agreed to leave the booth door ajar, and with that, I had won my first battle of the day by getting him to significantly alter his "Standard Operating Procedure." During the test I was ordered to hold a gray plastic gizmo with a little red button on it. When I first heard the high pitched sound I was to push the red button and then release it when I could no longer hear the tone. When I first heard the sound I left it in place until it was piercing my eardrums before pushing the red button. Then I held it down until long after the irritating sound had faded away. I kept doing this until the technician told me to leave – my hearing test was over.

Following a sort of pink line, and knowing what came next, I found the nearest bathroom to purposely hyperventilate myself before offering a blood sample. Holding my breath, I watched in pale fascination as the medic inserted the point into my bulging vein. He pulled the needle from my arm, and still holding my breath I stood up quickly, let out my breath, rolled my eyes, and instantly passed out from the sudden drop in blood pressure. When I came to, I was sprawled out on a pale green bench with a cold compress on my forehead. "Uh, what happened?" I muttered. The medic frowned and ordered me to follow the green line until I came to a white ceramic room. Once there, I was brusquely ordered by an old man in a rumpled lab coat to "turn around, bend over and spread your cheeks!" He didn't mention my documents and came at me from behind. Gazing up my sphincter, he rudely shoved his gloved fingers halfway up my rectum and rooted around a bit. Then he played with my testicles, ordered me to cough twice and without ever looking me in the eye, sent me down the pale green corridor following a poorly-painted crimson outline.

The thin red line led me to a metal trough under a pass-through window, where an anonymous arm handed me a glass beaker to urinate in. Standing next to me at the urinal was an East L.A. Mexican-American conscript with a pomped-out jelly-roll on his head. As he casually relieved himself he looked over at me with a smile and asked, "Hay essay, u wansome hepatitis?" and offered me a squirt of his blood-tinged pee! This sudden maneuver really wasn't part of my tactical plan, so I declined his generous offer, and moved on down the line – documents to the left – benzedrine, watch, wallet and comb to the right, when I came to a desk marked: "Evaluation Thus Far."

After reading my crumpled and incorrectly held documents, the career desk sergeant asked, "Just what is it about your left and right hands that you don't understand?" I responded by saying that I didn't understand his question! The Sergeant made a face like he had just tasted some canned dog food, handed me some additional documents and ordered me upstairs, with instructions to follow the orange line to a classroom where I was to take my "pre-induction personality test."

Upstairs, a dozen or so degenerate types sat picking at their desktops or just staring off into space. I took a seat by the window to await further instructions. A staff sergeant came in to distribute more #2 pencils and illustrated test booklets with enlarged print. He told us that we had one hour to finish the test of personality, and sat down at his desk to read the newspaper. I scribbled my dyslexic name and began the test, which consisted of picture situations, such as,

"Hammer, Saw, Screwdriver, Beach Ball," and I was to cross out the inappropriate item in each example. I scratched out everything except the Beach Ball. On others I scratched out the correct picture, erased the scratch and then drew a line through everything. I tore one page halfway down the middle, and skipped a frame or two. I sharpened my pencil until is was just a nub with an eraser on it and then asked the sergeant for another one, which I immediately broke and needed to re-sharpen. I finished just after the lunch buzzer, turned in my test booklet rolled up like a discarded flier and called the sergeant "Bob."

Following a brown paper lunch, I was ordered to "visit the Psychiatrist."

As I climbed the grimy, pale green staircase, I reflected on some of the more legendary actions taken by other unwilling conscripts, such as taking psychedelics cut with horse tranquilizers, refusing to wear underwear, or, ingesting laxative cubes before the exam, becoming incontinent along the way and then playing with your faeces as you begin calling everyone Bob. "Hi Bob, you want some of this?"

The upstairs desk sergeant ordered me into a small green cubicle, where behind a gray metal desk sat my psychiatrist. He was obese – wore a sweat-stained, short-sleeved Dacron shirt and smelled horrible.

I stared him directly in the eyes (something I would rarely do during the interview), and calmly said, "Hi Bob."

"That's not my name," he said, and asked me to shut the door behind me.

"I really don't like being in close places Bob," I said. "Couldn't we just leave the door open?"

After scanning my increasingly stained and rumpled document file, he ruefully agreed to leave the cubicle door open. He then ordered me to sit down and I filled in yet another form using my dyslexic alias and remained silent. (My primary mantra of the day was: Never Volunteer Unsolicited Information!). Then, my repugnant psychiatrist began his questioning.

"What's your father like?"

I told him the truth. "He's a Criminalologist."

"What was that relationship like?"

"He's a spy, we don't see much of each other." I replied.

"What does your mother do?"

"How the hell should I know! She abandoned me when I was four and left me to rot on a fuckin' horse ranch." I offered.

"How do you feel about that?"

"Good riddance!" I said

"Have you ever been to a child psychologist?"

"No, but I went to an adult psychologist when I was thirteen."

My psychiatrist flinched. "Are you homosexual?"

"I don't think so," I replied, "but I let the kid down the road suck my dick once, does that count?"

"Do you masturbate?" He responded.

"Sure, sometimes twice."

I started sniffing the putrid smelling air, rapidly bounced my left knee up and down and asked him if I could use the bathroom. I persisted, and when he finally agreed to let me relieve myself I went into the toilet, splashed water on my hair, chewed up three benzedrine tabs and pretended to masturbate into the sink, half hoping that someone would walk in on me. Thus refreshed, I felt ready to complete the interview.

"How often do you get these headaches?" he continued.

"Two or three times a month," I lied again.

"How long do they last?"

"Two or three days and I puke a lot." I answered.

"Have you ever been mean to animals?"

"Oh sure! I lived on a ranch – I know all about the fuckin' animals!"

From this point on, I began to blink more often, bounce my knee up and down – and professing to have "cotton mouth," I asked to use the bathroom again. He ignored me and went on.

"So, how do you feel about joining the Armed Services?"

"I don't care one way or another just so long as I gotta have a gun." I told the officious slob.

My psychiatrist scribbled at length on the document, handed the rumpled folder into my left and still incorrect hand, ordered me out of his cubicle, and to "follow the brown line to the duty clerk downstairs." As I exited his rancid sty I smiled at him for the first time, and said, "Thanks Bob!"

The geriatric duty clerk downstairs berated me for carrying my documents incorrectly, and after reading my orthopedist's letter, diagnosing my "chronic water on the knees," he feebly ordered me to follow the double yellow line to: "Go see the bone doc." Once there I was poked and fiddled with by an elderly osteopath. He commented on my doctor's pronouncement, and I told him that I didn't "give a fuck what the letter said" – I was perfectly willing "to jump around and lift all sorts of heavy shit," but added meekly that I had "never run too good." The doctor asked me to touch my toes and I asked "Bob" if he would open the door because I was "getting uncomfortable in your exam room." He protested, but after checking my messy document folder he opened the door, and then forgot about asking me to touch my toes. Scribble, scribble again, and off I went along a well-trod white line to the Classification Desk.

I handed over my incorrectly held documents for review, and the non-commissioned desk clerk read through the various reports. Finally he initialed my folder, checked some boxes on his clipboard and told me that my classification was 1-Y.

"Uh, what's a one-why?" I asked.

"You will be called up for service just before the women and children" he said with an expression of contempt.

Swelling inside, I returned to my wire basket, dressed and walked out a deferred man onto Broadway, where I tossed my remaining of benzedrine tablets into the path of an oncoming truck and made my way toward the Greyhound Bus station with a glowing sense of emancipation.

A Gathering of Tribes

Following my temporary deferment from military conscription, my room mate Chip, who actually attended his classes, and had realistic plans for himself, moved back home with his well-placed parents to better accommodate his future – leaving me to my own devices. Shortly thereafter I read an article in a magazine about the supposedly dangerous effects of marijuana, and I knew immediately that I wanted some. Knowing the secrecy surrounding illicit drug use, I contacted my ex-cadet buddy, Mike in Newport Beach, who I suspected either smoked the "dangerous weed" or at the very least, would know where I could get some. Mike as it turned out was well versed and receptive, saying he could "score a lid for ten dollars" from his older brother, Nick. Twenty minutes later I was back at my place with a packet of rolling papers and a sack full of what Mike called Acapulco Gold. I had never tried rolling a cigarette before and my first attempts produced dismal results. Following numerous failures I was finally able to light one up and I smoked the entire thing without feeling any effects, so I smoked another one. This gave me a headache and a slight buzz, but nothing like the phantasmagoria described in the magazine article, so I called Mike.

"Hey, what's the deal here? I smoked two sticks and nothing's happened!"

Like an over-enthusiastic appliance salesman, my friend said he would be right over. Shaking his head at my pitiful product, Mike pulled out a neatly rolled cigarette of his own.

"Here," he said, "smoke this, *that's* a joint."

I lit up, inhaled and blew out the smoke. Mike laughed and pointed out that nothing would ever happen if I didn't hold the smoke in my lungs for a while.

"Joints," he said, "are not smoked like cigarettes," and then showed me the proper way to toke and hold the hit.

I tried it Mike's way, and halfway through the joint I was walking around my house backwards, speaking in tongues. From his prone position on the floor, my pot guru proclaimed, "Now you're getting the hang of it!"

Through Mike and his brother Nick I met Danny. Danny's pot was a little different than Nick's Acapulco Gold, with weirder sounding names like Oaxacan and Michoacan. The other significant difference with Danny's product was that he always included a pack of rolling papers and a tinfoil covered roll of cross-white bennies (benzedrine tablets). I started buying all my pot from Danny.

My generous fresh connection lived just south of Costa Mesa in the seaside town of Laguna Beach, a favored tourist mecca for those in the know, which I was quick to learn was also a laid back colony for bohemian artists and other fringe types. Due to my frequent trips to Danny's, I enthusiastically began exploring the city's rather fascinating neo-Beat underbelly. The main street through town was lined with clay pot bazaars, sea food restaurants, curio shops, shack coffee houses and realtors surrounding a diminishing number of elegantly rustic beach-front homes. A curious fixture at the northern edge of town was an aging, Gabby Hayes-like character the locals called "The Greeter" (his real name was Eiler Larsen). A gentle charismatic eccentric, Eiler held forth daily with an eternal smile, waving his gnarly old cane at the passing cars and welcoming everyone who drove by the best of stays in Laguna. "Just an old crazy guy," I was initially told, but long after our entertaining conversations of desert prospecting and hobo literature – when Eiler passed away in his lonesome hill-side shack, thousands of dollars were found stuffed inside his death-bed mattress.

During one of my intrepid strolls around Laguna I found a minuscule record shop known as Sound Spectrum that specialized in imported rock'n'roll. It was a drug friendly environment, and I visited often to listen to the music and chat with the clientele. Following a number of these visits, and numerous Black Afghani hash enhanced joints, I was befriended by one of the owners, Jimmy the Clerk. Jimmy was one among several surf-friendly acid-head investor types, all a few years older than myself, who seemed to spend much of their freely scattered time on the beach in Hawaii. Following a moon-lit, tandem LSD trip down to the "Orange Sunshine" shore one moonlit night, Jimmy introduced me to his discreet, though hardly silent fold of partners. Jimmy the Clerk and his friends had a small but expanding communal set located in a hidden canyon behind Laguna. In those days they lived quite happily, well away from outsider scrutiny, in a series of shanty boxes amid a luscious grove of aromatic trees, along with their quite beautiful girlfriend-attendants (male chauvinism had yet to be clearly defined), broken down VW vans, copious amounts of psychotropic drugs, feral cats, a flock of obese hens and a number of seriously bewildered dogs. My new companions called their resourceful redoubt "Bluebird Canyon."

Much too much has already been written about this group of beatific surfers, and what hasn't been exposed in the media or by ugly rumor is best left unsaid. Jimmy and his fun-loving band smugglers, at the time uncommonly referred to as The Brotherhood of Eternal Love, and eventually shortened to simply The Brotherhood, entered the Psychedelic Hall of Fame for opening one of the original eastern import gathering centers for the underculture known as "The Mystic Arts," located on Laguna's main drag. Among their numerous humanitarian acts, Jimmy and crew became the West Coast guardians for Dr. Timothy Leary's Pandoric stash box. The subterranean action swirling around Jimmy the Clerk's set in Laguna was, unfortunately for them, becoming rather notorious, but by then I was keeping more to myself, miles away from Bluebird's oncoming history – though due to Danny's complimentary speed and Jimmy's powdered LSD, I was most certainly not sleeping.

A "Gathering of The Tribes," akin to the now famous "Human Be-In" held in San Francisco's Golden Gate Park occurred in Los Angeles that brought together (at least for the afternoon) the diverse factions of LA's underpublic, then living in and around Echo Park, the Silverlake district, and in what would come to be know as "Mondo Hollywood." The Elysian Fields are located near Dodger Stadium and it was in this scenic locale that the colorfully diverse, and ill-documented gathering was held. I wanted to be well equipped before heading north to play in the Elysian Fields so I stopped by to visit my friend Jimmy the Clerk to pick up a powder box full of Orange Sunshine. Jimmy suggested what a trip it would be to be the first Being at the Be-In, so, I took his comment to heart, and set my alarm clock for 4 am.

I arrived well before dawn, and was infinitely pleased to find that I was indeed the first quasi-tribe member to light up a joint, and began wondering about the dew covered grass in the early morning fog until I came upon an old growth oak. I took this to be a perfect redoubt for my Be-In look-out post, so, I spread out my Navajo blanket to observe the anticipated Tribal arrivals. As I sat there contemplating the vast whatever I noticed a gossamer-like figure strolling in my direction, and waved him over. As he came closer, I discerned that the gossamer was actually a head-full of Anglo-electrified hair, and that the Being was body-suited in a full set of well-worn leathers with a Tibetan shoulder bag slung across his chest.

"Whooah!" said the Being, "I thought for sure I would be the first one here!"

"Hey – let's call it a draw," I returned, and pulled out my powder box to offer my new acquaintance in the fog some Orange Sunshine Love Dust, which he quickly gobble/snorked with uninhibited Tribal glee.

"Whooah!" he refrained.

As we chatted away in the rising dawn, my guest told me that he wasn't part of the LA set, and had driven down from "The Haight" to scout out the Tribal scene in Hollywood. I remarked that I periodically visited the city.

"Whooah! Stop By Anytime Man!" he said giving me his address with and preparing to Be-On his merry way.

"On second thought," he added, as he pulled out a plasmic vial from his Lama bag. "Here man – Whooah! Share this with your friends," and handed me an eenie-meany little joint before disappearing into the bushes.

"Whooah!" I thought, staring at the paper twig before firing it up, thinking that I'd be lucky if the eenie-meany thing had enough material to get me high, much less my "friends." Match lit, I sucked in really hard on the pin-like object – nearly consuming the entire thing in one enormous inhalation. The second the smoke surged its way toward my unprepared brain I knew I had terribly misjudged my blanket buddy's offering – this was an eenie-meany joint full of DMT!

When I came back to reality, I was staring up and into the sunshine faces of a dozen or more Tribal Gatherers who had formed a rotating OM circle around me! It was now late morning, and the Gathering Of Tribes had obviously been underway for some time. I struggled to sit up, and I remember thinking that being the first "Being" at the Be-In hadn't exactly worked out the way I had anticipated. Navajo blanketless, I stood up to join the OM circle, and one of the gathered commented that they thought I would never wake up – OMMmmm.

The morning incensed into afternoon and a freely formed diversity ruled the day. Hundreds of smiling Tribe People wandered about the Elysian Field clad in their beady finery, macrame dresses, proto-tye-dyes, and loin cloths as pounding waves of Acid Rock spewed from not-much-of-a stage over the vibrating heads and into the multicolored foliage. Many of the local groups played the play that day, including (to the best of my fainted memory), Clear Light, The Peanut Butter Conspiracy, The Seventh Son, and The West Coast Pop Art Experimental Band. Folk Singer Barry McGuire was on hand – but due to the condition his condition was in, he refrained from singing. Instead, and smack dab in the middle of the Elysian Field, he covered his barely-clad self, and a lovely young woman in a blanket (not my donated Navajo), and quite uninhibitedly made Love-In with her. This is one of the few events that day to make the national papers – and over the years, the photo documentation of Reverend Barry's underblanket consummation has been reprinted in numerous publications.

Gypsy Boots, the Mojave Desert Vegemaniac with a blender, and health food promoter well before his time ran around wearing a suit of animal pelts, handing out his marvelous "Energy Bars," followed by lengthy excerpts from his never-ending story. Gypsy was quite a guy, and his grandiose, emotive humor is sorely missed in the stoic vegan world of today. Among the many intriguing characters I met that day was a blind poet-composer by the name of "Moondog" (Louis Hardin). Dressed in his Viking garb, he introduced me to a locally blind group of "psychedelic oil painters" who had a small gallery near the Silverlake District, where they exhibited their "LSD influenced visions" on canvas. Along with his many avant compositions, the late Moondog was the madrigal composer of "All Is Loneliness," slightly revised by Janis Joplin, and recorded by Big Brother and The Holding Company on their debut album.

By mid-afternoon my powder box of Orange Sunshine give-aways had long gone into the minds of others, and I danced the dance of dancers gathered every which away in the California sun. Patchouli oil, frankincense and marijuana ruled the air – hundreds of watermelons were delivered by the Digger Free contingent and a psychedelic water melon toss ensued – the bands played on into the late afternoon, and all was well and good in the Elysian Field. That is until the motorcycle gang "Satan's Slaves" decided that the Love-In was over! Without warning, the hairy minions of Beelzebub roared out of the bushes on their screaming hogs, and rode over the meadow spinning donuts in the sun, causing an immediate Scattering Of The Tribes. The Beings at hand were panic stricken, and I ran to the shelter of my Ford Fairlane and locked the doors – it was time to go home.

A few weeks later I happened to be in San Francisco, so, I decided to pay my Elysian DMT donor a visit. My fuzzy haired friend was chipper as ever and perfectly glad to see me, "Whooah!" he said when I told him about my daze following his departure in the field. We went into his neo-Victorian kitchen to get something to drink, and when he opened the refrigerator, there sat a lab tray holding what looked like a hundred or so ampules from Sandoz Laboratories in Switzerland! "Whooah! Here have a soft drink first, we'll drink some of that later," he gleamed – and then the door bell rang. Before we could get to the front door in tromps a group of wildly dressed long-long-long hairs, and my friend introduced me.

"Hey Hammond meet my friend John Cippolina and The Quicksilver Messenger Service."

"Whooah!" and the rest is sweetly remembered history.

Laguna – Hollywood Transition

The entertainment quotient in Costa Mesa however was severely depressed, so on Fridays I would roll up a pocket full of joints, gobble a handful bennies and head northward in my two-tone (lawn-green and white), four door, 1964 Ford Fairlane (on long-term loan from my ever-generous grandmother) and drive to Hollywood for a few days.

As a rule I would leave the car in a coin operated "All-Day-All-Night" parking lot near the freeway end of Hollywood Boulevard, smoke a joint, ante up two or three bennies (perhaps mixed with a smidgen of LSD), and then head out on the weirding path.

Hollywood Boulevard has most likely always been a safe haven for the disenfranchised factions of an otherwise sunny Southern California lifestyle. Ever curious on my weekly trips up and down this historic Boulevard, I would come to meet other nomadic experimentalists who turned me on to the hot spots for diverse weirding. Places such as the soon-to-be-closed Coffee House of the Rising Sun, The Blue Grotto, The Bizarre Bazaar, Ben Frank's Cafe, and the berserkian Fred C. Dobbs, where I met an astonishing array of oddly framed yet wonderful people, including Bunk Gardner, one of the multi-instrumentalists in Frank Zappa's Mothers of Invention. On the whole they referred to themselves as "Freaks" and belonged to a vague something-or-other they satirically called The United Mutation Front. (I immediately applied for membership.) One of the more mystically-apparent non-leaders of this unwinding group was a Beat elder and studied sculptor turned bizzarro dance-guru by the name of Vito Paulekas.

At the time, Vito held court within a tangle of wildly attractive lithe-bodied acid-bunny proto-groupies, and a smaller group of polymorphic male impresarios known collectively as The Fraternity of Man. The Frat-family and their gossamer clad women, who looked like the psychedelic brides of Dr. Frankincense, sported some of the most colorful clothing this side of the Munchkin Wardrobe from the Wizard of Oz. The group's interpreter and mephisto-jester was a ringlet-eared Mediterranean fellow named Carl Franzoni, who dressed like a rainbow-clad Oscar Wilde, right down to the crimson-skin tights and brass-buckled, patent-leather Artois shoes – a footwear named after the shoe-designing brother of France's King Louis XVII. Frank Zappa dedicated the Mothers of Invention double album *Freak Out!* to the outermost Carl, and the Fraternity band would become legends as the composers of the reefo-musical pearl, "Don't Bogart Me", later to be included on the sound track of Dennis Hopper's ground-breaking, though to my mind oxymoronic, biker film, *Easy Rider*.

When you take benzedrine and stay up all day and night for three or four consecutive days spelunking the Underground, your peripheral vision gets a lot wider, and your normally in-sync-with-reality perceptions quickly begin to record, replay and filter your many experiences almost before they happen to you. With a set of pin-pointy pupils inaccurately scanning up and under side-streets of constantly split decisions, time becomes quite irrelevant, until your frazzled psyche requires more benzedrine. You get wired and you stay wired. On one of these safari-morns, absorbed in the workings of the inner-tinsel set, where breakfast, lunch and dinner was little more than an endless cup of coffee retro-boosted by a handful of mega-vitamins and speed, I pocketed my comb, ball-point pens, the ever handy safety razor, and my stash, feeling that I was equipped and fully-qualified to confront the long unwinding whatever.

Lower Hollywood Boulevard near the Hollywood Freeway was then lined with laundries, fading pawn shops, repair stores, end-of-the-line agencies and a number of all night triple-feature movie houses featuring B-grade exploitation films. One theater would run films like *Mondo Cane, Mondo Pazzo* and *Mondo Mondo* – while another would have a Russ Meyers Festival of soft porn celluloid like *Vixen, Super Vixen and Well-Beyond the Valley Of The (next-to-last?) Super Vixen*. The price of admission was a dollar which was then good for 24 hours or until the theater's post-industrial janitor swept you out with the condoms and uneaten pop corn. Much cheaper than a motel, the movie houses were safer (and warmer) than sleeping in the Ford. They had relatively clean washrooms, and if I was there at the right time, I could play Mondo Bingo! (the lucky winners were paid in silver dollars). It was on such a Grade B morning that I headed out for what could be called: Mondo Hammondo and The Technicolor All-Night Movie.

After inhaling a 99 cent breakfast, freshly combed and sufficiently wired, I strolled up the boulevard, zig-zaging in the general direction of La Cienega. Without detours, this is an easy walk that would take just about anyone thirty minutes – but due to the interactive nature of benzedrine and the curious-sparkle of the weird, it took me nearly six hours of outside-down work on the captivating up-streets, heading specifically in the direction of lord knows what. I persistently distracted myself with the fascinating diatribes of the many other victims and pheromonic interventionists typical of Hollywood Boulevard and its immediate environs. To quell the increasing frenzy building up inside my nervous system, I meticulously scanned the directory listings in the lobbies of anonymous buildings before entering the offices of the probably transient and curiously titled. My scattered attentions focused on places such as: Bzerpt's Induction, 1st Temple of Zymphonic Transference, The Process Church of the Final Judgment, Grand Templar of the O.T.O., FulaVita-VitaVita, Silva Mind Control, Scientology and Overnight Squilbitz Removal. "Hi there! Can I have a brochure?"

Continuing my walk on the wired side, I merged with cheap arcades, near-empty cafes, used bookstores and odd exhibits long-gone, such as the eerie Witchcraft Museum, and Hell Bent For Leather where I would later purchase my fringed leather everythings. Candidly, I browsed among the lace and padded undergarments at Fredrick's of Hollywood, at that time largely catering to almost-starlets and full-bore transvestites. Without purpose, I toured myself through the professionally equipped Magician's Supply Store of illusion, Jaynes Auto Park (a truly curious palm-tree and small mansion rest stop, once a private finishing school, now sadly demolished), then across the street from Fredrick's, and into the wondrous lobbies of The Egyptian, The Pantages and, finally, Graumann's Chinese Theater – where I stuck my vibrating hands and feet into the fixed-cement impressions left by the illustrious stars.

Finally reaching La Cienega I wandered onto Sunset Boulevard, where the somehow dated weirdness turns into a flashing cacophony of freakdom. In Ben Frank's Coffee Shop I learned about the nearby Fairfax District, past the closed in the afternoon Silent Cinema, where I would later sit watching Harold Lloyd hang from the hands of an enormous clock, while the theater's realtime piano player charmed me and the empty-house silhouettes of other moviegoers painted on the aging walls of a nearly bygone era. Further along Fairfax was the Los Angeles FreePress Bookstore where I would occasionally find crash pad housing, and across the street Cantor's Delicatessen always sported a long line of Freaks, would-be rock stars, fluorescent groupies and government agents in trench coats standing in line. Along with the delicate kosher fare Cantor's provided a wondrous late night haven for a very strange set of patrons. The schizophrenic though oddly endearing street-singer Larry "Wild Man" Fischer would often come in to perform one of his aberrant ten-cent songs by running around the restaurant in ever decreasing circles, making awkward sounds before ejecting himself out the front door. Only Frank Zappa would recognize Larry's latent-croon potential by issuing a double album of the Wild Man's greatest ten-cent hits titled: *An Evening With Wild Man Fischer* on his Bizarre

Records label, which included a lovely photo of Larry standing next to his petite, grandmotherly-looking mother on the album's cover.

Back on The Strip I used my well-worn Marine identification to get into a burlesque house across from what was to become country-crooner Gene Autry's Grand Hotel. Inside the club, I continued to up my ante by washing down more benzedrine with a gin and tonic, watching the aging strippers twirl fluorescent pasties under the black light gloom of booze-hound, bar-fly and washed-out patron. Much like an out-of-work scientist I combed through the many night clubs of the time, such as The Sea Witch, The Trip, Pandora's Box, The Whiskey-a-Go-Go, Gazzari's listening to Iron Butterfly play the only song they knew. In the ill-fated den of iniquity known as The London Fog – an early sub-public watering hole catering to a dark and suspicious crowd – I would soon catch my first case of 'the crabs' from one of the waitresses.

As I stood in front of the Whiskey I remembered sitting upstairs in the club's VIP lounge one night and where during the show I became ill from VIP substance abuse and went outside for some fresh air. Free of the Whiskey's claustrophobia I became pale and ran across Sunset to purge myself in the bathroom of a service station. Just as I reached for the handle the person inside opened the door to ingraciouly receive the full frontal spew of my stomach contents all over his new leather suit! The guy was so aghast he ran off screaming into the night – and when at last I finished with my ugly business and feeling much better for it, I calmly went back to the Whiskey to hear Procol Harum's set closer, "A Whiter Shade of Pale."

Back from my pale reverie and needing a break in my current continuum I headed back down the Strip to the experimental Cinema Cinematique near Pandora's Box and watched the current underground movies, including Warhol's, *I A Man*, oddly featuring Valerie Solanas, Andy's future would-be-assassin, along with a blinding piece of celluloid by Conrad Brooks called *The Flicker*, which probably caused seizures in some fixated moviegoers.

The Fifth Estate

Renewed and out on the pavement again, I stuck out my thumb and within seconds I got a ride from a guy driving a battered blue Pontiac Sedan. He said his name was Barry Something, and as I got adjusted to the recently torn seat he asked, did I "mind riding in a stolen car?" Before I could answer, Barry told me that he stole the Pontiac from a used lot in Pittsburgh on his way out to California, having tired of his TransContinental bus ride. Talking a mile a minute, the disheveled Barry said he was "working in a greasy spoon, to kip enough smash to go on up to Frisco." I began to get the speed shakes when he asked me if I "liked Wyamines?" "Y-ya-whats?" I asked, and without answering, Barry pulled out a plastic inhaler, cracked it open on the steering wheel and pulled off a strip of sticky looking foil. Handing me the slip of supposed narcosi he cautioned me to "cook it up real slow" before injecting the yellowish goo into my veins! In a near state of speed shock I thanked Barry profusely before jumping out at the next red light. "Tell'um hello in Pittsburgh," I said. I beat the light across the boulevard and dumped Barry's proffered foil into the first bush I came to. To avoid the obvious I ducked into the darkened courtyard of a quasi-subterranean establishment called The Fifth Estate.

Inside the spacious coffee house I immediately ran into Bernardo, whom I had met on a previous junket to San Francisco. Bernardo, who spoke with a slightly effeminate whisper, stood a good 6 foot 4 inches tall, plus another 6 inches of naturally electrified Afro, and dressed like "The Spider From Mars" long before singer David Bowie became a world-scene Face. Ugly rumors circulated around Hollywood that the reportedly well-hung Bernardo had carried on a week-long menage a trois with Brian Jones of the Rolling Stones and Miss Mercy of the all-girl group, The GTO's – but in order to "protect the guilty" Bernardo refrained from spreading what he referred to as "lovely rumors." After the requisite set of hand configurations and brotherly jive, Bernardo introduced me to his "good friend, Moses-Two" – another Afro-wired spade in his mid-to-late twenties with an infectious smile, and who graciously offered to give me the fifty-cent tour.

There was a room in the back for folk singing, and another housed a small art gallery. The main salon had an espresso machine and a diverse lending library with a small fireplace, off which was a cinema room where silent European films were shown. The clientele at the Fifth Estate was a much more eclectic group than the frenetic crowd over at Fred C. Dobbs. Everyone from over-qualified psychiatrists to under-employed grave diggers hung out at The Estate, and on subsequent visits I would learn from this intriguing group about the jazz scene at Shelly's Manne-Hole and The Icehouse out in Hermosa Beach where Art Blakey's Jazz Messengers frequently played. Numerous other underculture clubs would appear within my spectrum such as Bito Lito's where Arthur Lee and his soon-to-be discovered group LOVE was the house band. Or I would wander into The Psychedelic Supermarket's Bizzar Bazzar to smoke huge joints of complimentary 'Bananadine', naively certain that Donovan's song "Mellow Yellow" contained a cryptic message about getting high on baked banana peels. According to the club's founder, Tom Kelly, the name Bizzar was coincidentally later used by Frank Zappa, Tom's silent partner in the Psychedelic Supermarket, for the name of his record company.

The Cheetah on the pier in Santa Monica was another favorite hangout of mine at the time. Formerly The Aragon Ballroom, hosting the likes of the Lawrence Welk Orchestra, The Cheetah was a psychedelic-friendly venue, where, on many a night I would swing from the scaffolding high on acid. Above me, there were moving sheets of mylar screens and liquid projections by the light show crew – reportedly led by an ex-chemical advisor for Timothy Leary. Memories of concerts featuring the early sound and pyrotechnics of the Electric Prunes, The Byrds playing eight miles high off the stage, The Peanut Butter Conspiracy along with The Jefferson Airplane – and being kissed by Grace Slick, afterwhich I did not wash my face for a week! Syd Barrett's Pink Floyd stopped there on the *Pipers at the Gates of Dawn* tour, and Jim Morrison of the Doors repeatedly fell from the stage shouting "this is the end," but The Fifth Estate, founded by Delores and Albert Mitchell, and where Art Kunkin would soon initiate the *Los Angeles FreePress* in the coffeehouse basement, was far and away the hippest scene I had encountered.

Back at the table, Moses-Two and Bernardo were leaving to go to a party and asked me if I wanted to go along. "Does a horse have hooves?" I asked, and off we went, zipping around corners and skittering down unlit side-streets with Moses-Two at the wheel like a nervous mole burrowing his way home, and when I noticed the Watts Towers roll by I started to get the speed shakes again. Moses-Two finally pulled over in front of a row of tenements with the remains of an old sedan in front. "We're here!" he exclaimed and hopped out of the car.

Bernardo and I followed him up some stairs and down a grimy hallway to an unmarked door where Moses-Two rapped the secret rap. When the door opened we were quietly invited into the dimly lit living room by an older black woman Moses-Two referred to as "Mom." Fresh Motown was playing softly on the radio, and as my eyes adjusted to the lack of light I saw that six or seven people (all of them black) were lounging on the numerous sofas lining the walls of Mom's apartment. Everyone appeared to be on the nod and didn't acknowledge our arrival until Mom introduced Bernardo (who took up much of the room) and me as being friends of Moses-Two.

Mom disappeared into the bathroom and when she returned, she spread the paper napkin she was carrying on the coffee table, exposing a large pile of multi-colored capsules, and everyone in the room, including Bernardo and Moses-Two took a handful before going back on the nod. I didn't recognize any of the pills but knew that it would be seen as bad form to refuse, so I scooped up a fistful and popped one of the big red ones in my mouth. Soon I was getting rather edgy if not outright paranoid about the set, when Mom came over and sat beside me on the sofa. "Lissen here Sugalamb – why yu be sittin in ma houze ain't nuthin bay-go-hatten, dig?" I felt better after her reassurances and accepted the joint she offered me. Mom said it was Panama Red, and true to its reputation, the stick took the top off my benzedrine enhanced head! Around 2:30 a.m. we thanked Mom for the hospitality, and Moses-Two and Bernardo drove me back to my all-night-movie motel on Hollywood Boulevard Moses-Two gave me his phone number for the next time I was in town and they let me go, stumbling blindly into the loge section where I fell into a Panamanian-Seconal-Benzedrine fugue. I awoke a few hours later. On screen, naked Mondo women rubbed fresh wildebeest manure on to the sides of their pathetic huts. Crying out in starvation, emaciated children with large festering ulcerations on their bodies nursed futilely at the mottled breasts of their mothers and huge bottle flies swarmed. Clear of my previous haze, I stormed out the Mondo theater, got to my car and drove back to the relative sanity of Costa Mesa where I slept solidly for two days.

I continued these weekly forays into Hollywood and its canyon environs, meeting so many intriguing would-be artists, writers and exotic-drug enthusiasts. I came to know, and at times loosely sit in with, some of the local groups, such as The West Coast Pop Art Experimental Band, FM radio pioneer Tom Donahue, Skye Saxon of The Seeds and most notably, Richie Furay (now a devoted Christian minister) and Stephen Stills of Buffalo Springfield, commonly thought of at the time as "the too good to be true band."

Backstage with the Buffalo was always a friendly, and at times hilarious scene. One memorable night, after hitch-hiking five miles in the wrong direction, I arrived at one of the band's concerts in Santa Monica playing along side Blue Cheer, who at the time utilized more Marshall amplifiers than anyone thought imaginable. Also on the program that night were the blues masters Sonny Terry and Brownie McGee (spitting blood into a tin can at his harmonica dancing feet). During the opening sets the Springfield backstage area was filled with Buffalo friends including drummer Spencer Dryden in his coy cowboy outfit, and Mike Love, lead singer for The Beach Boys. Away from the fray there was a long row of urinals separating the dressing rooms, and as Stephen Stills and I peacefully relieved ourselves in walks Neil Young sporting a Cheshire Cat grin. "Watch this!" Neil exclaimed, as he hit the flusher on the urinal closest to the door. His action caused all of the urinals to explode rather violently from their drains, spraying Stills and me with the force. Neil just laughed, brushed his hands together, and left us to our unfinished business.

Nascent guitar stars and garage rock groups aside, my own spirit quest was becoming much too self-absorbing for me to get overtly involved with the burgeoning Los Angeles art/rock scene, though I had many opportunities to enter into the questionable side-world of "The Other Crew." This was a debilitating quasi-profession where amplified wires, long hours, women, VIP drugs, and backstage passes take you mercilessly down the road of privileged excess – where the mystery in life is not your own – and furthermore, in those days, no self-respecting group wanted somebody in their band whose primary instrumentation was playing the drugs.

To branch out I began invading the elevated enclaves of the Silverlake and Echo Park Districts, finally extending my walk of the wired along Wilshire Boulevard past the La Brea Tar Pits and into the heart of downtown, where I stretched my young psyche by hanging out at the infamous Pershing Square. This is where the already weird go when their regular routines become pedestrian. Ghostly figures wandered these nearly indifferent streets at all hours, muttering into a trash-strewn eternity from out the subcortic bowel of writer Charles Bukowski's rummy world of butt-ugly barflies, flimflam artists and failed magicians on their last legs amidst a plethora of squalid bug-infested rooming houses perched ominously above Elbow Room bars. The whole area was a six by twelve block sanctuary, where a shifting population of bohemian out takes, Synanon drop-outs, confused perverts, stiletto-toed queens, and rather literate drug users went to get away from it all. To keep abreast of this sordid scene I would occasionally spend the weekend in one of the area's less than accommodating hotels where I had three heavy metal slide-bolts on the inside of the door. A short view that looked out onto a steam vent spewing vaporized grease and grime over Broadway and the nearby Greyhound Bus terminal – home to a bustling glory hole and tea room trade.

After a few weekends living among and observing this truly lost and limping generation I knew it was time to pack it in, go back to Costa Mesa and get my act together – Los Angeles was a condemned city.

The Golden Bear

"Getting my act together" proved to be more complex than I had imagined, due to my friends in Laguna Beach and my continuing experimentation with an exotic pharmacopoeia. Danny's free Benzedrine had morphed into Dexedrine tablets, which turned into yellow Desoxyn pills, and then 200 mg. Methedrine cross-hatches before finally rediscovering itself in the form of pure-crystal Meth-amphetamine sulphate. When you start using this amplitude of speed, you have quite a lot of spare time on your hands, and many a dazed night was spent sitting up with other rapid transients engaged in multifaceted conversations while stringing together strands of colorful beads, or repeatedly making nothing out of lots of something, which everyone prized as indigenous treasure.

Along with my constant-pot and weekly-speed allowances, I was also enthusiastically testing a number of Acronymic drugs. Standardized doses (200-500 mg) of soon-to-be illegalized LSD-25, the mystifying effects of which seem to last somewhere between eight hours and a life time, along with the occasional dose of DOM (STP), a proto-strobic substance which is best taken out in the desert, because this extremely powerful little pill will light your psychofuse for about forty-eight hours – DMT, (N,N-Dimethyltryptamine) which when smoked or injected instantly produces a phantasma-intensic acid peak lasting about twenty minutes – DET, (Diethyltryptamine) smoked on mint leaves which brings out the hallucinogenic "Lions and Tigers and Bears, Oh My!" and the government funded (via Dr. Sydney Gottlieb M.D. and the CIA.'s Operation Artichoke) incapacitant JB-39, a truly wacked-out psycho-pharmaceutical (perhaps a forerunner to agent BZ) that renders normal speech a useless tool, temporarily flipping the user's common reality into a slow motion dough boy world with an echoic sound track. Whatever my reasoning at the time, in lieu of the more classical education, I sought out the auto-didactic program, where I majored with celerity in the Anatophysics of Inner Space, with a strong minor in Adventurous Follow-up.

Since I wasn't going to Hollywood with any regularity, I satisfied my musical cravings by hanging out in Huntington Beach in an early folk rock club called The Golden Bear. A truly wonderful and original place, The Bear would eventually take up the entire block, but in those days, it was an intimate, minuscule venue, seating about eighty people at red checkered tables, with a dozen or so (myself included) seated at the foot of the stage apron. The Bear was more than a friendly venue for me. It became a socio-musicological education and I was lucky enough to hear and briefly hang out with some fantastic musicians – Chicago harpist extraordinaire Paul Butterfield and his East-West group of musicians including Michael Bloomfield, for whom I would score ounces of pot whenever they hit town. The Canadian duet Ian & Sylvia who were more than friendly, Sam Andrew, lead guitarist for Big Brother and the Holding Company, and folk singer Richie Havens to name just a few.

Richie played the Golden Bear often, and over time we struck up what has become a lasting friendship. Whenever he came to town, he would usually call to invite me along on one of his habitual walks around Huntington Beach, and on at least one occasion he spent the night at my house. It was such a treat to cover one of my folk heroes with a blanket half his size, when Richie fell asleep on my couch in lieu of the bed in his hotel room.

The Bear was located almost on the sand near the now demolished Huntington Beach Pier, always a source of after-Bear groupie entertainment. For the more 'reforming crowd' the Reverend David Wilkerson (author of *The Cross and The Switchblade*) had the West Coast branch of his ecumenical Teen Challenge just around the corner, and despite their good efforts and prayer, I wasn't to be saved.

The Bear, Huntington Beach and its neighboring sands provided a much needed release from my chemical studies at home. At the time, I was living in a newly rented 3 bedroom faux adobe house with 'A Speed Dealer Named Mike' and a UC Irvine physics major by the name of Ken who did little more than beat holes in the carpet with a pair of old drumsticks reportedly thrown to him from the stage of the Shrine Auditorium by Ginger Baker. I moved in with the dynamic duo because my father cut off my monthly stipend and recycled my grandmother's Fairlane, when he and my step-mother Arlene paid an unexpected visit to my original den of ubiquity – and found the barely conscious me coming down from a three-day methedrine run. I could hardly protest.

Living with 'A Speed Dealer Named Mike' did have its advantages. Like getting to lick the speed plate after his deals were consummated. Since I was going to be up all night anyway I got a job on the grave-yard shift in a local vacuform plastics factory, making those gray plastic tubs used by the bus boys and dishwashers of the world. For female companionship I dated Vickie, a sexful raven-haired beauty formerly among my Bluebird Canyon friends. Vickie had moved along from her deeply bohemian roots, forsaken all drugs, and was trying to make a go of it at a straight job. Completely tolerant of my own intake, Vickie said she enjoyed the ever-changing contact high she got from being around me. To establish the proper psychic connection in such a relationship I would occasionally double dose myself with Orange Sunshine tabs on the full moon, under which Vickie and I would copulate like a pair of landed porpoise on the locally named Victoria's Beach well into the colorful dawn. Vickie said I was her surrogate entry into the familiar (and somewhat missed) netherworld of her now passed period of psychedelic excess – Vickie was a true Acid Queen. We continued seeing and fondling each other until I met Wendy, the woman who would become my first wife.

Wendy and I met in the Student Union of Orange Coast College (from which I was at the time officially banned). First I stole Wendy away from the drummer of a rock band, and shortly thereafter from her parents. Her father was a balding civilian engineer in the U.S. Army Corps, and Wendy had grown up in the Cinecitta sector of Rome's international community. As an elegantly trim, blonde, full breasted, calendar hopeful, Wendy's teenage windows looked out onto the back lots of Italy's cinematic foreground, where classic films such as Fellini's *Juliet of the Spirits* and *8 $^1/_2$* were made. She spent her romantic evenings high on diet pills working as a paid customer, shilling the bar at trendy discos in Rome, such as the Piper Club, until her movable father was transferred to Southeast Asia, and relocated the rest of the family to Orange County during his absence. Aside from her adventures with me, Wendy's prime directive was to get out of Orange County, and if possible go back to Europe, where as she astutely put it, "Life actually lives."

PART TWO – SAN FRANCISCO

"Yes, and..."

Ready for a location change myself, I pulled the dead flowers out of my hair and decided to move us both to San Francisco. I switched from early morning vacuform flunky to injection-mold product delivery guy on the day shift. I trucked loads of tiny plastic do-dads to places like Mattel Toy Co. in the city of Hawthorn, and managed to save most of my meager salary. Wendy got a part-time job scooping ice cream after school and secretly did the same. When at last he visited the family, Wendy's father Norm immediately took a hatred toward me and the length of my hair. He thought I was a bad influence on Wendy (which I was) and forbade us from seeing each other. We of course ignored his unreasonable demands – we were in love, and Norm soon left for Saigon. Wendy's mother didn't exactly care for me either, and less so after she caught us screwing one afternoon in Wendy's bedroom.

Over the next few months I made numerous artificially enhanced forays north to hunt for an apartment, and eventually secured us a third floor walk-up on Gough Street near Market. Upon my return to Costa Mesa I convinced 'A Speed Dealer Named Mike' to borrow a functional car (vs. the dead 1953 Studebaker playhouse in our faux-adobe car port) with a small trailer in tow, and around 1 a.m. on the appointed night of my quasi-elopement, Mike and I drove over to nearby Westminster where I tapped on Wendy's bedroom window. She passed out a few boxes and five pieces of luggage, and while I packed her belongings into the trailer, Wendy gave her mother the unexpected news. She was moving to San Francisco with me and that was that. As 'A Speed Dealer Named Mike' drove us away, her nightgown-clad mother stood under the yellow porch light in tears, shouting at us that "Norm will kill the both of you," and, I might have added, "just as soon as he gets back from Vietnam."

The City by the bay was new to Wendy, but I had been visiting San Francisco since the early 1950s. As a child I would annually stay with my father's sister Catherine and her husband Uncle Jack in the East Bay village of Orinda. They were childless for many years and I was a surrogate son. On these lovely and thoroughly spoiled vacations from rural life, Catherine and Uncle Jack would dress me up in stylish new duds and take me to all the great restaurants at the time, places such as Caesar's Palace on Telegraph Hill, Venito's near Fisherman's Wharf and Des Alps in North Beach. During the summer days, Aunt Catherine would take me to play in Oakland's Fairyland Park or to dog paddle and splash in the enormous Fleishacker Pool in the City, at the time the largest swimming pool in the world, requiring three lifeguard towers with rowboats at the ready! After fun we would invariably go for a late afternoon Rob Roy for me, and one or two of Catherine's habitual Old Fashioned with extra bitters, siting in the old world charm of the Cliff House when it housed the world's largest Camera-Obscura, and overlooked the tide-crumbling rock and algae filled remains of the famous Sutro Bath House.

At the time we didn't know many people in the City, but on one of my speed-enhanced apartment hunts I met someone I planned to look up right away. On this previous visit I was without funds for a hotel room, so I stayed up all night, riding the bus lines (the Muni), periodically switching from one line to the next – and all for fifteen cents. On one particularly long route I met a guy who was a few years older than myself and a bit exopthalmic. He was wearing the pieces from three different sets of eye-glasses held together by colored rubber bands. He sported a long ponytail sprouting from a rapidly balding pate and plainly operated on his own frequency. Much like myself, my companion was practicing his own form of Rapid Transit Yoga and together we launched into an all night discourse on the Joyous Cosmologies of Speed. We didn't worry about our destinations because we were already there. My new friend's name was Del Close.

Wendy and I secured the new apartment, stocked the larder with frozen TV dinners, as neither of us was much of a cook, and made our way up Gough Street and through the Broadway tunnel to the North Beach district where Del had a studio apartment. Del remembered our transit yoga well, and after offering us the hospitality du jour – some dynamic pot, he walked us over to a little theater on Broadway, where Del was currently the director of a satirical review/

ensemble known as The Committee. Wendy and I sat in on the evening's performance, and Del introduced us around to the cast and crew. I struck up friendships that night, that, save for deaths in the family, have endured for over three decades. Wonderful characters such as actors Bruce Mackey, Gary Goodrow and the late actors John Brent and Morgan Upton. All of whom further introduced me around the neighborhood as a young up-and-coming artist. I got my first taste for improvisation and poetic courage on the Committee stage during the routine break prior to one of their midnight shows.

It is a standard practice today, but these madcap sessions were some of the first improv skits to be based on suggestions from the audience of an earlier performance, who were then invited to stay on to enjoy their suggestions being put to satiric use. On that evening, Bruce Mackey walked though one of the colorful doors that made up the Committee set and announced (without asking me) that during the break "they" (the audience, made up largely of people from someplace like Nebraska), would be "further entertained by a local poet." Momentarily stunned by the roving spotlight, I got up from my table and went backstage to find Bruce, Del and John Brent satirically smiling at me. Del looked me squarely in the eyes and with an emotive sweep of hand he said, "Take your moment and pick a door!" With these few words from the theatric wise, I indeed, "took my moment" and walked into the world of live improvisation, as I didn't have a word of my work with me. Supported on stage by Gosling Trauma on piano I made my way onto the boards for the first time with some success.

The Committee ruled the roost in those days, along with the many other talented members of the immediately post-Beat Underground. Luminous-beings such as Larry Hankin, Ed Greenberg, Howard Hesseman, Hamilton Camp, Hugh Romney (aka Wavy Gravy), Mimi Farina (singer Joan Baez's beautifully petite sister and partner to the late singer/song writer Richard Farina), folk singer David Blue and so many other talented individuals roamed the Committee's lobby. Among my friend Del Close's peers was Scott Beach (voice-over impresario, Hurdy-Gurdy/Bowed-psaltry player and Lord Mayor of the Renaissance Pleasure Faire). Then there was Alan Meyerson (director of the film *Steelyard Blues*), and writer/director Carl Gottlieb (co-author of singer David Crosby's autobiography *Long Time Gone*). They all fine-tuned their theatrical skills and honed their rebellious teeth directing the formidable talents of protege and alumni of Chicago's Second City review and Julian Beck's Living Theater. The cast and crew encouraged, cajoled and astonished me all along the way, and remain some of the truest individuals I have ever had the pleasure of knowing.

I think I can say without exaggeration that Del Close dramatically affected the lives of everyone who encountered him. One of these days someone will write his phenomenal biography, and I sincerely hope it is published in Braille Esperanto. I think this bit of surrealism would please Del, who always maintained, along with his contemporary Emmett Grogan of the Diggers, that "notoriety, unnecessary publicity and taking credit for the things one does is for the complete square." I am thankfully not the writer who will transcribe Del's biopic – that writer will have daredevil nerves of titanium, with a background similar to that of Aleghieri Dante. Here I can only offer a few anecdotes from my own experience with Del, along with some second-hand reports from other first-hand friends of his.

Del was an avid urban spelunker who loved to roller skate through the dry concrete maze of underground aqueducts beneath the Los Angeles river basin high on LSD (long before it became an Underpublic staple). He would do so with a flaming miner's cap atop his head, and his extensive collection of charcoal rubbings taken from ancient manhole covers is worthy of the Smithsonian Institute.

While he and a few others from The Committee were in Los Angeles being toured around a theater, Del suddenly disappeared. The tour continued without him and everyone went back to the hotel thinking Del would be there. No Del. They called the theater manager. No Del. A few hours later the worried group got a call from the Hollywood Police. "Does anyone there know a Del Close?" they inquired. It seems that Del, with his stealth-like curiosity crawled under the theater's stage where he found a large heating vent. Ever the intrepid traveler, Del crawled in, around, and up and down the winding tubes of sheet metal, until he broke through a wall and set off the burglar alarm in the offices of Warner Bros., located in the building next door to the theater! Before he began consuming nearly all of the world's meth-amphetamine supply, Del was the "LSD connection" for Aldous Huxley, Alan Watts, and their literate circle of voyagers in the late 1950s.

From time to time Del would go missing in action. On one such occasion actor Bruce Mackey and the late folk singer Tim Hardin went to Del's place to check up on him. They knocked, and from within Del yelled out, "Go Away!" "Come on Del," they said, "let us in." To which Del replied, "No! Go Away, I'm busy!" Knowing full well Del's penchant for the outer limits of the highly questionable, they broke in to find Del dressed in a Spiderman suit, suspended in mid-air by an intricate web of thick ropes. Caught up in a tangled section of web six feet off the hard wood floor, Spider Del looked at the stupefied duo of Close rescue and screamed, "Look! I'm just trying to work some things out! Now go away!" which they did, leaving Del to his arachnid improvisations.

A true astronaut of the beyond, Del's astute knowledge of all things obscure and his quiet consumption of inspiring narcosia were prolific. Ever the improvisationalist, he cured his monstrous addiction to cocaine "through Witchcraft and became the coven's Warlock." One of Del's first notable film roles was as the conjurer Svengali, and he was a member of The Compass Players ensemble along with Elaine May, Mike Nichols and the illustrious Severn Darden. Over the years he played many interesting bit parts on stage and in films such as George Lucas's *THX-1138*, *American Graffiti*, and Brian De Palma's version of *The Untouchables* starring Sean Connery. In the early 1960s Del and the late poet/actor John Brent recorded an hilarious album titled, *How To Talk Hip*, and in the late 1980s Del was responsible for Saturday Night Live hosting writer William Burroughs, who exquisitely drawled from his cut/up novel *Nova Express*.

As a director Del was spontaneous and very creative. During an afternoon workshop in the Committee Theater he suddenly (Del did and said everything suddenly) announced, "Let's have a little lesson in trust." He lined everyone up beneath the flies and then hoisted himself a good ten feet above the stage to a little platform. His glassy eyes smiling down at us on stage he said, "Now get close together and catch me," where upon Del turned around and fell backwards into our stage struck arms – we quickly put him down. "Now that's trust!" he said, and then directed each of us to do the same – "Otherwise," he added sternly, we were to "leave the theater at once!" – most of us complied.

The odd-ball anecdotes and legendary tales epic and small could go on and on, and many of them would simply stop traffic. His final theatric gift to the boards was the further development of "The Harold," – a form of improvisational exercise that he and writer/director Carl Gottlieb invented in the early 1960s. On March 4th 1999, (following his own wake – attended by many friends) my dear friend Del Close passed away in a Chicago hospital bed. In his last will and testament, true to his satiric word, he bequeathed his skull to the Goodman Theater, "for Yorik use during productions of *Hamlet*!" At last sighting, Del's skull-bone top-knot sat atop a velvet cushion in the Chicago landmark, patiently awaiting the next curtain rise. Truthful, if not satirical to the end, Del's parting words were: "I'm tired of being the funniest person in the room."

On The Set

Back on Gough Street, Wendy and I started looking for jobs. In those saner, less complicated days before the advent of computerization and faceless encounter, job agencies, much like the satirical "Cosmodemonic Agency" where writer Henry Miller once worked and which he so articulately described in the *Plexus* volume of his trilogy, *The Rosy Crucifixion*, were the ticket booths for employment. From street sweeping to part-time archaeology, these client-friendly agencies were usually to be found nestled above Market Street, next door to the likes of Dr. Campbell "The Credit Dentist." The kind ladies at the agencies would patiently thumb through boxed 5x7 cards of handwritten job descriptions, valiantly searching for a place to send me for an interview.

My qualifications at the time were, shall we say, minimal, and I was sent on some of the most arcane appointments to places such as leather belt factories, smelters, can companies, and felt manufactures. The felt factory has to be the strangest job interviews I've ever been on – it took place in a dense pre-earthquake warehouse down on Howard Street.

In a dingy fifth floor office I was greeted by the two felt proprietors, who were dead ringers for the old comic strip characters, "Mutt & Jeff." First thing, they wanted me to take a typing test, and to accommodate them I sat down at a small wooden desk with a well-worn Dashiell Hammett typewriter. I inserted a clean sheet of paper into the archaic machine, while Mutt and Jeff looked over my shoulder.

Mutt looked at Jeff and said, "Let's have him type the quick brown fox jumps over the lazy white dog."

"Why that's a marvellous idea," replied Jeff, "Let's!" and I proceeded to type the alphabetic scramble with perfection and flair.

"Well I don't know," said Jeff to Mutt, "Now what do we think?"

"Let's have him do it again twice," replied his partner, and I again typed the jaunty phrase.

"Well!" they chimed in unison.

Mutt looked at me through his wire-rimmed glasses and asked if I could "please type it again."

I was beginning to understand just why Lewis Carroll's Hatter had gone mad as I again typed "the quick brown fox jumps over the lazy white dog" with perfection. Completely ignoring my efforts, Mutt looked at Jeff, Jeff looked at Mutt and as though I were no longer in the room they began to debate whether or not I should type the by-now offensive phrase yet again. In their confusion, I got up from the desk, put on my coat and made for the office door while Mutt and Jeff, oblivious to my impending departure, questioned my spelling of the word "brown" and continued debating the merits of having me go on typing the continuing saga of the lazy white dog.

I laughed all the way back to the Cosmohilarious Job Agency.

After some weeks of searching the edges of gainful employment I managed to get a position as a micro-film processor. I was to work in a small micro-film laboratory, independently owned by its founder, a Mr Black-Something. The now archaic database business was staffed by the two of us and Mr Black-Something's silent wife Debbie. Mr. Black-Something drank more coffee than anyone on the planet and chain-smoked at least three packs of unfiltered cigarettes a day. The claustrophobic lab was located next to the Glory Hole bathroom of a Foster's Cafeteria and just across the street from the electric streetcar terminal on Lower Folsom Street. Why Mr Black-Something hired me in the first place has always been a mystery, because I knew absolutely nothing about micro-film and most certainly had never processed any. I learned the trade by the ever-pedagogic trial and error, overexposing everything, putting the films into the wrong spool containers and then delivering them to the wrong owners – companies like The Sumitomo Exchange, The Chartered Bank of London, Standard Oil and The American Can Corporation – companies that really hated getting their micro-imagery all goofed up. Nevertheless, I somehow passed muster, and once I got the routine down, Mr Black-Something would chain smoke and drink coffee, Debbie silently secretaired, and I spent most of the day in the darkroom.

Wendy got a job as a sales clerk for a photo finishing shop in the heart of the Financial District on Montgomery Street, and we would ride the streetcar to work, often taking our lunch breaks together, before meeting after work for the ride home. With our finances thus secured we set about enjoying our freedom from parents, schools and my pharmaceutical habits. Speed was out of the question and LSD had finally been criminalized, with much of the remaining product adulterated with psychotoxic by-products, so I refrained. Wendy and I stuck to smoking high grade pot (still $10 a bag) with the occasional dose of government issue mescaline or psilocybin.

Food was rather inexpensive in those days and we could buy a month's worth of groceries for about $50. Our rent was only $75 a month and we didn't have a car to worry about, so after taxation and household expenses we were doing all right. We even had the extra cash for an evening's entertainment, usually to be found in the many cafes and bookstores that dotted North Beach, where the 1950s glow of beatitude and bohemianism still hung in the subterranean air.

Mike's Pool Hall on Broadway, made famous by Kerouac and crowd, was still in business, along with Coffee and Confusion, Cafe Roma, The Shylock Shop and The Poster Mat on upper Grant Avenue.

After a cheap meal at Little Joe's or veal cutlet and fried eggs at the U.S. Cafe, it was on to the Committee for the late show. Wendy and I would usually close our evening at Cafe Trieste on Upper Grant for espresso and the operatic voice of the Trieste's owner Johnny, who fell paternally in love with Wendy. Johnny would sing, backed by the cafe's jukebox orchestra, the most angelic arias for her. We became great friends with his large family from Trieste, Italy and attended marvelous parties at the cafe. Johnny is a man of truly gracious hospitality.

On my own I would periodically visit Del Close in his mystic studio apartment, filled as it was with odd psychic props and the brass, candle-powered magick lanterns from his 1950s proto-light show research. Enlarged newspaper clippings and theatrical posters covered the walls, and Del would regale me with stories from his cryptic past, filled with anecdotes of great import, perhaps quoting at length from the comic strip Odd Bodkins, drawn by our mutual friend, cartoonist Dan O'Neill. I don't think of Dan as just another underground cartoonist. Dan is what I would call an Anarcho-Surrealistic Draftsman, and beyond his Bodkins strip, he has drawn alongside his countrymen, from inside the hostile trenches in Northern Ireland, and from the semi-illiterate back worlds of these Disunited States during periods of bigotry and civil unrest.

Through my friends Del Close and actor John Brent, I met Beat artist Bob Levy, and through Bob the poet Lawrence Ferlinghetti. Everybody was openly friendly in those days, and Wendy and I would often go with Lawrence and his wife Kirby into the Mission District for Mexican food and talk of things literary and not. Then they began having marriage troubles and we didn't see much of them as a couple anymore. One day as I was walking along upper Grant Avenue, I stopped in at Lawrence's little studio above City Lights Press, where 'He' was pretty much living at the time, estranged from Kirby. Tenacious to a fault, I sat down on the couch and started rambling on about a benefit I wanted him to organize for my newly-formed Poet Unity group. Lawrence, who couldn't be bothered, thrust a coffee-stained manuscript into my hands and said, "Here, read this and shut up!" I was holding the original hand-written pages of Jack Kerouac's *Scriptures of the Golden Eternity*! I didn't say another word, and sat humbly rereading one of my favorite pieces of poetic prose. The precepts and allusions to the Tao that Kerouac spoke so eloquently of in this work were becoming great influences on my own life as I began to determine the nature of my earthly purpose through creative abstraction and spiritual investigation.

16mm Moxie

I dearly wanted to become a writer, but came to see early on, by way of an Ernest Hemingway interview in the *Paris Review*, that "before one can write, one must first live." I was just twenty years old, and wondered just how much "living" could I have possibly done up to that point. Some to be sure, but barely a drop in the bucket compared to the experienced company I was beginning to keep. So I refocused my auto didactic studies on experimental film, now that I was "in the business" so to speak over on Folsom Street, and on painting. Oil painting was something I had been wanting to get back to since completing my first canvas at the age of eight. My vaporous mother's mother, Fay Hammond, then Fashion Editor of the *Los Angeles Times*, took my naive picture along on one of her frequent trips to New York, and had it framed by the Metropolitan Museum of Art. This was to the utter dismay of the rest of my family, who largely discouraged my pre-adolescent creativity. I didn't paint again until I took my first and last art class in college. When the instructor insisted on keeping my second attempt at oils, rather than being complimented, I was furious and asked him to return it. He refused, and I defiantly left art classes forever.

I began my real education by hanging out with other artists, reading art history books and film journals at the main branch of the San Francisco library, going to the Art Museum, and joining The Canyon Cinema Co-Op, where I attended showings of the Underground Films being made at the time by east and west coast filmmakers such as Harry Smith, Stan Brakage, Bruce Connor and Kenneth Anger. One day I answered an ad in the *Berkeley Barb* for a film class being held in the Fillmore District. The class was directed by a wire haired black guy by the name of Carl Mayberry-McKissick, who said he wanted to produce "three-minute 16mm comedies del arte," but mostly Carl wanted to get to know the women who came to his class. One of his more creative side-gigs was to get women to "star" in his three-minute porn films, and he was always on the lookout for fresh talent. Carl would advertise, in the *Berkeley Barb*'s adult section, the opportunity to "direct your own porno film." Carl would then charge the aspiring filmmakers fifty dollars to act as his "assistant directors" by positioning the sexy young "stars" for each take. The kick was that Carl almost never put any film in the camera for these licentious shoots! He would tell any disgruntled customers that the film didn't develop well and to come back to his studio "with another fifty bucks to try again." It was during one of Carl's more comic three-minute movie sessions that I first met fellow art film enthusiast, abstract portrait painter and writer Max Crosley. He had recently transplanted his family from Ft. Wayne, Indiana. The bespectacled Max, who habitually wore a striking ensemble of used corduroy everything, and sported a pair of robust mutton chops, was living with his blonde ash-haired wife Ruth and her nine year old son Mark in the well-hidden coastal colony of Bolinas. Twelve years my senior, Max (and Ruth before him) had come up through the jazzy be-bop abstract expressionist world of the early 1950s. Ruth, who at one time had her studio directly beneath that of artist Willem DeKooning, was a talented painter in her own right, and a venerable expert with a charcoal pencil. Max, aside from enjoying his substance of choice, "Next to Whatever," possessed an addictively wild sense of humor attached to a prolific knowledge of art and literature. We quickly became best new friends.

With Wendy and Ruth in tow, Max and I would go to the Surf, the Powell, and the Canyon to watch an astonishing array of rarely seen films. An abbreviated list of these films would include: *A Dream of Wild Horses*, *Flaming Creatures*, *The Zaragossa Manuscript*, *Finnegans Wake*, Cocteau's *Blood of the Poet*, Genet's (silent) *Chant of Love*, Bunuel's *Exterminating Angel*, Jodorowsky's *El Topo*, Fellini's *8 $^1/_2$* and *Persona* by the master of B&W, Ingmar Bergman. Haunting the Cedar Alley Cafe & Cinema off Polk Street, Max and I read our poetry for popcorn change and absorbed underbelly gems such as Kenneth Anger's *Fireworks*, *Inauguration of the Pleasure Dome*, *The Bed* by local poet James Broughton, and the kaleidoscopic imagery of fellow Bolinas-ite, Ben Van Meter. Max and I even sat through eleven hours worth of Andy Warhol's interminable **** film, which in its entirety runs for twenty-four hours. Our film appetites became insatiable, and soon Max and I, both wanting to make a more poetic brand of three-minute celluloid, left Carl's comedic/porn group to branch out on our own. We bought a case or more of negative print stock at an army surplus store and borrowed a 16mm Bolex camera with a tripod. Max began focusing his cinematic eye on close-ups of early morning Bolinas surf, sand and fog, while I turned my superimposing lens and negative stock upwards, to the thin slices of urban sky irregularly notched between the buildings and alley ways of Chinatown. Splicing the collective images together at random, we called our six to twelve-minute film blurts, *The Black and Whites of our Eyes*.

About this time, my friend Richie Furay and his band Buffalo Springfield came up from Los Angeles to play at the Avalon Ballroom. They were on the bill alongside folk singer Richie Havens and The Muddy Waters Blues Band. During the Buffalo set Muddy Waters, Richie Havens, who I knew from The Golden Bear daze in Huntington Beach, and I got to talking about independent films. He said he had an idea that I might like to write up as a screen synopsis.

Richie's idea involved a series of sumptuous parties, given for groupings of unknowing actor/members of each of the astrological signs. The parties were to be designed, he said, with the appropriate colors, room accommodation and party favors most closely associated with each particular sign. From behind two-way mirrors and with hidden microphones the festivities would be filmed and recorded. After editing the footage and tape, the finished product he said, was to be preceded on screen by the accumulating astro-sign information with a superimposed constellation representing the guinea pigs being filmed – fade in fade out. Richie wanted to know what would happen under those circumstances, so Max and I set to work until we had a reasonable facsimile of a film synopsis, or at least our idea of same. I mailed the draft to Richie in New York for approval and he was delighted, suggesting I take it down to Hollywood to look for backing. I conferred with Del about my impending adventure and he gave me a few "secret phone numbers" that he said might come in handy, and I headed for Hollywood. One number in particular which Del had marked "Call this one first!" turned out to be the private line of a notorious drug dealer, and after congenially inviting me over to sample his hospitality and to receive the Del Close update, he generously filled my pockets from his cache of psychotropic everything with all that I might need for my rather naive attack on Tinselville – "Try some of this!" my gregarious host kept repeating.

I stayed in the $6-a-day motel that was later used as the cover shot for an album by the rock group Spirit. In the photo you can see the phone booth at the foot of the motel stairs where I toiled away with my stack of Mercury head dimes, calling anyone and everyone who might invite me a step closer to the inner sanctums of film production. I really was green to this set but over the next week I managed to inch my way forward, convincing a number of types including comedian Tommy Smothers to read our synopsis. Most of the types wanted me to "add lots of SEX! to the script," but Smothers said he was "working on a computerized astrology project with Marshall McLuhan" (author of *The Medium is the Massage*). T.S. seemed genuinely interested in Richie's party concept, complimented Max and I on our ideas for the film, and asked me to send him a more detailed script, which I did. But after numerous phone calls where I was placed on terminal hold, I was informed by an anonymous Smother's Brothers' droid that "Tommy is no longer interested in your little astro-party film," and that as they say in the business was that.

Three years later, in London, as I was riding a red double-decked bus up Kensington High Street I noticed Richie walking along the sidewalk in the opposite direction – he's hard to miss. I jumped off the bus, caught up to him and, without breaking stride, he looked over at me as if we had never been apart and asked, "So what ever happened to that film script?" We had a great laugh over my doings in Los Angeles and enjoyed the afternoon together before he left for New York. Richie Havens is unquestionably one of the most knowledgeable and among the gentlest human beings I have ever had the pleasure of knowing.

Back in San Francisco I was beginning to realize that "real film making" was going to be an expensive if not equally frustrating vocation, so Max and I went back to the drawing boards. I went from job to job within the local film community, having left the microfilm business to develop more artistic celluloid for Palmer Films. Palmer's optical department was where the original Kinney camera was designed for news room work, and old man Palmer, though not among my favorite individuals, was highly revered by the major Hollywood studios as an optical effects innovator. After I was fired by old man Palmer himself (for being an active artist vs. a company drone), I went to work for Multichrome Labs, where they still had 3-D cameras on their shelves and continued to operate with the original wooden vats they used to develop film for Republic Pictures. At Multichrome I was the new guy among a time-tested crew of old school cinematics. I worked in the darkroom all day with an archaic printing device as a "special effects" man, super-double exposing footage. That is until Herb, the old boy owner of the cliquish lab came in to the break room one day and announced for all to hear, "Hammond, I don't think you're going to cut the mustard."

Following this lovely recommendation, I got out of the motion picture business altogether and went to work on the basement crew at Brook's Camera store on Kearny Street. At the time, Brooks was the most complete camera supply store in the nation, and many top photographers of the day such as doily-hatted Imogen Cunningham, then in her eighties, and Jim Marshall, one of rock's premier photographers, bought their supplies there. Even the F.B.I shopped at Brook's.

Artistically I was moving away from films and back to writing, via the "PoetUnity" sets that I was hosting in our newly rented railroad flat on Duboce Street. It was an open reading without critique, for writers only, and over time the Tuesday meetings drew quite a mix, including Joe Buttone, Martin Mosco, Richard Brautigan, Liam O'Gallagher, and even Gregory Corso stopped by once in a while to hit everyone up for cash. Liam O'Gallagher, a talented, innovative writer and close comtemporary of author Aldous Huxley, became an especially good friend, who has over the course of my life played a most generous role through his encouragement of my work and by introductions to other, more accomplished artists. Those he has introduced me to include painters Robert LaVigne and Muldoon Elder, writer Claude Pelieu and his partner Mary Beach (whose mother published James Joyce and invented the modern brassiere), San Francisco Earthquake publisher Jan Herman, *Grrarh!* poet Michael McClure, Robert Creeley and his lovely wife Bobby (whose visual work resembled my own at the time) and the angelic Greek surrealist/ avant-philosopher, Nanos Valaoritis.

Bohemian Rhapsody

Aware of my growing interest in all things Mayan, Liam suggested I visit his friend "Hube the Cube" Leslie, who, as Liam explained, possessed some rare prints taken from the Mayan temples at Bonampak. Located deep within the jungles of the Yucatan Peninsula, Mayan priests used these Pre-Columbian venues for original calendar research and to perform intentionally terrifying Permutation Rituals which helped to keep the uninitiated Mayan population submissively working in the maize patch. Hubert sold the *San Francisco Chronicle* from a worn yellow kiosk in North Beach at the corner of Columbus and Broadway, and lived among the infamous and never-to-be knowns at the Swiss American Hotel. This establishment was publicized a few months previously when comedian Lenny Bruce fell from a second story window during a drug-induced accident that left him with a few broken bones. This inadvertent stunt was memorialized by singer Grace Slick, then with The Great Society, in her well-composed song "Father Bruce."

Entering the labyrinthian flop house I was immediately hit between the nostrils with the unmistakable aroma of Toluene – the brain-frying ingredient in model airplane glue. I signed the coffee-stained register, and the squinty-faced Mongol desk clerk led me through a maze of grim-encrusted hallways to Hubert's room. Once alone, I explained through the door who I was and who had sent me, whereupon "Hube the Cube" began unlocking the many latches and bolts he used to "keep the riffraff out." Hubert was then in his late fifties, wore his long stringy hair tucked under a beret, and his bearded face simply beamed with original beatitude. His room was sparsely furnished with a more than rusty sink and few sticks of odd-ended furniture surrounding an old wrought-iron bed frame, where amid his tangled mass of dirty sheets lay a well-worn copy of Rene Dumal's *Mount Analog*. The floor of his habitat was strewn with strategically placed newspapers to accommodate the persistent droppings from his pet parrot, perched at the time on the back of the room's only chair.

Paradoxically, the equally encrusted walls of Hubert's tiny pad were covered with museum quality Tankhas, hand-painted by Tibetan Lamas! "What's the bird's name?" I asked. Hubert replied that it didn't really have a name but that he called it "ShitHead" or "FuckFace" when needed. "Hey, FuckFace, say hello to Hammond." With this introduction, the bird looked at me like I was dinner and began squawking and flapping about until Hubert threw an old shoe in its direction. Hube then went into his closet and pulled out the Bonampak material along with a shoe box full of strained weed. Thoroughly engrossed, the three of us spent the afternoon getting to know each other better, discussing Mayan insect rituals and getting high on his seemingly endless Pre-Columbian dope.

"Hube the Cube" was a jewel of a man. Honest to a fault, he was an intuitive-life curator bar none; innovative, wildly humorous, and exceedingly well-read. I would sit for hours listening to his East Coast escapades, where among his many oddball endeavors he helped film pioneers Len Lye and Harry Smith make hand-painted films. Crazed tales in and around the East Village in the early 1950s where he was a well-known speed freak who took to shooting "chicken speed" (an egg-laying chemical) when he couldn't score the human variety of artificial propellant. "Back in the daze," he would cackle behind the smile and fragrant smoke, as Hubert no longer tolerated the white powders of doom, preferring instead, his double espresso Romano laced with packets of ginseng. One of his most unusual stories involved an ovarian speed encounter with some of New York's Finest, where Hubert wound up becoming incarcerated in the lock-down ward of the dreaded Bellevue Psychiatric Facility. Over the next few weeks, and without his consent, Hubert received the treatments du jour: drug induced Sleep Therapy, Insulin Shock, Electroshock and painful Metrazol injections were applied in an attempt to calm his frail nerves. When these treatments failed to produce the desired result (whatever that was!) he was subjected to the Hydrotherapy. Hubert said that twice daily he was lowered into a king-sized ceramic tub filled with scalding water and then with just his head sticking out, he was "zipped into place with a thick canvas tub cover." After a time the attendants would lift Hube the Cube out of the bath, truss him up like The Mummy in tightly wrapped ice cold sheets, and then leave him bound to dry under the stark white noise of the observation room. The funny thing was, Hubert actually liked the iced sheet treatment! He said he "found them meditative" and refrained from telling the hospital staff, in fear that they would "stop the dunk and wrap for other therapies."

However, due to Hubert's firm inability to conform to hospital guidelines he was placed on a prefrontal lobotomy ward. At first strapped into his bed, Hube the Cube contemplated, as he put it, "the plus/minus quotients regarding cranial deflowerment." On one of his early morning trips to the toilet Hubert noticed one of the other lobotomates tinkering with the steel mesh on the locked bathroom windows. "Hey Buddy," Hube exclaimed, "If you ever get that window open let me know." A few nights later the guy woke Hubert, "Remember that window?" Hube the Cube was up in a flash and jumped to freedom, and without missing a beat hitchhiked (still in his hospital gown!) across the underbelly of the country until he finally resurfaced in North Beach, where he got the job selling newsprint at the corner of Columbus and Broadway.

Hubert never made much of it, but he was rather close early on to a number of then nascent Beat writers – Bob Kaufman, Jack Kerouac, Neal Cassady, Allen Ginsberg, Taylor Mead, Ray Bremser, Philip Lamantia and Gregory Corso, just to name a few. I was visiting with Hubert one day, getting high with him before making my way over to the Brazilian Embassy where I planned to stand in protest against their country's recent imprisonment of Julian Beck and Judith Malina of the nomadic Living Theater. As I was about to leave, Hubert said his "old pal Allen Ginsberg" was going to be there and suggested that I "say helloyou!" His unexpected introduction was a great honor for me, and I felt no reservations in approaching Ginsberg now that my credentials were in order, an important factor at the time when it came to Beat protocol.

When I arrived at the embassy Allen was already there, the local media shoving microphones into his well-known face.

The hairy poet looked me up and down as I came up to him and muttered, "Hubert says hello."

Ginsberg frowned and asked, "Hubert who?"

"Hubert Leslie," I replied.

With this Allen cracked a beatific smile and shouted out, "Hube the Cube?"

Just then a reporter asked him another silly question and before he answered, Allen handed me his well-fondled Tibetan dorje.

"Here," he said, "hold this for me will you?" and then turned to the reporter.

After a minute or two of holding the curious object an almost numbing energy surged through my arm, and my hand spasmed out in front of me like a humanoid dowser's wand! Ginsberg laughed, reached over and took the mysterious energy magnet from my hand.

"That's quite enough of that. Let's us go over to the American Express office and check the mail." He said

We sat for an hour or so in the Express, reading Allen's correspondence and chatting. Allen was quite friendly in a strictly non-sexual way, and after catching up on Hubert we exchanged on the spot poems and mailing addresses, giving me his in Cherry Valley, upstate New York. Regrettably I never got the chance to visit, though we began a periodic postcard correspondence and our intrepid paths would cross numerous times in cities around the world. Back in North Beach, Hubert was pleased with my accounting of Ginsberg Meet and fired up another one of his Pre-Columbian joints before launching into a pre-discovery discourse on the finer points of fiber optics (which had yet to be clearly invented!).

Sometime in the later 1970s, the fumes at the Swiss American ignited and the historic hotel burned itself down. Hubert simply moved around the corner to another flop, this one above a coin-operated striptease parlor. The hotel fire unfortunately destroyed much of Hubert's Mayan and Tibetan iconography, along with Baby Jane Holtzer's collection of antique razor blades. When I first visited his new room, Hubert was busy cleaning the soot from some Afghani carpets with images of Russian helicopters woven into their borders. One well-documented 'Hube-ism' is that he was once hired by Henri Lenoir, founder of Vesuvio's Cafe, to sit in the window seat and drink espresso so that when the tourists walked by they could exclaim, "Look Honey, there's a real Beatnik!" This was particularly funny in lieu of Hubert's maxim that "the only successful Beatniks were the ones that got away." Hubert and I remained close friends until his passing on May 27, 1986. I miss him beyond words and count myself lucky to have known him so well. One of my most privileged moments came one afternoon when he invited me to spend the day with him, sitting inside his faded yellow box to help him sell *The Chronicle*.

Closing The Draft

The dreaded military's reclassification attempt was about due, and in my case, their timing was impeccable. One year later, to the day, I received a call from my silver-toothed friend Alan in Los Angeles informing me that "The Letter" had arrived. I used Alan's house near MacArthur Park as my cut/out address to the Selective Service System, which had no idea that I was living in San Francisco. A few days before I was to be re-examined, I cropped my hair for hopefully the last time, dug out my fake spectacles and flew to Los Angeles, sans benzedrine tablets, to reunite with Alan and prepare for the test.

The day after landing at Alan's place an official "Peace March Against The War In Vietnam" marched en masse down Wilshire Blvd., shouting among other crescendos: "Hey, Hey L.B.J. How many kids did you kill today?" and ending the parade of protest in nearby MacArthur Park. First things first, Alan and I smoked a potent joint before wandering down to check out the disenchanted throng. Ho Chi Min's name was in the air as we sat down on a store front window ledge and I commented to Alan that although I empathized wholeheartedly with the protesters, I felt no incentive to join in their demonstrations. My resistance was an internal affair, and my personal fight was still with the government's policy of mandatory conscription. I felt that this Southeast Asian conflict of ours was patently illegal – a War of "hearts and minds" that I would at all cost resist participating in, and that the numerous problems of the Vietnamese governments were simply not my concern.

As we stood up to leave Alan and I glanced inside the store's picture window and discovered an unsettling tableau. In front of us, the center-piece for the stained arena was the blood-let carcass of a steer hung from a stainless hook, gently swinging over the random gore and left-over entrails in the butcher's back room. Alan and I stared into that crimson-stained mess for some time before slowly walking back to the house in silence.

The next morning I put on my fake glasses and Alan drove me to the forbidding Induction Center. I walked up to the desk sergeant who asked me my name. "Guthrie, Michael, H!" I replied sharply. Startled by my military spark, he asked me to spell my last name and I slipped into dyslexia. He couldn't locate my file and asked me to spell it again which I did. "G-U-T-H-R-E-I, Sir!" His mood souring, the sergeant located my document file and was about to order me what to do next, when Alan came in to the building wearing strands of Hippie love-beads and a multi-colored headband. Without a nod to me, Alan scattered Anti-War leaflets around the lobby and shouted out to no one in particular, "Repent ye Sinners Before Its Too Late!" I looked at the desk sergeant and said, "Somebody ought to shoot that Hippy scum bag!" He looked at me like I was an alien and ordered me upstairs to the wire basket room while he went to deal with Alan, who was loudly proclaiming his involvement with the Second Coming and asking if anybody wanted "Backstage Menus!"

Upstairs in my BVD's and socks, I clutched my documents and valuables in my perpetually incorrect hands, and entered the all too familiar maze of pale green corridors. I remembered my lines perfectly, and even without the benzedrine lift, it looked to be a 'deja' vu' exam. The Blood Pressure Check was the same as was the claustrophobic Hearing Test, the clear glass Vision Test, the untainted Urine Test and the Blood Test (yes, I purposefully hyperventilated and passed out again) were the same.

The colored lines painted on the floor and the stony amorphic faces ordering me to carry my documents in my right hand were all the same. Everything was the same. Everything that is, until I left the pale green, stinky psychiatrist's cubicle. I was sitting on a side-line bench waiting to have the level of my knee water checked by the osteopath – in fact, I was next in line. Suddenly the door to his office flew open and out barged an enormous black medic, just spitting with anger. He grabbed up my incorrectly held documents and those of the guy next to me and brusquely ordered, "You and you come with me. The rest of you go home and come back tomorrow!" Adrenaline panic set in as he led us down another pale green corridor into separate rooms.

The uncharted exam room with its pale green/red curtains, a little footstool on chrome wheels and the frightening concept of Chance Improvisation was not part of my thespian arsenal and I was beginning to wish I had brought along the benzedrine. Just then my "doctor" rolled into the room. He was at least ninety years old and needed an aluminum walker on wheels to get around. He wore thick coke-bottle glasses but he couldn't see – he had a set of double hearing aids but couldn't hear a word I said. Ignoring my pleas for transfer, he told me to take off my shoes and socks, after which he measured each of my legs from the knee to the ankle. At each point he put a mark with a black magic marker and then put my knees together. "Well, the lines meet," he intoned in a Mid-western drawl, and without so much as another drawl he rubber-stamped my orthopedic form with a blood red "Re-evaluate in 60 days." The doctor handed me my document folder and then rolled himself away without telling me where to go next.

I went straight to the nearest latrine, locked myself into one of the pale green stalls, and tried to calm down. Sitting on the toilet I remembered one of the Berrigan Brothers, who tore his pile of documents into shreds, flushed them down the toilet and then slid down a drainpipe in his underwear to escape further induction. I wanted to scream, "There will be no further evaluations!" at the top of my lungs but restrained myself and spread my documents out on the tiled floor in front of me.

Searching through the paper work I found a plain brown envelope containing some induction information I was relatively certain would not be scrutinized, inserted the offending sixty day orthopedic dictum and sealed the envelope. I then carefully arranged the remaining documents into an order that would hopefully lead the reader chronologically through my two exams, with one exception. I took the original osteopath's report from the previous year, changed the date as best I could and put it in with the rest of my current documents. Holding my breath in fear this time, I walked along the same single white line to the classification desk, although this time I didn't call the sergeant "Bob!" The iron-faced noncom meticulously read through my file, lingering for just a moment over my orthopedic evaluation before continuing on to the decidedly pro-deferment psychiatrist's report. My heart was about to implode when he finally checked some boxes, signed the folder in three places, tossed it into a wire basket and said, "Next!"

"When do I have to come back?" I asked.

He looked up at me with his cold pin-prick eyes and said: "Son, you don't ever have to come back."

Within hours I was back in the City, an officially deferred man.

The Intersection

Safely back in our Duboce Stret flat, my friend Liam O'Gallagher, author of *The Blue Planet Notebooks*, and his life partner Robert Rheem called one evening, inviting Wendy and me to go along with them to visit astrologer, Gavin Arthur, who was then living in a soon to be demolished Victorian on the southern edge of the City's Fillmore District. At the door we were greeted by a scruffy, somewhat hobbled middle-aged man who politely introduced himself as "Cappy, Gavin's main-servant." Cappy looked just like a biped Tasmanian Devil on LSD, but as it turned out, the wiry haired Cappy was a gentle soul, who indeed performed as the devoted Sancho Panza to Gavin's at times demanding Quixote persona. Born in 1901, Gavin (Chester Alan Arthur III) was the grandson of the 21st U.S. President, Chester A. Arthur, and stood in direct philosophic lineage to poet laureate Walt Whitman, having studied at length, and slept with Walt's protege, the late Edward Carpenter. Gavin called himself a "Whitmaniac," and a "High Priest of OM in the Order of Shasta." Among his many claims to the greater bohemian lore he was chosen to draw up an astrological chart and which thus determined the (cosmically appropriate) date for the first Human-Be-Ins, held in Golden Gate Park. During the 1950s, much like my friend "Hube the Cube," Gavin sold newspapers in San Francisco, only down on lower Market Street, where he exhibited an uncanny eye for the often-Beat and hidden genius lurking just below the humanoid surface. He also had a homoerotic propensity for "young nautical rough trade." It was this extra-curricular interest that brought Gavin to the attention of the noted Sexologist, Alfred Kinsey. Gavin said Kinsey was too frightened to actually go into the area's seedy proto-leather bars, so he used Gavin as his surrogate into the predominantly gay and kinkier sets around the City.

Gavin also worked for a time as a psychotherapist in San Quentin Prison where among his patients was one Neal Cassady, the frenetic hero of Kerouac's *On The Road*, serving a set-up stint for possession with intent to sell. Like everyone else who encountered "the fastest man alive," Gavin was fully enamored by Neal's intellect and profound sexual aura. Gavin would later publish the now (unfortunately) long out-of-print book *Circle of Sex*, covering the astrological indications for preferred sexual behaviors.

I spent many an evening with Gavin and Cappy, drinking cheap red wine from green gallon bottles, soaking up articulate knowledge and personal anecdotes from one of the heartbeats of astrological phenomena, reincarnation and early bohemian lore. Our friendship grew and Gavin gave me the distinct honor of performing his first marriage ritual for Wendy and me in the Shakespeare Garden of Golden Gate Park. With Gavin's spiritual blessing our marriage rite was attended by our well-dressed sets of seemingly bereaved parents and many of our closest friends, including Taxi Tommy, our pot dealer, but per Gavin's stricture, Cappy was forbidden to attend.

Following the reception Wendy and I, along with my best man and hometown friend Dennis (of Dennis and The Delmonics), went back to Gavin's aging Victorian, where he was going to give us his wedding gift: our astrological charts with Gavinized darshan. When we got to the house Gavin realized that he didn't have his door keys, so Dennis perilously climbed up to the third story window and managed to get inside. When he let us in downstairs we were not at all prepared for the multi-colored spray paint surrounding but not touching every object on the walls of every room in the house! Cappy had swirled the graffiti in protest of his ceremonial exclusion from our wedding and Gavin was livid. We eventually found the whimpering Cappy hidden under Gavin's bed, clutching something to his breast. He held out his hand to me, tears streaming down his face and said, "Here's my wedding present. It's a crystal tear from the chandelier used on the set of *Gone With The Wind*." Gavin finally calmed down, and commented that he actually had great tolerance for Cappy's shenanigans because they had been together "over many lifetimes of Bardic travel."

My dear friend Gavin Arthur left his body in 1972 at the physical age of 71. The lesson from him that I most enjoy came about one day as I was washing the dishes in his kitchen. I dropped a plate on the floor and it shattered. Gavin came in, looked at the mess and said, "Youngman, if you want to be a successful dishwasher, do it with the consciousness of someone doing dishes!"

The last time I saw Cappy was some ten years later as I was entering the main branch of the Santa Barbara post office. I heard a strange hiss come from one of the bushes near the door, and there squatted Cappy, dressed in rags with his ruddy hair all askew. He looked up forlornly and said, "Gavin's gone and dead; I don't know what to do." He looked so pitiful. I gave him all the money I had on me and told him to go back to San Francisco if he could. He thanked me for the cash and then happily skipped down Anacapa Street unseen by anyone but me – and perhaps Gavin!

Bolinas

Filled to the shouting point by the straight forty hour work week at Brooks Camera and artistically bored with the burgeoning counterculture, the City became claustrophobic and suffocating for Wendy and me, so on the weekends we took the Greyhound Bus to Bolinas to stay with Max and Ruth. Our new friends had lived at least two lifetimes before meeting up with us, and the saga of those drug- and job-worn days are evocatively described by Max in his unpublished novel, *The Ballad of Fagan Stone and Mary Carter*. A Midwestern tale of personal woe set in the state of Indiana circa 1958 and written under the influence of codeine-laced cough syrup, to which Max was thoroughly addicted at the time. Max and Ruth moved to Bolinas, following the trail blazed earlier by Ruth's former husband, Philo T. Farnsworth III, Philo is the son of Philo T. Farnsworth II, inventor of television, circa 1914. The profile of Philo's mother, Pim Farnsworth, was the first-ever televised image.

Philo came to Bolinas from New York following years of inventive (like his father, Philo was a genius), musically experimental (he once threw minimalist composer John Cage out of his studio), and much amphetamine-bolstered research (he had a 6 foot three Sudanese body guard named Freddy). Now, Philo was living the not quite drug-free vegan life in Bolinas with his second wife Diane and their ever-expanding brood of spiritually named children: Maya, Krishna and Baby Matthew. Philo's oldest son Mark lived with his mother, Ruth (now a Crosley), in a tiny two room bungalow overlooking the Pacific Ocean from the Bolinas Mesa, with Max and a lovable hound by the named of Poochie. The clapboard house sat specifically atop one of the lines defining the San Andreas Fault, for which Max would write a satirical ode entitled "Living the Fault." Philo's place was on the other side of the Mesa next to an old convent and overlooking the bird sanctuary and Bolinas lagoon. Here Philo worked relentlessly on the models and blueprints for his geodesic, though curved home for the present, the "Yantra House."

"If you extend twelve cones from any point in space you get a spherical orb. At the orb's outer edges there are twelve circles and each circle is separated by a tetrahedral space." (P.T.F. III. circa 1968) Philo discovered that by constructing (from foam core) a tetrahedron, gluing three of them together and then linking them all up, a spherical dodecahedron was formed. Philo's "Space Age Ball of Light (the 12 circles were filled by polarized lenses) is intended to house a modern family of four" (*SF Chronicle*, 1969) and was designed to be built "from the inside out." Resting atop a concrete cone, the prototype for Philo's vision took up just twelve cubic feet of land area. Dymaxion designer and chief geodesic theorist R. Buckminster Fuller personally complimented Philo on his take of Fuller's own straight line principles for geodesic structures.

The Farnsworths, the Crosleys and the Guthries became the best of friends, and these weekends represented some of the happiest days of our lives – living and breathing the creative moment in the salt-sweet air swirling atop the Bolinas mesa – delivering up our dreams, drugs, and polytonal songs of life-living now to the golden eternity's logbook.

Bolinas is a sleepy little hamlet nestled against the hidden shore of poet Lew Welch's "Spacific Ocean," twenty-eight miles north of San Francisco, and over the top of Mount Tamalpais. Actually finding Bolinas for those out of the loop was nearly impossible because the local residents repeatedly took down any and all markers leading into Bolinas to protect their jealously guarded anonymity – you either knew the way or you took the bus. Nowadays the bus service has stopped running, and even the locals have a hard time finding Bolinas.

Downtown consisted of two shops and a bar, called Scowly's, Snarly's, and Smiley's respectively, the Bolinas General Store, a minuscule post office, and a one horse gas pump. A very few rickety old boats bobbed eternally in the inlet harbor – seagulls and stray dogs roamed Wharf Road, and most everyone lived on the Mesa in rustic shacks and half-constructed homes hidden among the eucalyptus groves overlooking the ocean's expanse to the west and protected bird sanctuary with its quiet lagoon to the southeast.

Max and I would stay up late into the night getting higher, reading, recording, and over-dubbing our writings with multiple playback under the influence of William Burroughs, Bill Evans, Charles Mingus and all the cannaboid products we could find. When these enhancements weren't available, Max would simply bring out a bottle of his codeine-laced syrup to treat our nagging minds. Wendy and Ruth on the other hand would nap, read, sew, bake treats and take Mark and Poochie for long walks on the beach.

Our intrepid literary explorations led Max and me into the cross-over realm of "Happenings." We called them "Event Rituals," and began absorbing the documented works of earlier event-blazing artists such as Allen Kaprow, Claes Oldenberg, Jim Dine, and Red Grooms, all from the New York scene; along with Wolf Vostel from Germany, and the reclusive Swedish artist, bengt af Klintberg. In the process we met a group of woodshedding Jazz musicians, also living on the Mesa, who collectively referred to themselves as The FreeArts Workshop. We got together regularly to jam and mix up our WordSkramblings with the band's FreeArt sound. Their music was (for the time) a unique blend of original composition and jazz standard medleys played around a creatively structured, though to the uneducated ear, chaotic set of improvisations which formed the basic vocabulary of ideas for us to work around. The resulting tone poems came from the eclectic group's arsenal of bar room pianos, flutes, contrabass, alto-tenor sax, vibraphone, trombone, clarinet, trap set and percussionist's everything referred to as "The Eternal Machine." Spread over two picnic tables, the spontaneous machine harbored a sonic obscura produced by ten penny nails, pocket combs, serving spoons, baby doll squawkers, castanets, red rubber enema bags, Tibetan gongs, Japanese chimes, noise-making wind-up toys and a variety of woodwind reeds attached to industrial grade garden hoses.

Max, who always carried at least one portable tape recorder in his taped together briefcase, would record everything, and after the session he and I would repair to the bungalow to overdub the tapes with further lip-splice and tuck manipulations. Ever the connection to non-Ripley's esoterica and its unusual by-products, Max was always on the look-out for the odd-ball groupus artisticus. One day he took me over to nearby Point Reyes where he had located a group of "tree people" – a truly odd-looking collective of loin-clad, long-haired families with a bevy of naked children of multiple origin. They all had permanent grins on their faces and lived in a series of tree houses amid a grove of eucalyptus near the Point Reyes lighthouse. As a group they practiced what they called, "Self-discoverering Tree-atric Yoga and Dance Meditations." I thought it was all very weird but Max insisted that along with the FreeArts Workshop, we invite "the tree dancers" to help us stage our first Event Ritual: "Art, Ancestrical, Xanadude, AsIsOrIsn't."

I convinced the unknowing pastor of an old church near North Beach to agree to our five weekend run of shows, which we dedicated to the expression of all Art Forms, and to preserve the ritual aspect of our production, we served up a home cooked meal to the audience after every show. Our event's title was a splay on words influenced by the 1936 study of James Joyce's pre-Finnegans Wake, *Anna Livia Pleurable* subtitled: *Our Exagimination Round His Factification For Incamination of a Work In Progress*. Without description, this wildly minor success led Max and me along with our FreeArts friends to write and perform other Event Rituals within the hallowed walls of the old church, which we renamed *Intersection For The Arts*. The upstairs portion of our newly christened venue was used by the gifted composer Bill Mathieu (currently known as Allaudin Mathieu) as a rehearsal space for his spirit-vocal ensemble *The Ghost Opera*.

Our events included a participatory homage to the late collagist and Mertzbau constructionist, Kurt Schwitters, titled You, Ye, You, Your, I, Your, You,

My, We?" after a Dada poem written by the German artist, and another honoring "All Poets" – an interminable piece of work Max and I chaotically dubbed: "Ananthologically Historic Poem." For this 'epic today', we worked individually at the library, combing through and sampling lines and words from the great poetics of the past, beginning with the *Egyptian Book of the Dead* and continuing through time to Bob Dylan. Max and I then chronologically combined our collected past to present, present to past versions into one work, which we intended to read on stage, by randomly interchanging the stanzas of the newly constructed poetics. It took us months to compile, and nearly four hours to read, yet absolutely no one came to this historic event except our wives, Ruth and Wendy, who grudgingly sat through the laborious reading as our audience.

Among others, we involved the well-known yoga instructor Walt Baptiste and his lovely belly-dancing wife Magana in our activities as well as the poet/actor Jack Tiebau, inner-space composer Jeff Beach (son of publisher Mary Beach), and numerous Bolinas-ites in our freely-formed doings. Max focused on the musical-dance prop end of things and I started writing Event Rituals for our friends – for example: "Bamboo for Martin Mosco."

This piece (based on an idea of Martin's) involved dense patches of potted bamboo placed on stage with a performer and a microphone hidden inside. Amid the theater's audience were placed a variety of bamboo bird cages filled with "borrowed song birds" trapped inside. A number of rotating fans were suspended above the stage and seating to provide air current, and as the tall bamboo gently amplified about and the borrowed birds sang, the hidden performers uttered tiny (amplified) sounds. And there was, "The Great White Leader" (for Max Crosley). We charged a two-dollar entrance fee to watch 1,000 feet (300 minutes) of opaque white film leader, all spliced, scratched, smeared on and fiddled with by me. The FreeArts Workshop provided a live sound track for the Event and at the conclusion of the film, or whenever anyone left the theater, they met Max standing at the door with a sign around his neck that read: "Hi I'm Max Crosley." He thanked them for coming and gave each them back a dollar bill as they left.

I had a penchant for buying old tape recorders, especially ones that played their tape backward or recorded onto rolls of wire instead of tape. I had about 15 of these relics and placed them in a large circle around my studio (and later on stage at Intersection). I hooked them all up to a central microphone on/off switch, ran a long tape-loop Mobius strip through the tape heads, some on playback and others set to record, with a last recorder to capture the results. As the spools turned I would stand in the middle of my circle and shout out a couple of words, such as "God?" or "Dog!" and then lay out as the studio filled with the repeating "BackForWord Text." Eventually a consistent blur of Just Intonation, in the school of composer La Monte Young, would be all the issued from the speakers.

A welcome addition to our ritual doings was the arrival of piano player and Jazz composer Eddy Sears, who was a major part of Max and Ruth's extended family of underbelly artists in the Mid-west. Eddy was a musical prodigy who studied composition at the Berkeley School of Music on a scholarship provided by big-band leader Stan Kenton, with whom he toured for a season. After which, he married a registered nurse named Jennifer (how better to acquire the medicines Eddy habitually abused?), and having tired of the Mid-west set, moved the two of them and his multi-tiered piano act to Bolinas. Eddy was a handsome man in the vein of the late actor Sal Mineo, and an impresario at the keyboards, both electric and acoustic. He would rework his polytonal compositions using numerous tape decks, proto-phaser gadgets of his own design and delayed tape loops (preceding bandleaders Don Ellis and Miles Davis), in much the same manner that Max and I composed, read, and then reassembled our own recorded tracks.

As Max and I were influenced by writers Joyce, Beckett, Burroughs, Hemingway and Kerouac; Eddy was influenced by avant-composers such as Joseph Jarman, Rosco Mitchell, Bill Evans, Cecil Taylor, Archie Shepp and Charles Mingus. With improvisational elan, Eddy could play atop, under, over, around the corner and behind our improvisational phrasings in a free flowing swarm of original ideas. Max might recite the word "blue" and Eddy would play "Aquamarine Blue!" I might toss out a "my-oxford shoes," and Eddy would come on like an English pedestrian. Exclaim Coltrane! Monk! or whisper Miles, and Eddy would be all over their melodies, altered poignantly by his own open figured approach to cinematic dissolve and juxtaposition of genre. One of our most outstanding practice sessions involved a long chain of extension chords running from Max's bungalow down the face of the Mesa cliff to the shore, where the three of us blew wildly with sea spume, Farfisa piano, wordwrithing and tape-playing on the sand. Sadly, Max and I, along with the Jazz community in general, would lose another extraordinary player to the same self-destructive tendencies ending in wasteful suicide that has robbed the world of so many talented musicians. Eddy was a wonderful friend and gifted man of hip letters and credentials, who walked the walk, and talked the talk but who didn't always think the think.

For example, one evening Max, Eddy and I were working in Max's outdoor studio on an ethereal composition Eddy called "Heaven and The Stars" – a tribute to Philo's father, written as a suite of songs for twenty pre-recorded pianos and text manipulations. That night we were recording to the live radio reports from the first landing on the moon. Eddy wanted beer so he got ten dollars from Jennifer and went off to Smiley's. An hour later Eddy came back high, six pack in hand, but he couldn't find the change for Jennifer, who was now calling Eddy "a juiced-up liar!" He shuffled a swift denial that he must have lost the change, and this sent Jennifer into a wife-blown frenzy. Eddy soared into spontaneous combustion, picked up the pot of boiling camomile tea from the camp stove and threw it at Jennifer! The tea scalded her arms badly, and in a panic, Ruth and Wendy rushed her to the Bolinas medic for burn treatment. Ten minutes later Eddy found the change in his overcoat pocket.

The three of us, along with the FreeArts Workshop forged ahead at The Intersection, with Event Rituals such as "Not Another Thing Doing", "Warm Moments," "Pro-Laxification," and "Don't Get Foiled Again!," a participatory Ritual for which we used over a mile of semi-toxic tin foil. One of my solo Events ("Pig-Nailleon") got us thrown out of the church for quite a while. During the "Abstract Expressionist Ritual," I mixed a gallon of sow's blood into my PigMents and then painted a large canvas, using a number of freshly butchered pig's feet for brushes. When the work was complete, I nailed the collection of colored feet to the canvas, and the event was over. (Almost!) Somehow, unbeknownst to me, my PigArt was left inside the church, and a few days later I got a call from the irate pastor, who demanded to know what "the ungodly smell" was. I went over to Intersection, where the chapel air was now permeated with the odor of rotting pig meat. I tried to explain what had happened but the irate reverend went over his top, calling me "a demented artist with distinctly Pagan tendencies," and announced that I was summarily "banned" (albeit temporarily) from my own theater.

Max and I went on to other venues such as the basement of Moe's Bookstore (a truly alter-radical hangout), and Pacifica Foundation radio station KPFK in Berkeley, where our briefly alive and uncensored material managed to get the program director, Charles Amirkhanian, into all sorts of hot water. Our hour-long program, *TalksBack* came on the air just before (now Senator, then radical), Tom Hayden's talk show on Friday nights. Max and I were thrown off the air for "obscene language" (Max loved to quote Burroughs' *Naked Lunch*, and Henry Miller's *Opus Pistorum*), and for refusing to tape our programs so that they could be screened by the station management.

For lack of a venue we went back to negative film making, and for our next three to six minute epic du jour, *Dreams The Dreamer* I got a friend of mine from North Beach to take on the dual roles of the Grandfather and The

Wizard. Hank was a wizened elder Beat in his late sixties, with a Gandalf beard and infinitely-blue eyes who lived in a flop on upper Grant Avenue. As a rule, Hank wore a straw boater that had real owl wings sprouting out of the hat band, and some will remember him as the mystic proprietor of a once upon a time incense & button shop on Columbus Avenue called: In Search of a Ripe Persimmon.

Hank and I would sit around in his tiny pad, which was piled high with assorted used clothing and costumes as my well-spoken friend was something of a Scarecrow when it came to fashion. Always wearing several pairs of pants with unmatched combinations of shirts, socks, sweaters and boa scarves regard-less of the season, one day Hank invited me to come along with him to "visit a friend" who had just arrived in the City. On the way, Hank began telling me how he hadn't always been a vagabond. In fact, he had been a physicist! He explained all of this to me, he said, because "we were going to the Palace of Fine Arts to meet with Dr. Frank Oppenheimer," brother to Dr. J. Robert Oppen-heimer, with whom Frank had worked on the development of the hydrogen bomb. Hank said he and "Oppie" were old friends, and that Oppie was going to "create the first Museum for the Senses" in the classically-domed structure, built in 1915 for the Panama Pacific International Exposition.

We arrived to find the palace as echoic and cavernous as a recycled blimp hanger, with the exception of Dr. Oppenheimer's bullet-shaped aluminum house trailer. "Hey Oppie!" echoed Hank, and from out the trailer appeared a balding man in a rumpled brown suit, swigging yellow elixir from a Mason jar. "Hey Hankie!" replied Dr. Oppenheimer, who then handed Hank the Mason jar. "Here try some of this!" said Oppie with enthusiasm. "Hankie" tipped it back, introduced me, and then handed the mysterious Mason jar back to Oppenheimer who quickly stuck it in his jacket pocket. I later learned from "Hankie" that the yellow elixir was in fact aged absinthe – Oh Great Spirits of Missed Opportunity! As we wandered around the vast empty space of the future exhibition hall, Hank began telling his friend about our negative films and Ritual Events. He further suggested that the good doctor might like to have us perform in his proposed "Sense Museum," or as Dr. Oppenheimer put it: "a Museum of Science, Art and Human Perception". Thus was born the Ritual version of Eddy's memorial to Philo's father, *Heaven and the Stars* – which we and The FreeArts Workshop performed for the opening of the now well established Exploratorium.

Dr. Oppenheimer loved our presentation and was so enamored by our close ties to the Farnsworth family that he asked us to put on another Event for the opening of the museum's soon to be constructed theater. His invitation led

Max and I to produce what would in years hence come to be known as The San Francisco International Video Festival. For our "VideoVent" (The Philo T. Farnsworth II Memorial Video Festival), we brought in Philo's mother Pim Farnsworth, who arrived from Salt Lake City with the original cathode ray tubes invented by her husband while living in a former pasta factory near The Embarcadero in 1914. We also invited The Ant Farm Collective of "Cadillac Ranch" fame and other artists to participate.

After words: Unconsciously following each other in 1992, my compatriots Max Crosley (director/composer of the film made for Lawrence Ferlinghetti's poem, *Assassination Raga*), and Philo T. Farnsworth III (inventor/designer of "Yantra House" and one of the first prototypes for the ultra-sonic toothbrush) sadly and quite unexpectedly passed away in their sleep from consumptions. Ruth Crosley still lives in Bolinas with her grown son Mark Farnsworth, (Poochie died of old age), and we remain the best of friends.

Carmen Mcrae In The Rain

Back in San Francisco, I was just ahead of an impending storm front, sidewalk down on the lower end of Polk Street, making for the warmth of our third floor walk-up, when a torn scrap of paper scotch taped inside the window of a dingy little bar caught my attention. Curious, I walked over to read the note. The joint was completely dark inside and pad-locked tight, but the childish pencil scrawl read: "10 p.m.– Carmen McRae." I laughed as rain began to fall, thinking how improbable a performance that would be, and made for home. But I couldn't get Carmen's voice out of my head. The City was then in its psychodramic era du Trips Festival, and though I enjoyed the ballrooms and their condiments as much as the next person, I took a more personal interest in the sets happening in clubs such as the Jazz Workshop in North Beach and the Both/And in the Fillmore District. Free Jazz was beginning to come around, and my focus at the time was on musicians such as Thelonious Monk, Sun Ra, Ornette Coleman, Bill Evans and John Coltrane.

In order to get up with this kind of music, and that of The FreeArts Workshop, I had spent a considerable amount of time (via Max's extensive library of rare LPs) listening to the work of earlier players – Coleman Hawkins, Lester Young, Charlie Parker, Art Tatum, and to the incomparable big band sound of the Benny Carter, Charlie Barnett, and Count Basie Orchestras. It was during this background education that I first heard the uniquely vibrant voice of Carmen McRae, the younger contemporary and eventual confidant to the great Billie Holiday, who recorded one of Carmen's earliest compositions,

"Dream of Life." Hence my reservation that the formidable singer would be performing in a nasty little dive on Polk Street at 10 p.m. on a wet Wednesday night. As the evening progressed throughout one of the worst storms in memory, I kept thinking about Carmen McRae, played Billie Holiday albums and, without any affirmative results, called a couple of jazz clubs in inquiry. At nine o'clock I gave in, still doubting that the seedy little tavern would even be open for business, put on a sport coat under ten pounds of rain gear and made my way back to Polk Street.

To my surprise, the missive had been removed and in its place a small neon blinked "Open." After depositing my slicker at the door, I let my eyes adjust to the bar's campy interior. I felt soggy and a little out of place when the overtly gay bartender swooned by my table for my drink order. I just couldn't bring myself to ask him if there was a cover charge – the unremarkable bar didn't have a stage or a piano. I brightened a bit when four or five other patrons, including a black couple, filled up the remaining tables. Just before ten o'clock, as I sat nursing my whiskey and doubt, the flamboyant bartender rolled out an old upright from behind a heavy curtain and returned to his perch at the bar. What little light there was dimmed, and without prelude beyond saying, "Good evening, everybody," Carmen McRae herself sat down at the keyboard. She sang one glorious standard after another for a good forty-five minutes to a completely silent (if not stunned) audience of a dozen or so very lucky people.

During a casual break Ms. McRae commented that twenty years before, the bar had been a great after-hours hangout for jazz players in transit. She and the owner had remained friends, and whenever she stopped in the City, she said she liked "to fall in, relatively unannounced, and sing for a while." Carmen went on for another intimate thirty minutes, mesmerizing the tiny house with her classic interpretations of Billie Holiday songs, including the rarely performed "Don't Explain." Following our applause, she quite unexpectedly closed her impromptu set with an amazing piano skat take on Charlie Parker's version of Ray Noble's composition, "Cherokee."

Carmen thanked us for listening (!) and joined some friends at one of the tables. The bartender rolled the piano back behind the curtain and, except for her anomalous presence, the bar returned to its unremarkable condition. Following a night-cap I gathered up my rain gear and repaired to the nearby Cedar Alley coffee house for a double espresso to guide me home. When I ventured out again, the storm was at its most furious, and I stopped to catch my breath under an awning next door to the bar where Carmen had performed. Just then, a door opened behind me, and out walked Carmen McRae! She stood there a moment taking in the torrential downpour, and I addressed her with as much courage and decorum as I could muster. "Excuse me, Ms. McRae, I was here earlier this evening and thoroughly enjoyed your performance, but, really, you shouldn't be out here by yourself on a night like this!" I then innocently offered to escort her to wherever she was going. She smiled a smile I will never forget, and as her cab pulled to the curb, she said to me with all sincerity: "Young man, you are a gentleman – if I was just a few years younger and didn't already have plans, I would take you up on that offer." As she got into the back seat, she paused for just a moment – her indelible eyes took me inside so tenderly, and she waved me good-bye from the rear window. Truly flattered, I stood there forever, actively blushing in a precipitant wind as the image of Carmen McRae's unlikely presence in my life disappeared in the rain.

The Cost of Freedom

In the once-upon-a-time Haight Ashbury District, what had been no longer was, and what might have been never happened. Heroin, crystal meth and paranoia were now the drugs of choice, and a parasitic breed of psychedelic doggerel ran the area's honeycomb streets. "The Hashbury" was originally (by bohemian standards) a well-kept experience, bordered by trees and city parks on three sides. Her lanes were lined with a variety of historic architecture, colorful lofts, Victorian railroad flats and turn-of-the-century storefronts. Originally the area was occupied by first generation immigrants, African-American families, and then ever so briefly, by a brigade of post-Beat/proto-Diggers, musicians, dealers, poets and post-graduate chemists along with their families, fiends and fidos. They didn't call themselves much of anything but "Free."

Later, with the help of other cosmically adventurous and infinitely creative souls, an ever-expanding tribe of afterBeat-hippies inhabited the Haight environs just prior to the unfortunate release of singer Scott McKenzie's flowers in your hair song (written by Papa John Phillips). This was before the tidal waves of adolescent runaway and psychedelic scam artists invaded the surprisingly quiet neighborhood, and long before "No-Name Maddox" and his early zombette followers hit the set.

Just one long multicolored year after the lemming run had begun, the Haight Ashbury District and its left-over minions were no longer protected by creative naivete, openly-private chemical experimentation, peaceful communal life and internal discovery. A death knell was in the air and it was doubtful if the music, personal freedom or even the planet itself would survive. The scene in North Beach was changing as well. The Jazz Workshop and Little Joe's Cafe closed their noted doors, following a regrettable lead established earlier by Mike's Pool Hall. Tourists from the great wide everywhere appeared in unqualified schools and over-the-top topless bars were becoming ad infestus. There was a topless shoe shine parlor next to City Lights Bookstore, and to even things out, a well-known poet's daughter became one of the City's first XXXX hardcore porn stars.

The City air became unusually tense and favored last-Beat hangouts like Coffee and Confusion, the M.D.R. (Minimum Daily Requirement) and Morey's Delicatessen closed up shop. Poet-friendly biker Free Wheel'in Frank and local friend Chocolate George, along with the spirit of Digger Frodo were dying or on the nod. Gonzo journalist Hunter S. Thompson was selling tickets for the Mitchell Brothers at the cocaine-friendly O'Farrell Cinema, and Odd Bodkins cartoonist Dan O'Neill was living in the projection booth. The "Summer of Love" was undeniably over and Darkniks roamed the previously friendly alleyways running between Van Ness, Fisherman's Wharf and North Beach, where the idle remains of the earlier set seemed content to hang out anywhere – preferably nowhere, doing as little as possible. They were quite satisfied to toss back drinks at spots like Vesuvio's, writing predictable poetry – remembering, and then just as quickly forgetting why the City was an interesting scene. The local image banks were over-extended on their loans, and many of yesterday's players were now hanging out like bohemian supernumeraries holding someone else's spear. The message of the moment seemed to be that if you dressed up like Christopher Columbus, you just might discover "Amerika" – I wasn't convinced.

The Golden Gate was terminally oil slicked, and the once arboreally diverse Angel Island was now a toxic waste dump – Social Service was in a deplorable state and the City's homeless were becoming a nomadic nation unto themselves. Bay Area life was beginning to fail as factories leached death into the water table – hair-sprayists were wantonly spewing ozone depletion, and everything of consumer use, from ironing board covers to the glue on our postage stamps was bound together by Poly-Chlorinated by-products. Nothing was being used twice – television was, consciousness wasn't – our natural resources were threatening to eat us alive and the so-called "necessities of modern existence" were now being measured in thousand year half-lives. Further more, the indigenous government was illegally at war with most of Southeast Asia, and following the Century City police riot in Los Angeles during the Democratic Convention, it didn't take much to sense that a true Police State on the rise.

For my part, I was artistically stymied by the new set and spiritually disoriented by the multitude of sociopolitical and plainly civilian problems that the Pentagon, the CIA, the FBI and President Nixon were in many instances actually creating – and as seen in retrospect, blatantly lying about. A popular bumper sticker of the day read: "America, Love It Or Leave It!" and in disgust over the whole scene, Wendy and I resolved to follow the definitive advice into exodus. We set about saving every penny that came our way, and made plans to permanently relocate to Europe. The cost of freedom in America had become too expensive.

Max and I were now writing in a genre that left our audiences physically and theatrically threatened. An example would be "Cement Mixer" where participants were invited to a soon-to-be demolished basement room in North Beach. Following a five-minute period of behind the curtain silence, six portable cement mixers begin to churn ominously. After ten minutes of just-cement intonations, the curtain was opened by Max and me, and one by one we tipped the mixers to pour their contents of fast-drying liquid cement onto the floor (exit the artists!). The Ritual Event was complete only when everyone had left the room.

In order to expand our writhing and increasingly aggressive concepts, Max and I began absorbing hard to find scripts from the Theaters of Cruelty and the Absurd. We attended productions whenever possible, and as per usual, our tastes were decidedly off-beat: Samuel Beckett, Eugene Ionesco, Jerzy Grotowski from Poland and the transient anarchies of The Living Theater. Also, Pablo Picasso's "Desire Caught By the Tail," Fernando Arrable's "Groupuscule of My Heart," Luca Ronconi's "Orlando Furioso," and Artaud's mini-masterpiece, "Spurt of Blood." For character analysis I took 35mm photographs deep within the vice-riddled Tenderloin, and in the back alleys of the terminally alcoholic lower Mission District, using the morning's uremic light to capture the strangled lips of street sleepers, drooling a significant bile. Unshaven and ragged, I sat in a dead-end cafe at the corner of Leavenworth and Eddy, drinking miserable coffee, while surreptitiously taking my inner-urban snapshots of the rhinestone pimps, cruising like vultures in pitty-tink Cadillacs while their pitiful working girls ducked in and out of urine-soaked doorways to avoid the infrequent passing of an S.F.P.D. patrol wagon.

New and older faces began to appear in North Beach. The relentlessly on-the-make poet Gregory Corso seemed to be around more often, "Hobo" was still alive and sipping whiskey through a straw at Vesuvio's, poet Bob Kaufman spoke again after his lengthy self-imposed silence and poet Janice Blue, who wore a blue felt everything made her stunningly "Blue" entrance onto the crumbling set.

To help speed up our departure, I took a second job as the night attendant for Walker's Wonderful World of Wax museum at the far end of Fisherman's

Wharf. Visiting patrons were always breaking the fingers off Moses standing in awe of the burning bush, tipping Snow White's dwarves over or putting a baggie full of mint leaves into the hands of Jesus at the Last Supper. I found it gratifying when I gave my two weeks notice and the owner presented me with a letter of high recommendation regarding any future employment with "Wax Life."

During our final weeks in the City, Wendy and I ate most of our meals in Chinatown at our favorite noodle house, Sam Woo's. To get to a table at Sam's you had to go through the steaming kitchen filled with chattering Chinese noodle prep-ers, and up some minuscule stairs to one of the dining rooms above. The first floor was always full, so you automatically went up another flight to the room controlled by the honorable Edsel Fong. Edsel was unusually tall, weighed in at around three hundred pounds, and was notoriously rude to his customers. He would scream at prospective dinners to "Go on uppa stairs! I'ing gah-no woom!" even though there were obvious places to sit down. If a stranger actually sat down at one of his tables without permission, Edsel would come up to the table and demand, "Whayouwant? Whayouwant!" and if the person didn't answer immediately, Edsel would shout, "Come-on Come-on, I'ing gah awe-day!" If they dared to ask Edsel for a menu, he would roll his eyes, give them a dirty look and say, "I be right back," and then ignore them completely. If the intimidating waiter became truly impatient with a non-local or if he thought someone was staying at his table too long after their meal, Edsel would simply clear the table of plates and throw the befuddled customers out of the place without a bill! Wendy and I loved watching Edsel do his thing on unsuspecting tourists, although, truth be told, Edsel Fong was an extremely gentle and extraordinarily funny man. His serial rudeness was just a routine.

Wendy and I sold or gave away just about everything we owned, made a profitable dollars to yen switch on our savings before turning the bulk of our money into British pounds and prepared for the one way trip to London on a charter flight out of Oakland. As a precaution against instant rejection abroad, I wanted to obtain a status of journalist at large upon arrival in England, so, I hatched an editorial egg with the publisher of *Earth* magazine. With his covert co-operation, along with the generous recommendation of an acquaintance, I contacted *Time Out* magazine in London, and with the usual reservations regarding expatriot American artists, the fledgling magazine agreed in principle to have me loosely on board as a foreign writer in-residence.

The Wild West Festival

Just prior to our departure I got involved with a filmmaker acquaintance from Los Angeles by the name of Don Zavin. He was in the City to put together a crew to film the beginnings, middles, and ends of what was called *The Wild West Festival*. FM radio pioneer Tom Donahue, rock mogul Bill Graham, Ron Polte, and someone from the City's Music Council had the bright idea to put on, throughout the expanse of Golden Gate, what they were calling "The Event of the Century," that was to include every neo-Beat/post-Hippie band, poet and organization known to man. The festival idea was born out of necessity, and was to serve as the venue for The Rolling Stones who had offered to perform "a free concert" in the City.

As Zavin & Co we got the funds and the go-ahead to begin filming the many meetings and doings surrounding the proposed festival. We envisioned a cinema verite film with camera work a la Maysles Brothers (who oddly enough filmed the follow-up to the ill-fated *Wild West Festival*, calling it *Gimme Shelter*). We had the high hopes of using multiple screen projections as seen in the film *The Boston Strangler* starring actor Tony Curtis (also something the Maysles did with their film). Because of Don's connections in Hollywood we had excellent 16 mm and 35mm equipment and a carte blanc budget. If Max's and my, "Art, Ancestrical, Xanadude, AsIsOrIsn't" was our 'gesamkunstwerk' (a blending of music, plastic arts, dance and dialogue), the *Wild West Festival* was most certainly my "Last Waltz" with the counterculture before leaving the country.

The Wild West Festival never happened, and the following vignette describes the Town Hall meeting that took place in the Glide Memorial Sanctuary on Ellis Street. This telling and well-attended meeting of the minds was the deciding note that extinguished the last glimmer of hope surround the *Wild West* Fiasco. The cancellation of this historic event, aside from embarrassing the festival's organizers, gave the Rolling Stones and the remainder of the West Coast counterculture another kind of party. They called it *Altamont*.

The organizing committee and agents from the City Parks and Recreation Department, sat in their platform chairs before a balcony-filled SRO crowd of festive friends and associates. Members of the San Francisco Mime Troupe, Hari Krishna devotees in saffron robes, musicians, street winos, poets, dancers, the Diggers, and numerous egomorphic counter-faces were in attendance. I was in charge of a roving crew, which meant we could film anything we wanted. Right away, "Robert's Rules of Order" were tossed by the wayside. My crew and I started filming close-up to the spittle falling between the hairs of Tom Donahue's salt and pepper beard, and jumped full-frame on to the fire-breathing profile of Bagwan Bill Graham screaming into the face of a blissed out Krishna, whose spiritual eyes had rolled back into their charismatic sockets! The Casa de la Raza contingent stood up on their seats and demanded "more porta-potties!" The Black Panther in the house wondered aloud why the Black Community had been ignored, and The Diggers announced to all that the festival would be "Free!" The musicians in the house wanted more stage time and better time slots and the poets began reciting spontaneous verse – the Mime Band began playing "The International." Things were not going as planned, and The Wild West rapidly started to come unglued.

Zavin & Co ran around like ferrets, capturing the increasingly psychedelic and most certainly, omnidirectional chaos for posterity. At a certain point, The Diggers and the Mime Troupers took over the proceedings altogether. The befuddled organizers on stage, with the notable exception of Bagwan Bill, still screaming at everyone, were speechless. The room was expanding (quite literally!) as The Mime Band continued to explore their atonal Comedia del Arte song list. The Diggers began printing up and distributing colorful anti-*Wild West* Broadsides on the Glide Memorial Gestetner machine, and the Krishnas went into a full-blown vegetarian ecstasy. Amid the festive madness a disheveled Tom Donahue stood up to announce in his best radio voice that "the meeting, and *The Wild West Festival* is over!" The meeting however, partied on until we were finally ejected by the Glide Memorial Ushers. The only 'reel' product to come out of the *Wild West Festival* was the raw footage taken by Zavin and Co.

Note: Don Zavin suddenly and quite unexpectedly passed away in 1998, and his extensive archive of 60s material, including the exclusive Wild West footage, is being donated to the Oregon Historical Society by his widow, Ellen Thomas.

PART THREE – LONDON

Time Out in London

I made arrangements for us to stay temporarily with a childhood friend living in London's Chelsea District. Denise had moved to London a year prior from Berkeley, to be with her future husband Dermitt Cammell, brother to filmmaker Donald Cammell of *Performance* fame.

Denise and Dermitt were living in the family home along with Dermitt's mother and the family bulldog. It was agreed that Wendy and I could stay in the basement until we could "find proper lodgings." To make our transition a little softer I booked a room for our first nights in at a shady place called Gallagher's in Earl's Court – the emerging immigrant and all-night Wimpy stand sector of London. Just before departure Denise asked me if I would bring her "a canister of undeveloped film" that one of the Cammell's had left behind at a house in Berkeley, after which I blindly agreed to be her film courier and picked up the canister without question. We said our goodbyes to friends, and Wendy and I headed for the Oakland Airport. Baggage became a problem at the last minute because we were allowed just one hundred and twenty pounds between us, and along with our full weight of luggage I was hand-toting over thirty pounds of writings, notes and artistic obscura as carry-on. The flight Gestapo made me toss out much of the paperweight, which I simply stuck under my shirt, before letting me on the plane. Other than Denise we didn't really know anyone in England, but however naive our expectations were we were determined in our exodus from America, and as we lifted off in a twin engine prop jet towards Bangor, Maine, excitedly anticipating sixteen hours of stark polar flight, Wendy and I edged toward the unknown.

Upon arrival at Gatwick Airport I was immediately put under scrutiny by Customs. When asked how long I intended to stay in Great Britain, I told the official seven years. The agent of custom frowned and replied that Jesuit missionaries were only granted a six year visa and then escorted us into a side room, where we were joined by another agent. The pair inspected my passport and letters of transit several times before calling the offices of *Time Out* for some editorial verification. Still unsatisfied, they called the Bank of England to check out our financial position, after which they took my passport into custody. In return I was handed a mimeographed slip of paper with a rubber stamped signature, indicating that I was not in the country illegally. The agents insisted I give them a phone number in London where I could be reached, so I gave them the Dame Cammell's number, forgetting for the moment that one of her sons was considered to be a degenerate filmmaker by the British Board of Censors. They stamped Wendy's passport with a three-month tourist visa. They looked at me with cold expressions and said, "We'll be in touch."

When finally we reunited with Denise and Dermitt in Chelsea, we couldn't help but count our blessings, as my childhood friend enthusiastically unwrapped the "undeveloped film canister" full of powdery white nose emulsion that we had just unknowingly smuggled!

Once we had settled into the Cammell's' basement, Wendy and I began exploring the unincorporated borough of Chelsea during the just after days of Carnaby Street splendor. The well-documented clothing store Granny Takes A Trip and a few other lesser known shops selling hip accessories were still open, but a neon Americana was encroaching further down the King's Road with the opening of the pompous and fern-laden Great American Hamburger. The line to get in the alter-Wimpy eatery went around the block, but Wendy and I were repulsed by the glaring blemish on the area's historic charm.

One afternoon Dame Cammell invited us to tea and cucumber sandwiches, where she introduced us to her friend Patricia. Patricia was a tall woman then in her late 50s – prim and quite plain in appearance, much like a stereotypical school ma'm, but one who regaled us with semi-ribald yarns of war-torn postal service near Covent Garden. Patricia told us she lived in a large rooming house off Kensington High Street, just behind the Kensington Olympia Exhibition Hall. Having sussed us out she suggested, with the full encouragement of Dame Cammell, that if Wendy and I were willing to become her "cousins" she would rent us the attic studio in her building. This would reduce her own cost of living by twenty-eight pounds a week – not an unreasonable amount for

Left: Following the burning of photographs depicting my mother, this is the only existing photo of me actually touching both of my parents. Taken just before their divorce in Salinas, California, 1952.

Photo. author's collection

Right: Me on the ranch in Dinuba in my day outfit. *Photo: author's collection*

Bottom left: Cadet Guthrie in full dress uniform (Army Navy Academy). Note: The white cottage behind me is where Chip and I were relocated following the near riot with the Samonans from Oceanside.
Photo: author's collection

Bottom right: My Acid Test card.
Photo: author's collection

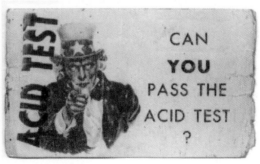

Top left: The Golden Bear in Huntington Beach, California (circa 1969) just before it was demolished, along with the rest of the 'Old Huntington Beach'.
Photo: Bill Anderson - Anderson Gallery Sunset Beach, California

Top right: Wendy, San Francisco, 1967. *Photo: Hammond Guthrie*

Right: Myself in San Francisco, circa 1967. *Photo: author's collection*

Bottom left: The Fifth Estate Coffeehouse in Hollywood founded by Albert and Delores Mitchell – and where Art Kunkin began the *Los Angeles Free Press*. *Photo: Delores Mitchell*

Bottom right: A warp of me done by Mike Hovancsek. I include it as an example of my typical condition in Hollywood and what LSD did to my help guide my future.

Above left: Del Close at Enrico's (1968).
Photo: Charna Halpern – The Del Close Estate (Chicago, Ill.)

Above right: Liam O'Gallager.
San Francisco. (1968).
Photo: Liam O'Gallagher

Left: Hubert "Hube the Cube" Leslie,
San Francisco (1968).
Photo: Hammond Guthrie

Bottom: A ticket stub from The Committee
Theater, SF. *Collection of the author*

Top left: Max Crosley, Bolinas, California. Drawing by Ruth Crosley.

Top right: Philo T. Farnsworth III with a model of his Yantra House.
Photo: estate of Philo T. Farnsworth III

Left: John "Hoppy" Hopkins, circa 1969.
Photo: Pamela Edwards, Studio C: Architecture

Below left: "Homage to Magritte".
Below right: "Tenement".

These early Letra-Set images on paper are typical of my artwork around the *Time Out* period in London, circa 1969. *Collection of artist.*

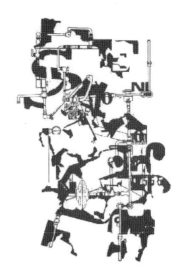

Above: Prince of Wales Crescent,
London (circa 1968) Arts Lab annex and
home of TVX.
*Photo: Pamela Edwards, Studio C:
Architecture*

Right: Cover of my first book, published
by the Bettiscome Press Dorset, 1971.
Author's collection

Bottom left: The author shortly after
arrival in London.
Photo: author's collection

Below right: The author in Lyme Regis
while living on the Allsop estate.
Photo: author's collection

URBAN
DISINTEGRATION...

(codex)

Hammond Guthrie

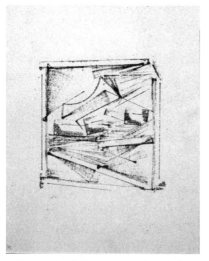

Left: "Apres Apres" typical of my work in Amsterdam. *Collection of the artist*

Below: The cover of my book *Belfast Insert* 1972 - Expanded Media Editions - Bonn, Germany. *Photo: author's collection*

Hammond Guthrie - Belfast Insert

Top: Jasper Grootveld through the lens of a video camera.
Photo: author's collection

Above: Self portrait in Amsterdam, circa 1972. It is ironic that I took this photo just hours after learning of Wendy's affair.
Photo: author's collection

Left: "Under Glass" typical of my oil painting in Amsterdam.
Collection of the artist

Top left: The area where the open air market was held each week in Asilah. Of special note is that the tree visible in the upper left is the same tree that author Alfred Chester had himself tied to. *Photo: Skip Stone, creator, Hip Guide to Morocco.*

Top right: Asilah – the shot is looking down the street where we lived. *Photo: Skip Stone, creator, Hip Guide to Morocco.*

Left: Wendy in Asilah.
Photo: author's collection

Bottom left: The Petite Soco in Tangier
Photo: Stacy Elko

Below: The author in an Amsterdam (Central Station) photo booth on my trip back to Amsterdam from Morocco.
Photo: author's collection

the time. Although Patricia was forbidden to actually take on lodgers, she was allowed to have relatives stay with her indefinitely. Sworn to secrecy, Wendy and I readily agreed to join her in Kensington as "cousins by marriage."

We thanked the Clan Cammell for their gracious hospitality, and moved in with "cousin Patricia" the next day. Our new fourth story attic digs were on a quiet, tree-lined, cobblestone street behind the formidable exhibition hall, and after depositing our luggage the three of us trooped down to meet Mr. Bompitts, the House Person. As we were about to exit the front door, Patricia instructed Wendy and me to look down to the basement stoop, to where an automobile side mirror was mounted on the wall. From our point of view it was momentarily filled by a fleeting pair of beady little eyes, peeping out from the lace-curtained window below our feet.

"That's Mr. Bompitts," she said. "He's a real nose-minder that one, so look for him to be spying about whenever you go in or out the building."

"Bompee," as I called him, was a troll-like curmudgeon who lived amid a dim-witted collection of overly-stuffed furniture with tatted doilies, newsprint portraits of the royal family on the walls and a multitude of porcelain knick-knacks barely visible through the gossamer and subterranean light. In a way he reminded me of Fagin from the Dickens novel, *Oliver Twist*.

Bompee was suspicious – encroning to Patricia, "Ann juss oo moight th' cousins by marrage bee related to?" Ever the improviser, Patricia spoke glowingly about the previously memorized Guthrie twig on her family tree, which of course included my "Uncle Angus Guthrie, who lived near the Scottish border on a profitable sheep farm!" Bompee bought Patricia's hilarious charade and hesitantly welcomed us in to the household. Dutifully, if not a bit proudly, he informed us that "everything en th' cooker en closet" was spurred into action by inserting large out-of-circulation pennies into the ancient brass-boxed meters positioned next to the kitchen sink and washroom tub. He said we could exchange our "contemporary coinage of the realm fer Victorian Alberts" with him. Bompee bid us "success and farewell," and the three of us retired to cousin Patricia's flat quietly howling with laughter. The attic studio with its spring bed, table and wicker chairs was suitably quaint, with a dormer window, and included an old easel which Patricia was willing to lend if I promised to be careful – as she was adamant that it had once belonged to the painter Augustus John. Wendy and I settled right into place.

Knowing of my predilection for cannaboid sustenance, Denise thoughtfully introduced me to her connection, Trevor. Underground credentials and such having been ascertained over the phone, I arrived at the door of his anonymous Chelsea flat. Once established a little more in-depth, Trevor pulled out a small gunnysack and ceremoniously poured the contents onto his Afghan carpeted floor. A dozen or so Nepalese temple balls the size of ostrich eggs spilled out.

"Ow's them fer rug bowlers?" Trevor spouted rhetorically.

He then wedged off an enormous crag from one of them and handed it to me. "Ere mate, this is fer oo en th' missis. Welcome tah London!" I was floored, not only by his unexpected generosity, but it was more hashish than I had ever seen. Arriving back at the attic with my prize, Wendy and I sat around trying to figure out how to smoke the stuff without benefit of a pipe. My innovative user's light suddenly clicked on, and we rolled up two balls of the potent goo about the size of large marbles and inserted them like suppositories into our rectums. Then we went out for a long, long walk down the High Street. I know this sounds like, and is, a rather privately medicinal method of absorption, but if you want to turn a common hashish-tinged afternoon into a mushrooming trek to Fandangoland, then this is your ticket to adventure.

A daze or three later I called for a meeting with Bickerton, my nebulous *Time Out* connection, and we arranged to meet at a public house rather than his office. This choice of location turned out to be a necessity for my alcoholic mentis connecti, and we didn't get to my quasi-functionary role until our third whiskey and ale. *Time Out* was founded by Keele Universtity student Tony Elliot after he wandered into the offices of *IT (International Times)* one day in 1968 with a notion to take over the "What's Happening" pages of the underground paper. Not realizing its importance and potential, *IT* editors, Graham Keen, Peter Stansill and Dave Hall were all to happy to let Tony take it off their hands – and as a result Mr. Elliot is now a multi-millionaire.

Bic squinted at me and slurred, "Well mate, just wot the bloody'ell do you want to write about?"

"Cutting edge films," I answered.

To my astonishment he agreed, offering me a monthly allowance of complimentary tickets before ordering up another round of doubled drinks. Bic accurately pointed out that he thought what I really wanted from the magazine was "visa security." Before I could lamely protest, he calmly slurred that I could turn in copy if I really wanted to, but that things might run just as smoothly if I didn't right away. He feared my foreign presence in print, at least for the moment, "might ruffle some feathers in the *Time Out* pecking order." Relying purely on the recommendation he had received from our mutual friend Hoppy, Bic didn't even ask to see samples of my writing. Following a final round of mind-numbing drinks my new supervisor bid me good day, adding that if I needed anything, "anything atall," to give him a call. I feigned sobriety long enough to wave him away before nearly blacking out on my first pub crawl.

When I finally sobered up I decided it was time for a reunion with the man who recommended me to *Time Out* in the first place.

Following UFO

I first met Hoppy in San Francisco when he came to one of my PoetUnity sessions on Duboce Street. When the bardic set broke up, Hoppy lagged behind, offering to "turn my head inside out!" After blast off he looked me squarely in the third eye and asked, "So, Hammond Guthrie, what do you steal?"

I protested that I wasn't a thief, but he insisted, "Look, mate, everybody steals something. Me, I steal information." Now here was a man after my own heart. Hoppy read some of my Event scripts and minuscule press clippings before he went on to tell me about his group of friends and their "Arts Lab" in London, describing in great detail his role in the British counterculture as a photographer and social activist of some renown. He said he and his fellow astronauts of inner space were then bivouacked in a place he referred to as Chalk Farm. I wanted to ask Hoppy if they actually grew chalk in London but restrained myself. We spent a magnificent evening together, and when he learned of our proposed departure from America he offered his support and hospitality once we were settled into our temporary digs in Chelsea. The only thing that prepared me for Hoppy and his Arts Lab crew was my peripheral association with Emmett Grogan, 'Emeritus Spiritus Sancti' of the San Francisco Diggers. I have to take a step in time to clarify this comment.

Back in San Francisco, my gregarious and exopthalmic friend, the late John Brent from the Committee Theater took me by the scruff one day and asked me if I wanted "to make a difference?" Not really knowing what John was talking about, I enthusiastically assured him that I did. "Then come with me, young Hammond," he intoned. John led me into the City's meat packing district, where we landed up in a dusty second-floor loft, occupied for the moment by dogs, Diggers, Mime Troupers, a leather-clad biker named Sneezy Hairy for obvious reasons, and our mutual friend, Del Close (then director of The Committee). Del motioned us over with a freshly-lit joint and John and I fell in with the free-form set.

After awhile, this New York banker type marched into the room (Wolfgang Grishonka-Graham, I would later learn) and then ordered, "Okay listen up!" I looked over at Del and knew right away I wasn't going to like this guy. Wolfgang prattled on about the psycho-logistics of benefit hustle and the prime directives of hipper-than-thou management surrounding an upcoming dance concert in the Fillmore District. To be honest, I wasn't really that interested in most of the on-team groups building up in the Haight Ashbury District, nor was I overly fond of over-crowded, mind meld rock'n' roll concerts, with the exception of the Family Dog's Avalon Ballroom and the Straight Theater in the Haight. It all seemed so limiting, with the sets cryptically posed hipness, over consumption of ill-defined drugs and flamboyant costumerie. The future of rock impresario impressed me as being an off-set character in dire search of a merchant – someone who counted plebeian shekels in a dank basement awaiting a pound of flesh, and as early psycho-culture history has shown (with all due respect), I wasn't too far off the mark.

Graham finished speeching at us, and everyone went back to smoking pot and laughing uproariously. John leaned over and whispered in my ear. "You see that guy over there? That's Frodo!" By this nom du anonymity, John was referring to the well-traveled writer and socio-philosophic activist, Emmett Grogan. I was never particularly close to the Diggers, although over time I came to meet most of them, keeping in touch via my North Beach acquaintance poet Richard Brautigan. The Diggers were regrettably all too unique, and it wasn't easy to truthfully interpret or fully utilize their philosophy at large. The plagiaristic counter-theatrics and self-promoting acts of the late quasi-activist Abby Hoffman are a good example of what I'm talking about.

I don't think I nor Emmett would have suggested at the time that I was a friend of his. I did however maintain a degree of credibility with him because of my close friendship with John Brent and Del Close. I'd also like to think it was because he believed I was sincere in my own self-centered approach to "life acting." Following this first encounter, Emmett and I got together haphazardly around the City, and occasionally spoke with each other in freely-framed references. Though my personal contact with this legendary man was minimal, he was always forthcoming with Digger tactics and philosophy. I respected Emmett immensely but couldn't accept some of his methods, which at times abutted the criminal edge of counterculture justification for the common good. "Karma is always," I would innocently tell him. I was especially enamored by his consciously plagiaristic use of Adolph Hitler's Mein Kamphian Diabologue at The Roundhouse in London, during the "Dialectics of Liberation" event, a counter-conference of hip dignitaries. At first he was vigorously applauded for his oration and then people cried out in staunch indignation when he revealed the origin of the words.

Emmett encouraged me to "take the moment without expectation," and to "act" from my "imaginative heart without representation or acclaim, in an increasingly nonverbal, anti-artistic world, infested with unyielding corporate greed."

I am honored to have known Emmett at all, and was deeply saddened by his lonely death on April Fool's Day 1978 at the end of a New York subway line. His only identification at the time was printed on the empty methadone bottle found in his front pocket, prescribed to "E. Grogan." Without Emmett's spirited counsel I could never have fathomed the anarchy surrounding the inner workings of Hoppy's crew.

Returning to Chalk Farm (Prince of Wales Crescent), crewman Cliff wired up an artistic and rather bulky transformer for my tape recorders and Wendy's hair dryer, while Hoppy gave me a tour of the Arts Lab community and environs. The area was largely taken up by falling-down council housing without heat, near Arnold Wesker's Roundhouse – a former railway turntable transformed into an underground venue. The Arts Lab itself was at the time sort of an annex, housed in a corner building across the street from an experimental Film Co-Op, and just up the lane from the well-ensconced and self-sufficient community's free organic food outlet. This was during the just after daze of Swinging London, when Hoppy, along with his accomplices, Arts Lab founder Jim Haynes, Barry Miles, Tom McGrath and Peter Stansill produced and edited (*IT*) *International Times*, an underground newspaper for anti-social comment accompanied by deadly serious prose and scathing agit-satire. Hoppy and his mates were wood shedding at the time, to borrow a jazz musician's phrase for polishing your chops in some obscure privacy before jumping back onto the set, perhaps blowing everyone away with your artistic changes. He and the Arts Labbers were quiet in comparison to earlier and headier times, and they seemed to genuinely accept me into their group-imposed anonymity as a "foreign research associate." Hoppy particularly appreciated my lack of desire to become any sort of new Face on the scene – I didn't want to exploit any of his considerable rock'n'royal connections, nor did I want any quasi-official affiliation with the Arts Lab beyond the friendly association we were then exploring.

Over the years I have experienced many instances of inner exploration and insider investigations with openly diverse groups of communally conscious and infinitely courageous people, such as my friends in The Brotherhood of Eternal Love, hidden in the triptic hills behind Laguna Beach, the Los Angeles Hog Farmers (when it was still just a hog farm), and the wonderfully Beat gathering of dome dwelling acid heads in the Drop City commune; to Steven Gaskin's Family and Lou Gotlieb's Morning Star Ranch. The only significant truth I was able to glean from this enlightening research was that I am simply not tribal material.

Much like Emmett Grogan in San Francisco, Hoppy was for all practical and impractical purposes the "Frodo" of London. Apart from his photographic talent and Arts Lab affiliation, Hoppy was co-founder of the London Free School, and the club UFO (pronounced, You-foe) at Tottenham Court Road, along with the co-owner, American expatriate/producer Joe Boyd. The all too brief life of UFO provided the initial springboard for a wonderfully diverse set of groups including Pink Floyd, The Soft Machine, Mick Farren and The Deviants, the Crazy World of Arthur Brown, and the lesser known Tomorrow – featuring (future Yes guitarist) Steve Howe.

One afternoon I described to Hoppy a rather impractical musical concept of mine for a curious form of composition involving five or more orchestras. Hoppy said he had a friend who might be interested in hearing about the idea and gave me a phone number to call. A few days hence I called the number, and a man answered. "Yeah?"

"Er, this is Hammond Guthrie and Hoppy said you might be interested in this quirky idea of mine," I stammered.

"Yeah?" the voice returned, "So, what is it?"

I explained as best I could the rather laborious process I had envisioned, where the individual notes of certain standard songs would be parceled out individually to the musicians in each of the orchestras. Each orchestra in turn would then play the assigned notations simultaneously, theoretically playing any number of songs at the same time, composing a linear set of enormous sounds. I though it might sound something akin to the fall of Finnegan on page one of *Finnegans Wake* by James Joyce.

Weird, I know, but the voice on the phone said he could see why Hoppy had thought to give me his number, as he was "currently involved with a little music project," and that "a scaled down version of the idea, using three orchestras in an empty blimp-hanger might add something to it." He asked what I wanted to do with the concept, and as I had no practical use for it, I offered it to him if he thought the idea had any merit. He thanked me, and before the voice could hang up the phone I asked his name. "Oh, sorry, this is Peter Townshend."

Sometime later, Peter released his "little musical project," calling it *Quadrophenia*.

In the manner of my friend Del Close, Hoppy could step off the set when he was with me and we would simply go on a quasi-anonymous tour about town. Hoppy was a wonderful guide and over the course of our strolls I came to learn more of my new friend's diverse background. To my great surprise he had read physics for his degree and was once seated as a nuclear scientist! In the mid-60s, Hoppy and his partner Suzy (Zeigler) Hopkins, formerly Suzy Creamcheese of

Frank Zappa song fame, were at the hub of a diverse melieu centered around the London Free School at All Saint's Church Hall in the Notting Hill district. Following this, Hoppy and his friends put on such memorable 'Roaring 60s' events as the illustrious "14 Hour Technicolour Dream," and the lesser known "Utterly Incredible Too Long Ago to Remember Sometimes Shouting at People" – benefits for the alternative newspaper *IT*, London's (and one of the world's) first alternative publications – an historic underground newspaper which Hoppy and (Barry) Miles founded. They held the launch party for *IT* at the Roundhouse, and it was also here that Syd Barrett's Pink Floyd (yet another of Hoppy's under-acknowledged discoveries), made its formal debut. The list of Hoppy's innovative contributions to the era is a remarkable one, yet with the presiding time's illogic of law, he was also judged to be "a menace to society" by the ruling magistrate after Hoppy was prosecuted and sentenced to nine months in goal for openly supporting the use of marijuana.

My heartfelt thanks go out to Hoppy, for without his friendship and generous advocacy I would never have received my papers of journalistic transit or my rather vague status with *Time Out* Magazine. This helped to free my passport from government hands, stamped as it was with a three-year residency visa, which among other benefits entitled Wendy and me to the National Health Service.

"Cousin Patricia"

Initially, Wendy and I got high and toured London's day and night life – got high, went to films – got high again, and wandered aimlessly about Kew Gardens, Regent's Park, and the stalls along Portobello Road, but eventually I settled down to work. In a semi-konkrete fashion, my writing began to focus on individual words and, eventually, the shape of the letters themselves – but they were so small! In my search for a new medium I discovered Letra-Set Ltd, and its headquarters on Gerrard Street in Soho. As I was soon to discover, Soho is a mobster's warren of pubs and more pubs, peep shows, music store/hock shops, cheap trattoria and curry houses, betting parlors, second-floor rent girls, subterranean clip joints, and some wild back-door casinos. Hordes of people flooded the area, where the influence of the infamous Kray Brothers still hung in the congested maze of switch back mews and dead end streets. The innumerable pubs were filled with buskers, businessmen, musicians, latent mods on uppers and failing rockers. Outsider Teddy Boys still preened in long black overcoats playing with their flick knives, and small but frightening packs of truncheon-fisted proto-Skins dressed in suspendered liederhosen and hobnail boots wandered the hoodlum paths of Soho. Scores of sloe-eyed characters and sanctioned heroin addicts waxed to a prolific pitch, and Gerrard Street was right in the middle of it. To get to Letra-Set Ltd, I exited the underground at Piccadilly Circus near the well-recognized statue of Eros. Notorious Soho is just across the street, and as if to solidify the sordid reputation of the area, as I exited the tube station I noticed a blonde young man with a scabrous face standing next to a bank of phone booths, idly stirring his cuppa tea with a glass hypodermic syringe.

Publisher John Mills had produced a soft bound edition of some of my earlier writings and illustrated the text with examples of my new work. I called the collection (long out of print) *Urban Disintegration(codex)*, and soon after it hit the seemingly minor racks, London University invited me to read from the work. I was honored by the invitation and sought out Hoppy's assistance in locating an avant-bassist to work with. I told Hoppy I wanted an accomplished player along the lines of my former accompanist Chuck Sheer in Bolinas – one who could intuitively finger and bow to a wholly improvised situation, and my friend enthusiastically recommended jazz bassist Barry Guy. I called Barry (a much sought after musician) at a studio session. He took to my idea and said he had the upcoming date free on his calendar, but no time in between for rehearsals. I told Barry that was perfect because I hated rehearsals, much preferring to just take the moment and go. He thought this brave but inspired of me, and we agreed to meet backstage on the night of the performance. My hosts at the University most certainly expected a regular type of poetry reading, perhaps delivered by a tailored pipe smoking suit sitting pompously in a direc-tor's chair. I must have neglected to give them a copy of my non-existent script, because when I requested equipment such as a large projection screen, stage monitors, microphones, tape recorders and slide projectors, the stage manager asked if I wasn't at the wrong venue.

Barry arrived, fresh off the train from an out of town gig just as the moni-tors and tape decks were brought on stage. Wendy and our friend Robert were up in the balcony setting up my quasi-light show, composed of close-up transparencies of shattered glass patterns, fragmenting road signs and my col-lection of expressive sidewalk stains. I loaded the tape decks with Mobius tape loops of pre-recorded avant-noise from the underground railway and snippets of poetic abstract. I ran the sound through the house monitors – with stage microphones set at bass, foot and mouth levels.

Barry and I rehearsed by consuming the massive joint I had prepared for the occasion, and Barry, much to his credit, looked to me and said, "I'll just take your lead."

"Right you are!" I beamed.

"Cue the curtain, cue the light show," which cued the bewildered scholars in the house that the "reading" was about to begin. I pressed the go button for the background intonation as rivulations of shattered glass and shields of transparency hit the stage. On cue, Barry and I launched into an eye-opening version of my friend Max Crosley's, "Sometimes I Wake Up Screaming!" As I moved about the stage from microphone to aside amid the overlay of colorful projections, the pace and texture of our improvisations well-accommodated the Mobius intonations and my amplified "Breath Poetry and Another Works from NowHere." I named Barry's ruthlessly professional and infinitely creative virtuosity, the "He Was Bowed to Prose Variations," and when at last we crescendo-finished with a lively little piece I called, "And You Thought We Were Done!" my hosts were a bit taken aback. But the general audience responded with enthusiasm and a short encore ovation. Preferring to keep them wondering, Barry and I settled for the appreciation and simply took a curtain call.

I truly enjoyed being in performance again, but my improvised set with Barry brought with it a level of visibility (as an expatriate American artist) that made me uncomfortable, so I contained the itch and returned to Augustus John's coveted easel in Kensington. Barry has gone on to become one of the world's premiere avant-bassists, improvising and recording with artists such as Fiona Campbell on her peerless recitation of Molly Bloom's final soliloquy from James Joyce's 24 hour duet, "Ulysses" – "Finnegans Wake."

From the Kensington attic, along with the occasional review copy for *Time Out*, I worked on my fragmented prose and Letra-Set improvisations at a steady pace, though distracted by the many libraries, parks, museums, clubs and available drugs. One concert in particular that stands out was the night Ricky Nelson came to town with his Stone Canyon Band. His new music was rather bland but what struck me directly between the eyes that night was the answer to a mystery I had long pondered. Upon entering the famous venue and seeing the numerous black acoustic discs suspended from the ceiling, I finally understood what John Lennon meant by "now they know how many holes it takes to fill the Albert Hall!"

Operation Dorset

London is an expensive town, and our bank account was beginning to feel the crunch. In search of relief, Wendy came across an ad in the *Times*, and without mentioning it to me she wrote to the box holder, thinking that the advertised cottage was just outside London. The ad had, curiously, requested a writer for a tenant, and Wendy thought it would be ideal for us. A day or so later a woman called with directions for what Wendy imagined to be a short train ride, as she had neglected to ask just how far "south of London" the cottage owner had meant. So without asking anyone or looking at a map we hopped on the train, and three-and-a-half hours later we arrived in the village of Crewkern, Dorset. At a minuscule railway station (only one track wide at this juncture) we were met by a well-dressed, middle-aged woman who introduced herself as Betty Allsop. Betty drove us in her blue and spanking-new Jaguar sedan through the immaculate hedgerows and idyllic country lanes between Crewkern, Beaminster and Cerne Abbas to the nearly non-existent hamlet of West Milton (one postage stamp post office/store and an ancient church), and then on, quite literally to the end of the road.

There a decorative wrought-iron gate opened electronically, and we entered a Lewis Carroll environment of sculpted garden and rivulets surrounding a refurbished mill house. Its antique water wheel churned away and a pair of honking peacocks roamed the numerous outbuildings of the lovely estate. Needless to say, Wendy and I were wide-eyed and completely speechless. Behind the large and lovely mill house (and, unbelievably, inside a white picket fence) was a story-book dwelling – a two-story stone cottage, with windows trimmed in lace, with its own rose garden, garage and babbling brook. Inside the cottage, the living room, dining room, and kitchen with pantry downstairs; and large bedroom, bath, and naturally lit studio upstairs, were all tastefully furnished, including an upright piano in the living room. Every room but the pantry and the bathroom had a quaint little marble fireplace in it, and there was a bin full of kindling and coal just outside the back door.

The distance to London notwithstanding, Wendy and I fell instantly in love with the place, but knew it would be well beyond our means. I asked Mrs Allsop the rental cost and she said that if we didn't mind looking after her dogs whenever she and her husband Kenneth were in London, we could have the cottage for thirty pounds. Wendy and I regretfully demurred, informing her that our attic apartment in Kensington was costing us twenty-eight pounds, and that we had hoped to save a bit more, especially if we were going to be so far from London. Without a blink, Betty then offered to accept twenty-seven pounds per month, as she thought us perfect tenants for their cottage. Wendy and I stood frozen in mid-breath, looking cross-eyed at Mrs Allsop like a couple of dolts.

I stammered, "I'm sorry, did you say twenty-seven pounds per month?"

Betty smiled and confirmed her price (a staggering saving for us of eighty-five pounds per month) and without another word of discussion or leaving a deposit, Wendy and I signed a twelve month lease. Before leaving us to discover the rest of the estate on our own, Betty invited us to a light supper at the mill and to spend the night in the cottage – "to get the feel of the place." As we roamed the Allsop's pristine acreage, dotted with sculpted topiary, lush flower beds, vegetable plots, and expertly pruned trees, we were awe struck by the seemingly natural beauty and scale of things. To us it was a garden of Eden, within an open aviary, complimented by exotic flora, roughly hewn sculpture and druidic-looking walkways bridging country brooks dividing the immaculately clipped lawns. As Wendy and I tried to take in the grandeur of our new environs, we happened upon Kenneth Allsop, laird of the mill house.

Wearing the proper walking attire, canvas hat and sporting a well used pair of field glasses, Kenneth enthusiastically waved his cane in our direction, and ventured toward us with what looked to be a permanent smile on his handsome face and a pronounced limp to his stride. A disability we would soon learn was caused by the prosthetic leg he obtained with Purple Heart equivalency, serving as a war time flier with the RAF. It obviously caused him a great deal of discomfort which Kenneth politely disguised with a not-quite-stiff upper lip. Perfectly groomed from hat to walking shoes, our laird seemed genuinely pleased to have us as tenants, and as we strolled together Kenneth pointed out varieties of prized flora and Dorset fauna with interesting anecdotes. It was obvious to me that Kenneth possessed a great deal of skill with the verbal art of succinctly phrased descriptives, backed by a well-educated, literate mind. Kenneth Allsop's literary credentials are impeccable. At the time of our residency he was the BBC's version of CBS commentator, Mike Wallace, and had his own *60 Minutes*-type of television show called *Man Alive!*; he regularly reviewed best-selling books and wrote a You Are Here column for the *Times* monthly supplement – traveling to interesting and diverse locales such as Borneo. Among his list of published works is a well-received book chronicling his travels in the late 1950s while riding the rails and living in deportee camps for a time along side hoboes in America. Kenneth had what I like to call "Beat sympathy," and before departing in the direction of the mill house, he welcomed me professionally by rhetorically inquiring, "It will be good to have another writer at hand for a winter's night and a bit of cheer, wouldn't you agree?"

After a modest meal, Wendy and I spent the night toasting ourselves with borrowed cognac and our own stash of smoke beside the roaring fire in our new living room. Wendy plunked away at her surrealist's version of "Chop Styx," while I browsed the cottage bookshelves. They were heavy with advance copy pressings, including lovely editions of Henry Miller's three volume opus *The Rosy Crucifixion*, Lawrence Durrell's *Black Spring*, and dog-eared first editions of Aldous Huxley's *Chrome Yellow* and Jack Kerouac's novel, *The Subter-raneans*.

Though bohemian-friendly and, according to Betty, "ready for occupancy," the cottage had been vacant for some time, and our first night of gentrified living was marred only by my face-spider dream. Lying beside Wendy in nocturnal REM, I felt the hideous face-crawlies and bolted upright and alert to find literally hundreds of semi-transparent arachnids scampering all over the bed and us. I threw off the covers in panic and ran screaming to the bath, followed by my thoroughly disgruntled wife. We rapidly de-spiderized ourselves and spend the rest of our first night downstairs next to the flaming safety of the open fireplace. In the morning, a mortified Betty Allsop promised to have the uninvited guests removed by the time we returned from London with our belongings – "a feel of the place" indeed!

The next day, back in Kensington, Wendy and I gently broke the news to Patricia that her rent had just returned to its previous "cousin-free" condition. She was understandably disappointed to lose us as tenants, but understood the economics of our decision and knew well the beauty of the Dorset coastline near Lyme Regis. Before we left town, I got blindingly drunk again with my editorial cohort Bickerton to advise him of the move, and he kindly slurred to me that bi-monthly submissions would be sufficient to keep me loosely on the magazine's roster – "Oye! barkeep, another round here if you please!"

We bid our goodbyes to "cousin" Patricia and the Clan Cammell, packed our meager belongings, and had a bon voyage celebration with Hoppy at the Arts Lab. But before embarking for Dorset I made a going out of town stop at Trevor's hideaway in Chelsea to pick up a healthy supply of his potent condiments – necessities of the trade that I was certain would be in short supply among the West Milton hamleteers.

Dorsetime moved at a snail's pace by any standard, and after purchasing a nearly-done, aquamarine Ford Anglia from the local "gare-Raj man," Wendy and I began taking long drives along the Dorset coastline toward Exeter, Cornwall and Bodmin Moor. One day we stopped for a drink just outside the rustic sea shanty town of Lyme Regis at a minuscule inn called The Yokel Publican. It was a very local establishment indeed where our alien presence stood significantly out of place and time. Nonetheless, after a pint or two from the house tap and a chat up with the jovial inn keeper, we were befriended by Yokel locals, Roger Sharpe and his wife Maggie, who upon learning of my pocket stash of Nepalese temple haze invited us back to their stone, cold water flat above a roperie, for further befriendment.

Roger was a former London R&B club guitarist who, once we were sufficiently raked on my hash, and with trademark boisterous aplomb, zeroed me in on the largely incomparable songs of blues innovators Elmore James and his fast-fingered cousin, Homesick James. I was at a loss to describe these pre-Clapton/Hendrix slidings and became an immediate fan of the originally fused bottle-neck genre of guitar playing. Roger was stout, with a fistful of thick calloused fingers, swollen tight from years of guitar pluck, and the pharmacologic afterburner from London's club scene had taken its toll on Roger's delicate psyche. Though his mindings were at times a bit like latent imagery shot from a self-educated verbal mix-master, Roger was a knowledgeable, humorous man and generous to a fault. Maggie was an attractive mystery, who under nom du anonymity had played a significant role in London's proto-psychedelic set, but left the scene when it began to popularize. Sporting knee length ebony tresses, Maggie wore exclusively black attire and hid much like Greta Garbo behind a pair of impenetrable owl-sized sunglasses. Quiet as a dormouse a good deal of the time, whenever she chose to articulate her astute two-cents into a conversation the talk usually shifted gears to accommodate the truth at hand. Our growing friendship with the pair offered Wendy and me the opportunity to loosen up and spread our terminally un-gentrified wings, temporarily pinned in place at the Allsop estate.

Roger and Maggie were living on the outer edges of the dole in near poverty, but they loved every second of their life together. Wendy and I made many a trip on gray, rain-soaked days to warmly chat and smoke our seemingly endless supply of Nepalese and Lebanese delights in their enjoyable company. Maggie would serve tea and whatever was a hand, after which Roger and I would retire to The Yokel Publican for quaffs of raw cider while the ladies indulged in some much needed girl banter. Another Dorset acquaintance was author/publisher Michael Gibbs in Exeter who became an especially good friend and thoughtfully invited me to co-edit *Ginger Snaps* with him – a one-time on-the-Beat journal for the pro-Burroughsian prose set. All of our Dorset friends lived in moderately large creepy-leaky old houses with little or no heat, and in this respect Wendy and I chose to remain Californians my nature and stoked the embers of our many fireplaces to a near constant pitch.

Our weekly shopping was made easy for us by the Allsop's class status, and on separate days, meat, veg and bread lorries would stop by our cottage to offer us their freshly produced wares. We had doorstep delivery of all dairy products, and due to Kenneth's literary position I could order without subscription a wide variety of daily, weekly, and monthly tabloids. The shops in Beaminster were also Allsopized for us by shopkeeper introductions from Kenneth's wife Betty, whereupon Wendy and I were granted instant credit with the village greengrocer, the pharmacy, the dressmaker, tobacconist, and spirits dealer. Even the coal merchant in Bridport offered to lorry over a fresh supply of smokeless fuel and tempered coke at the drop of a phone call. It was all rather mystifying, but we nonetheless charged ourselves silly as winter and my next round of artistic wood shedding approached.

All was well at the Cottage Guthrie, where we shared a tranquil ease – taking long Wellington-booted walks over mist-enchanted loam, purchasing our eggs, potatoes, sprouts, fresh garlic, and measures of honey-sweet mead from the West Milton farmers. It was so refreshing to stroll home, hand-in-hand along the hedgerows, to a fireplace and pipe, a glass of amber spirit, and thin slices of aged Stilton cheese. Our resident peacocks honked about the rose garden, and the brook behind our cottage babbled brookly. Wendy would read, cook, play at the piano or knit something warm, and I worked the work upstairs with my pipe, sitting at my desk beside the bay studio windows until called down to meals. Wonderfully cooked meals, prepared on the cosy kitchen's coal-fueled Aga stove. The well-cured, dual-oven stove also heated a large boiler behind the wall, simultaneously sending hot water to the taps and steam into the small wall-mounted radiators in the rooms upstairs. Rose hip and bud flourished outside our cottage dream, affording Wendy and me a sense of inner security and happiness that we as a couple would never share again. But in that moment, we felt our love for life and each other amid the sheltered environs of West Milton was eternal.

A Stringless Yo-Yo

It was through my friend Hoppy that I came in contact with Harvey Matusow. ICES (the International Carnival of Experimental Sounds), was an upcoming event at The Roundhouse, and Harvey, having been tasked with finding someone to design the festival's logo, turned to Hoppy for suggestions and my name dropped. The list of avant-performers for the event was rather notable, including Charlotte Moorman, Carolee Schneemann, and video artist nam june paik. To honor them with a bit of humor, I submitted my rendering of an ice cream cone with a human ear emerging from an oozing glob of cream. The sketch fell into the top three category, and I was subsequently invited to tea. Harvey and his wife Anna Lockwood lived outside London in the village of Ingatestone, where they occupied the garden cottage on the estate of the French sound poet, Henri Chopin.

I was greeted by a rotund, bearded and infinitely jovial Harvey. He introduced me to his lovely wife, who adjourned to the garden while Harvey and I sat down to the usual spot of tea. We spoke briefly about the festival and he perused the small portfolio he had asked me to bring along. Observing him, I sensed there was a great deal more to my host than festival logo design, and following the post-tea refreshments Harvey, an extremely articulate and well spoken man with an Orson Wells-like voice, loosened up a bit, and the fascinating saga of his quite infamous life began to emerge. Harvey was an occasional stand-up comedian who invented a little toy called the Stringless Yo-yo. I told Harvey about my childhood encounter with his fascinating invention.

The odd little up-and-down plaything was (and perhaps still is) on display at the Museum of Science and Industry in East Los Angeles, where, due to his association with my father, I was being docent-toured by the eminent scholar Erich Fromm and his wife, who called him her "Uncle Bunny Rabbit." Inside the display case, Harvey's befuddling toy rolled endlessly up and down the wire as Uncle Bunny Rabbit tried to explain its stringless theory to my preadolescent satisfaction. Harvey got a kick out of my interjection, and as he continued, his biopic took a radical left turn.

It seems that Harvey was once the trusted mole-de-camp to Senator Joseph McCarthy during HUAC's witch hunt trials during the 1950s. As Harvey told the tale, he "became a paid government infiltrator into the Communist Party, who then bore false testimony for the FBI." Senator McCarthy sent Harvey out as his personal agent, "to infiltrate and testify against suspected subversives," and Harvey came to be considered an expert on the Communist Plot to alter the innocent minds of America's youth. He even investigated Mother Goose! Eventually, Harvey's territory included the entertainment industry and my host said he really enjoyed all the attention, fancy clothes, beautiful women, and fine cuisine he was receiving in Hollywood, and as a result, he became addicted to the potent narcosium of seeing his name in newsprint. So he continued to spy and lie.

Ever the improviser, when Harvey ran out of facts to distort he fabricated his Senate and FBI testimony with stand-up material. That is, until he had a religious experience of sorts. Having sent numerous innocent people to jail as Communist conspirators, Harvey, with the aid of his priest, "resolved to confess his lies, tell the truth, and expose the government's conspiratorial use of paid infiltrators." He said many of his fellow quasi-agents were so psychologically unbalanced they could not have applied for a regular government desk job. Following several investigations resulting in great scandal and embarrassment to the U.S. government, Harvey found himself the subject of direct Senate investigation.

(This account is an abbreviated rendering of Harvey's turbulent and at times comic testimony as a false witness gone good. In the intervening years numerous books on Harvey's life have been added to the considerable U.S. Congressional Record and UPI accounts regarding his activities and direct Senate testimony. For an in-depth reporting of these bizarre events contact your local reference library.)

During the Senate interrogations, Harvey was asked by the Committee how he earned a living now that he was "no longer a paid government informant." Along with his stand-up comedy and other peripheral cash-producing endeavors, he told them he was "the inventor of the Stringless Yo-yo." The Committee, ever alert to possible Communist ploys, wanted to know who manufactured his stringless toys. Harvey refused to name (denounce!) the producer of the bent-wire, magnetically influenced curiosity as a Communist, and much of his comedic testimony (U.S. Congressional Record 1955) is taken up with judicial debates about whether Harvey "was or was not a stringless toy inventor." Off-street theater at its best. The HUAC Committee, utterly unable to determine when Harvey was being straight with them, did however determine that he was "deeply involved in a Communist plot to obstruct justice." They ensured that Harvey Matusow, the former "paid government liar," wound up being sentenced to five years in a federal penitentiary, essentially for telling the truth. Harvey spent much of his time reading in the prison library, and a few years after meeting Harvey (who ironically once interviewed Bertrand Russell), I discovered that there was another Prisoner of Conscience in the same prison at that time by the name of Dr. Wilhelm Reich.

According to one of his biographers, Dr Reich spoke to few people during his imprisonment except in his capacity as the prison librarian. Fascinated by their close proximity, I drafted a theater sketch titled, "The Danbury Library," in which Harvey and Wilhelm engage in (my imagined) conversations regarding truth, justice, magnetism, Orgone energy, toxic DOR containment, and the nature of freedom.

Completely over-amped on Harvey's epic, I went out to the garden, where I found his wife Anna squatting at a piano with its legs sunken into the ground. I looked around, and there were keyboards of all description literally planted in what she called her "piano garden." Mounted on the music stand of each was her three or four note minimalist composition. She confided to me that she was "obsessed with recording the songs of different rivers," and as I left she handed me a blank cassette to send back to her, in case I "ran across any with significant songs." Anna (now Annea) Lockwood went on to compose the highly acclaimed work "Sinopah," in which she used the recorded sound of erupting volcanoes and earthquakes. My ice cream cone with an ear wasn't chosen as the festival logo, but Harvey said, "it was used as the letterhead for something."

(Thirty-six years later)

I recently spoke over the phone with Harvey (long separated from Annea), who at seventy-three years of age (and now going by the name of Job) has taken a vow of poverty and devotes himself to Native American community service and public broadcasting in rural Utah. Though Harvey (Job) Matusow played a significant role in HUAC's witch-hunt by helping to put away any number of rather innocent people, he is also unbound by his time. He finally dared to expose the truth when such tactics were anathema to the politicians in Washington D.C. in their unrelenting search for subversion in America. When I asked Harvey about Dr. Reich's death in prison, he said he was in the adjoining cell, just five feet away from the renowned author/scientist, whose books and orgonotic inventions were the last items to be officially banned and burned by the U.S. Government. Harvey related to me that when Dr. Reich's lifeless body was discovered during the morning head count, the guard yelled out, "Hey Captain, this guy's dead. Call him a doctor!" Whereupon Harvey shouted out, "You schmuck! He is a doctor!"

Amsterdam On The Lam

One day I walked outside the cottage to pick up my weekly supply of tabloids when Kenneth popped in from nowhere, immaculate as ever, but uncharacteristically flushed and all a dither about something. He said he was up in arms about "the bloody tap-testing!" Kenneth went on to explain that the encroaching Dorset-soil invaders were in fact oil speculators from America in search of black gold under the village loam. I told Kenneth that allowing the oil scouts any leeway whatsoever would be a major mistake, resulting in hedgerow decimation by Ameri-sized equipment rigs and corporate disregard. I also confided to him that these same oil companies were poisoning everyone in the U.S. by encouraging consumers to use their toxic bug strips and other carcinogenic products. Kenneth was aghast. "That's nothing," I told him, "Who do you think makes all the Napalm and Agent Orange my country uses to dehuminate Southeast Asia?" Now Kenneth was really upset, and asked me to write a letter saying as much to the editor of the regional weekly, the *Bridport News*, which I regrettably did.

On the day of publication, Wendy and I drove to Bridport to get the early edition. Quickly scanning the "Letters to" column I found my words noticeably absent, and tossed the rag into the backseat. As we drove back to West Milton, Wendy said, "I don't think you looked the front page." She held up the bold headline, which read: "American Attacks Oil Companies!' The industrious editor had paraphrased my one page letter of warning into a full-blown article advising the local populace to brace themselves against the foreign invaders; and went on to condemn the oil companies (by name!) for indiscriminately poisoning Americans at home, and the careless decimation of most of Southeast Asia!

Back at the estate, Kenneth rushed over, newsprint in hand, and gleefully spouted, "Well done, old chap! Right out of the old Tell-it-like-it-is School!"

This was just the sort of notoriety we didn't need, and I certainly didn't fancy having any heart-to-hearts with the nameless and potentially hostile envoys of petrochemical doom. So, shortly before Guy Fawkes Day, Wendy and I decided to cool things off by taking a winter vacation to Amsterdam. I took the blasphemous article, spliced in some unrelated text to create sardonic cut/ups like "X on pest ship gas-sunk never ending," and "periodic tables innocent-Napalm Death mask sundae," as my final copy for *Earth* Magazine in San Francisco (then on its last legs), before leaving West Milton on the pseudo-journalistic lam.

In London, I mailed off some fresh copy to *Time Out* and left a stack of my "Works UnderGround" recordings on consignment at Compendium bookstore with Nick Kimberley, the bohemian friendly bookstore's underground what-ever man. My Letra-Set jacketed acetates were little 45 rpm jobs that I made in rustic coin-operated booths located in some of the older tube stations around London. For 50p I could record three-minute snippets of my work against the muffled sound of London's Underground whoosh-clanging and swoosh-buck-ling away behind me. Nick was a terrific guy, and to the Word World's great loss, Compendium Books has finally closed up shop.

As we walked toward our bank in Piccadilly a chauffeured Bentley pulled to the curb beside us. I glanced over as the rear door was opened by its liveried driver, and out stumbled a short man with brown shoulder-length hair. Oddly, he reminded me of record producer Phil Spector, and as he hit the pavement his heel must have caught the curb, because he spilled briefcase over tea kettle into my arms – the contents of his leather briefcase flew in all directions and the four of us scrambled around saving his papers from the Piccadilly wind. Then I recognized his voice. It was film director Roman Polanski, who once reorganized, sputtered his thanks without making eye contact with anyone and then scurried up the street like a well-dressed ferret toward the Circus rounda-bout. Wendy and I finished up at the bank and headed for the Harwich ferry.

The night train rolled into Amsterdam's Central Station around midnight, and we should have checked the weather report, because we arrived following an ice storm. Everything in town was frozen or covered with six inches of fresh snow and in my haste I hadn't thought to bring along any hard weather gear. I had also neglected to arrange for any form of accommodation. "Now what?" asked Wendy, shivering, and a bit put off with my lack of foresight. She was quite ready for warmth with a stiff brandy back. To this day I have no idea where the following tidbit of knowledge came from, perhaps Divine Intervention – most probably my Digger acquaintance, Emmett Grogan. I didn't know a soul in Amsterdam but told Wendy not to worry, that I knew right where we were going – I just needed to "ask for directions." I looked around the train station for my "guide," and found him dressed in stained outlaw leathers, leaning up against an empty news kiosk. As I approached, I could see him set his internal dials to "tourist hustle," but before he could initiate anything I said, "Excuse me, do you know where the Dutch boat with the American flag is?" He looked at me through a set of ponderous, probably junk-filled eyes and echoed my refrain, "...the Dutch boat with the American flag." "That's right," I said, "How do I get there?" Oddly enough, the nocturnal train-spotter knew exactly where it was, and gave me a set of detailed directions along with the owner's name, Kees Hoekert.

We trudged over the snow covered ice toward our vague destination with the nearly frozen Wendy asking me a raft of perfectly relevant questions about our intended host, whom I, unbeknownst to Wendy, knew absolutely nothing about. Close to one o'clock in the morning we located the Stars & Stripes hanging off the stern of an odd-looking boat. The wide canal was dotted by sheets of ice and a fresh snow began to fall as I banged on Kees Hoekert's cabin door.

A moment later a sleepy voice called out from below deck something that sounded like, "Hotferdommawhovasitnow?"

"It's me, Hammond Guthrie, and my wife Wendy," I replied.

"Harmon Gutree? Who is Harmon Gutree and Vendy?" asked the confused Hoekert.

Not knowing what I was talking about I said, "We've come from London and I was told you could find us a place to stay for the night."

The cabin door opened a crack and Kees stuck his fuzzy head out into the increasing snow fall. "Who toll you dot?" he inquired.

I answered truthfully, putting Wendy on red alert, by saying, "I have absolutely no idea who told me, but if this isn't the case, my apologies for disturbing you."

"No, no that's fine," Kees said, "Just a minute," and disappeared below.

Wendy looked at me as if confirming her suspicious. "You're making this entire thing up aren't you?" Before I could continue my blatant charade, Kees came from below and said, "Vollow me." He led us down canal to a much smaller boat with lights on inside and knocked. The hatch door opened and out came a dense cloud of hash smoke and the face of a very stoned-looking young man. Kees had a few words with the man in Dutch before assuring "Vendy" and me that we could "stay the night with the other crazy people!" He then invited us to come by his boat for lunch the next day, and scuttled back to his warm bed, having dealt with the uninvited "Gutrees!"

Inside the frozen-into-the-canal boat we found four very stoned people playing a game of hashish enhanced Monopoly in Swedish! Our bleary-eyed Dutch host invited us to play, and I said that we didn't speak Swedish. "Neither do we!" he replied, suggesting that Wendy and I could be "the shoe and the thimble," which for some reason broke everybody up.

Two hours of congenial warmth and many hash-heavy joints later Wendy and I passed "GO" for the last time before falling into Teutonic bankruptcy and a travel-weary coma.

The next day Kees woke us up at noon, announcing that lunch was ready. Wendy was beginning to believe that I really did know this older fuzzy-haired Dutchman after all, when we both stopped short at the gang plank of his now day-lit boat. Kees' canal boat was a floating marijuana garden and tea house called "The Lowland Weed Company!"

I looked at Wendy and said, "Look, you were right, I don't know anything about this situation. Let's just go with the flow, eh?"

"Fine," she said, "but tonight, we sleep in a hotel bed. No more incomprehensible Swedish Monopoly!"

Kees, who was ebulliently preparing our meal below, called us inside, where every square inch of space was adorned with exotic images and drawings of sadhu temple ball hieroglyphics amidst drying cannabis plants and gallon jars of pot seeds sitting proudly on the shelves. He handed us steaming mugs of fresh coffee and motioned us to the sofa in front of his large desk overlooking the frozen canal. He then proceeded to roll large joints of what he called 'binnenlander veed," meaning the local product.

"Vendy and Harmon Gutree, I velcome you to the Lowland Veed Company!", he said as we smoked his potent "veed". Kees informed us that he had dreamed of us during the night, and was shown via dream merchant that "Vendy" and I were "sincere creative people." Because of his dream, he said he would help us find proper lodgings after the meal, noticeably relieving "Vendy." As Kees served up three bowls of savory stew, he gave us Chapter 1 Verse 1 of The Lowland Weed Company Saga.

"High in the lowland," he intoned, "vee Dutchmen are spice explorers! When vee tried to bring the spice back to the Netherlands from The Dutch Vest Indies, vee found that it vould not stay dry (droog) during the long voyage home. Vee Dutchmen knew about the henep (hemp) plant and the vay it vould absorb moisture, so, on subsequent journeys vee wrapped our spice kegs vith henep roots and stalks, vitch kept the spices dry. Dry is 'droog' in Dutch, and this is the root for the English vord 'drug'. Vee have used the henep plant in this vay for centuries, and to serve as a vind break in our lowland fields; as rope fiber; and the henep seeds feed our birds. The laws surrounding the use of the henep plant," he concluded, "fall vithin the domain of the Dutch Opium Contract."

Kees pulled out a small blue book containing the Opium Trade proscriptions and pointed out the henep stipulations. He went on to say that the document did not specifically prohibit the sale of the henep plant or the consumption of its tea. Kees understood this to mean that he could legally set up shop as an Henep Merchant of plants who gave away marijuana tea aboard his canal boat. He began by writing letters to growers in Afghanistan, Nepal, South Africa, India and the Congo. Where he obtained these addresses was not explained, yet he did say they produced the contacts he needed to begin ordering kilos and kilos of pot seeds from all over the world – so far, no problems. Kees said he culled through the incoming gunny sacks, "looking for the perfect seeds" for immediate germination, potting, labeling, growing and final testing, before archiving the seeds and dried bud filled branches with detailed journal notations regarding the growth patterns, etc., of each breed of seed. Kees accumulated a canal house of information and thousands upon thousands of pot seeds. He then lovingly and with increasing botanical skill sprouted the seeds in the confines of his boat.

When the time was somehow determined to be "perfect," Kees moved his cannaboid nursery up on deck. Here, along with his start-up plants, he placed a large hand-painted sign with a huge marijuana leaf on it that read: Lowland Weed Company – Marihu Tee Huis / Plants 1 Guilder. Ceremoniously hanging the announcement off the starboard side of the boat and directly facing the busy Wittenburgergracht traffic, Kees and his Lowland Weed Company were open for business. His enthusiastic walk-in trade picked up briskly as word-of-mouth spread through Amsterdam's numerous proto-Underground anti-Movements of the early 1960s.

After a week or two of this influx of seed enthusiasts, Kees had to deal with two very imposing facts. First of all, he had ignored to ask anyone in charge of such matters if what he was quietly doing in the privacy of his boat would be equally acceptable aboveboard. Secondly, and most importantly, his Lowland boat was docked quite near the district headquarters of the Amsterdam Police Department (the Politi), and whose captain dispatched his emissaries to discuss the situation with Kees. Kees informed the officers of intrusion that he was completely within his rights by governmental decree as stipulated in section blah, blah, blah of the Opium Trade Act, which he theatrically began to wave under their noses. The Politi beat a fast retreat to report back to their captain, and Kees attended to the business at hand. The next day, the captain and his troops stormed the Lowland Weed Company, dragging a manacled and protesting Kees Hoekert down the street for interrogation.

From the intrusive captain's skewed perspective, the floating eyesore was obviously a front for a major criminal organization in its infancy and was to be shut down immediately. This vision of stupidity was sadistically played out in his treatment of our protagonist Kees Hoekert, who was brutally thrown into an interrogation cell and tortured. After reviewing the evidence and rereading the Opium Contract, the judge was sympathetic to Kees' cause and his victimization. The police captain was brought up on charges, while Kees was allowed to proceed without further intervention from the Politi with his Lowland Weed Company.

This quizzical turn of the great wheel along with subsequent post-Provo activities by Kees and his cohorts would lead the way for the current leniency regarding the socially accepted use of "soft drugs" in the Netherlands. Thus concluded the first of numerous trials by fire for the first legally sanctioned hemp dealer in the western world since George Washington, and as of January, 2002 Kees Hoekert was still aboard the Lowland Weed Company, culling "perfect" seeds for germination, floating on the same canal near the former politi-headquarters. His marijuana tea continues to be free and the potent binnenlander plants still sell for 1 guilder – now equal to about sixty cents.

Following lunch, Kees walked us over to the quasi-legal Brouwer Hotel on the Singelgracht near the 'Centrum' of town, and after "Vendy" and I checked in to the family-run inn, the three of us retired to our lovely antiquated room. Here Kees presented us with a large bag of binnenlander "veed" and warned us against the street trade, which at that time was rife with what Kees called "nephashish" – a noxious blend of brown shoe polish and camel dung clumped together with low-grade black-Pakistani hash. Wendy and I set about exploring the city's multitude of frozen canals, cafes, museums, galleries and bookstores, and I was particularly taken with the Stedelijk Museum of Modern Art. We spent the week idly roaming the open cafes, the Artis and Hortis (zoological and botanical gardens), the Albert Cuypstraat market bazaar, and the warren of narrow streets comprising the Jordaan, the oldest section of Amsterdam. We enjoyed sampling the naturally-aged cheese, sweet butter, freshly baked bread, along with slices of raw herring and smoked eel. We sipped the locally brewed beers (except Heineken!) and tall shots of young Dutch gin (jenever) served in original Brown Bar establishments. We walked in the lush Vondel Park, and into the only official hash club at the time, het Paradiso, located in a vacant spire-topped church near the Leidseplein, where over time, millions of joints would be smoked by cannabis heads enjoying live sets from some of the world's most cutting edge musicians.

Ogle-eyed, we visited the socially condoned Red Light districts and the amazing Tuchinski Theater on the Rembrandtplein, where an original Art Deco atmosphere set the scene for talented acrobats, who swung magnificently from velvet ropes high above our seats during the interlude prior to the film. A light snow continued to cover the slick cobblestones with a footpath veil of unending fantasy for Wendy and me as we explored the organized mass of bridge-connected islands (there are over 300 of them), mesmerized by the historic content. We watched at every turn, hoping that the puzzling 'Lieverje' (the Dutch prankster leprechaun) would come bounding out, and perhaps turn us away from reality to become Amsterdamers, as we tended to the fertile tulip fields of our perpetually stoned imaginations. The week went by far too quickly, and while "Vendy" went out exploring on her own, I set out for the Lowland Weed Company and further conversation with Kees Hoekert.

On board the frozen tea house, Kees listened intently as I told him about my visit to the Netherlands with my father as a child in 1958, and how deeply I felt about the consistent warmth and depth of Dutch hospitality. It was an anomaly to be in a society filled with pleasantry and open-minded sociopoliti-cal philosophies. I found it especially enriching to walk the Amsterdam streets, day or night without unwarranted apprehension, finding happy people who seemed to truly enjoy meeting strangers. Literally everyone in town seemed to have smiles on their faces, and I mentioned to Kees that I was somewhat reluctant to return to stodgy old England. Kees encouraged me to consider relocating to Amsterdam, adding that he would help "Vendy" and me find a canal boat to rent. He also said that I could help him with the spring planting, and tea service for the tourists that would be arriving in droves for the summer months in "Magic Amsterdam." I told Kees our lease in Dorset would be up in February and that I would broach the idea to Wendy.

My new friend seemed truly taken with the idea of our return and said that he had again "dreamed" of my spirit. In the dream he was told that I had the potential of becoming an alter-Amsterdamer after I had met with a group of his close friends. This departing vision pleased me no end, and my decision to abandon England was subconsciously made in that moment. If his group of anonymous friends were anything at all like Kees, I wanted to meet with them as soon as possible! With this possibility in mind, I departed the Lowland Weed Company with the beginnings of a fresh vision for Wendy and myself in the Netherlands, where all was below sea level and the cannabis factor was highly tolerated. We crossed the English channel and returned home to the Allsop's estate just prior to Christmas.

Return to Blighty

Upon our return we thought we were on our own for the holidays when the Allsop's thoughtfully invited us to spend Christmas Day with them. Decorated for the season by a fashionable London designer, Kenneth and Betty's restored mill house was tastefully furnished with an upper-crust sense of daring elegance. Past-era holiday decorations and antiques, Tiffany lamps and old marble table tops accented the living room. Kenneth's extensive library of leather-bound books was conservatively trimmed with classic hunting scenes expertly framed into the room's inlaid walls, polished to a reflective sheen by their maid. True to the Allsop's sense of class and position, the buffet on Christmas Day was ostentatiously presented on Revere serving trays. The elegant dining table was draped for the occasion with silk damask tablecloths and lit by Victorian can-delabra. Much of the wonderfully prepared food, however, was so gamy it was nearly inedible. Game pies, sweetbreads, ill-defined aspic, and plum puddings with sauce surrounded delicious servings of brandied venison, Beef Wellington and a robust pheasant under glass.

The guest list, though illustrious, was surprisingly short in view of the sump-tuous repast. Among the better known, were lute impresario Julian Bream and John Fowles, noted author of *The Magus* and *The French Lieutenant's Woman*. Fowles, who lived in Lyme-Regis, was quite friendly and became even more so when Kenneth informed him that I was "the American writer who attacked the oil companies in the *Bridport News*." I must admit that being introduced as a writer to the esteemed author was rather embarrassing, although Fowles, who along with Kenneth was decidedly against the intrusive American explorers, expressed his appreciation for my article. He kindly treated me as a comrade and thoughtfully refrained from asking me any potentially embarrassing ques-tions, such as who my other publishers were.

Fowles and I talked at length about writing in general, and when I asked him how he felt about being a best selling author, he laughed and said he felt that his level of success and that of just about any other living author was founded on blind luck rather than literary talent.

"It's like a monstrous crap shoot," he said, "where one shouldn't really care too much about winning."

He then went on to admit that he felt terrific about the current popularity of his titles, and that as far as he was concerned his books could go on selling millions of copies and he wouldn't complain a bit. Julian Bream on the other hand was shy and quiet as a mouse, and to Wendy's and my great disappointment, the lute virtuoso left just as anonymously as he had arrived, without playing his instrument.

The holidays passed and life in West Milton continued to be idyllic for Wendy and me, but my thoughts kept returning to Kees and his Lowland Weed Company in Amsterdam. I was writing steadily, but my erratic copy for *Time Out* was becoming so cut/up and abstract that they rarely published my submissions. Artistically I was tired of the woodshed, and Wendy was equally ready for change, so it wasn't long before we made up our minds to relocate to Amsterdam once the lease in Dorset was up.

Belfast Insert

In the mean time I increased my trips into London to visit with Hoppy at the Arts Lab and to pay my respects to one of my mentors. As with so many of the noted artists I have come to meet, I called upon "Mr. Lee" with an introduction from my San Francisco friend and advisor, Liam O'Gallagher. This was a formidable honor for me, as Lee's routines and courageous adventures into the largely uncharted frontiers of experience were then important agents of influence on my own humble attempts to rearrange the written world. On the phone he was most cordial and agreed to receive me the following day at his flat in Duke Street St. James. I wanted to get his take on my improvisations for a reader's pedagogic of the cut/up technique, which I called "Belfast Insert." Cut/up writing is an extension of Tristan Tzara's early Dada prose taken to a painter's point of view and then reapplied to the written word. The resulting texts of combined structure and newly formed contents offer an unusual approach to written space/time continuum.

Belfast Insert – Improvisation 23
(Secondtense behind the mortared street) "I got out the bed 3:00 a.m. night to drop fresh air. The bureau clock seemed still ahead of the pain in my left thigh – Good God! – I'd been shot clean through the balls!"
(Behind the mortared wall) 'robed in seepage from the hall. Father cried so loud

I ran from the sound-like air hissing through a pipe – I've disoriented today, what with Father's blood, and the baby gone from her crib" – (Six or seven canisters landed) "Father still-holding that blood gushing handkerchief between his legs – It seemed like hours before I got him into hospital."

(Slaughter-housing dissonant sub-titles in the back) "Reports flowed into long hours" : Tortured troop diffractions without water supplies Yesterday. "Mother reminded we could be sent to Belfast any day now." (sub-scorched by earlier attacks landed)

"News came with the morning post and we were on a north bound train."

BELFAST: (insert two hours later.) "Twin-storied troops mingle apolitical light at the end of a long iron tunnel – Nothing had arrived from London except for the baby's crib and Mother's old robe, I only had the clothes on my back – not even a bloody handkerchief to wipe my nose. Gunfire echoes in the distance and I knew it would be a long night." (Send & Receive)

Duke Street St. James is just off Piccadilly Circus near Mason's Yard and what was then the Indica bookstore and gallery run by Beat-biographer Barry Miles. With an expectant finger I rang Mr. Lee's bell and was duly admitted to climb the carpeted staircase to a #23 shoe-polished door, where I was warmly received by one of the most innovative, overly criticized and highly praised authors of the twentieth century, William Seward Burroughs III. (aka, William 'Bull' Lee.)

Poised, immaculately groomed and dressed in his classic attire, Burroughs invited me inside with a slight bow and sweep of hand. The sitting area also served as his sleep chamber, with its Murphy-like bed coming off the rear wall of the apartment. I was quick to notice the econo-sized jar of petroleum jelly at the bedside, as I sat down in the room's only visitor's chair. The adjacent wall contained a collection of books by authors such as Joseph Conrad, Colin Wilson, and George Ade, along with copies of some of Burroughs' own pub-lished works. A Scientologist's E-Meter and an Alpha-device with a dual set of headphones sat atop the book shelves, but otherwise, his room was the penul-timate example of the direct experience philosophy, pedagogically described in his essay, "The Adventures of DE."

After directly exchanging pleasantries I brought Burroughs up-to-date on our mutual friend Liam, and asked him if he had a slide projector handy, as I had brought along some 35mm slides taken at my friend Hube the Cube's place in San Francisco. He did, and was curious to boot. When I flashed the first image onto his wall, Burroughs guffawed with a spontaneous gesture of Mid-western delight.

"Where on earth did you come by these?" he exclaimed.

I explained their origin as I continued to change the colorful and detailed mural images of Mayan priests conducting insect permutation rituals and tongue hole manipulations, while standing over the prostrate bodies of young adepts about to undergo cranial trepanation. Burroughs asked if I would allow him to make copies of the slides and I offered him the second set I had brought along, correctly anticipating his enthusiasm. There is little in the life of an artist to compare with pleasing an influential mentor, and I was gushing with youthful pride.

After my slide show of Bonampak murals we had a cup of black tea, and I offered to get us high on the opiated Kashmir hash I had purchased at Trevor's place just prior to my arrival at his hallowed door. "Excellent idea," he beamed with little expression, and then watched me like a telescoping hawk as I rolled a mind-numbing joint of the potent Kashmir with Navy cut tobacco. Once this was rather dryly consumed things loosened up quite a bit, and we started playing around with his dual alpha set, endeavoring to "blend our alpha patterns." I'm not sure if this mergement actually took place, but Burroughs seemed to be satisfied with the results and we moved along to the E-Meter, an auditing device I was familiar with from my benzedrine-dazed research in Hollywood.

I did not then, nor have I ever subscribed to L. Ron Hubbard's Dianetic philosophies, but Burroughs (an ousted adept) was truly taken aback when I tested "Clear" on the first try, laconically suggesting that I was a "Nomadic Thetan!"

"It's all in the wrist," I told him.

I must have been entranced by this first-hand experience of what both T.S. Eliot and Burroughs meant by "the third who walks beside you." Before taking my leave, I asked him what he was currently working on, anticipating an inspiring or at least intellectually complex project. Now it was my turn to be taken aback when he replied in his famous St. Louis drawl, "Not a god-damned thing."

That evening as I was relating my experience to Hoppy, the Arts Lab phone rang. A moment later Crewman Cliff called out, using my Arts-labby moniker.

"Hey Hammer (a pun for Hammering It Out), Billy Burroughs is on the phone for you."

"Yes," I queried, and was met with the voice of an apologetic Burroughs! He politely admonished himself for not asking to see the writing I had brought along that afternoon.

"I lost the script after the first whiff of that incense you brought over. Why don't you come back tomorrow and I'll have a look, if that's convenient." He added.

I was completely floored that he was interested enough to call back, as I had forgotten all about showing him my exploratory cut/up material.

When I arrived the following day, Burroughs was somewhat agitated, though elegantly polite as before, and I noticed that his bedside jar of petroleum jelly had moved during the night. I produced my "Belfast Insert" improvisations, and rolled us another opiated joint while Burroughs sat at his writing desk, perusing my nascent cut/splice offerings. When finished, he asked me a few questions regarding my methods, and what percentage of the writing was my own versus purely cut/up text. William advised me regarding a passage or two but overall he was quite complimentary, encouraging me to "continue manipulating the piece until it disappears from the page altogether!" I know this is great ego-boosting material for a young writer, but I was oddly miffed that he liked it so much. In retrospect, I can't really fathom why this was the case (perhaps I thought he was just being kind), but that's how I felt nonetheless. Burroughs and I got high again and enjoyed another lovely afternoon together, ended by a knock on his door from an expected guest. Preparing to leave I thanked him for critiquing my work, adding that I would send him a few things after my forthcoming move to Amsterdam. As Burroughs opened the door, I became momentarily trapped behind it, and there I saw what has become my most vivid image from visiting with "Mr. Lee." On a wooden stool behind the entryway sat a weathered yet lively brown fedora, waiting patiently to cover the exquisite pate of the man whose writing, as Jack Kerouac once put it, "will drive us all crazy."

Shortly after arriving in Amsterdam and ensconcing ourselves aboard the canal boat "Alcina," one particularly wet and windy night there came a gentle rapping at our 'woonschip' door. Sliding back the hatch, I was confronted with a raven-black apparition, pelting rain running off his wide-brim hat, who intoned, "My name is Udo – Burroughs says you have a book." Not knowing what Udo was talking about, I invited the uninvited inside for a warm drink and dry surroundings. Apparently Burroughs had thought enough of my work to send one of his publishers to my door, in search of manuscript! I pulled out the now-abandoned "Belfast Insert" improvisations and handed the jumbled manuscript to Udo Breger, of Expanded Media editions, who without reading the coffee-stained pages, tucked the disorganized work into his ebony colored case, and asked if a sizeable edition with half in a German translation would be acceptable!

Astounded by this unlikely turn of affairs, I agreed out of hand and Udo soon took his leave, just as mysteriously as he had arrived. At first I imagined that I would never hear from the mysterious publisher again, but six to eight weeks later I received a package in the mail containing twenty-five limited copies for my signature. Udo arrived a few days later to hand deliver fifty copies of "Belfast Insert" and while he was at it, invited me to design the jacket cover for his Expanded Media edition of Burroughs reading selections from his work titled: *Call Me Burroughs*. (I used a Chicago Police officers badge with a ticket stub from the Nova Theater in its center.) After Udo left the Alcina, I looked back on my insecure feelings after last seeing Burroughs, whereupon I sat down to write my gratitude for his thoughtful recommendation. We corresponded a few times thereafter, but I would never visit with "Mr. Lee" again – his brown fedora stuck to my memory like pilot gossamer on a soft pink underbelly.

West Anglican Breakdown

Having dispensed with the formalities regarding our lease, Wendy and I set about packing and saying our farewells. The stone cottage had come to represent all that Wendy and I dreamed of receiving from life's destinies, but the upper class structure with its pompous, vaguely spoken tongue was now thoroughly tiresome to the both of us. All was going to plan until I took a good look at the Anglia and found it listing to starboard in the tiny wooden garage. The rear axle had dislodged under the weight of the thing and would need replacement before we could get any further than out of the Allsop's long and winding driveway. This was a problem indeed, as our financial situation couldn't withstand paying for a proper mechanic to fix it, and I knew absolutely nothing about car repair.

I ventured forth nonetheless, using Kenneth's lending card to the library in Bridport where I borrowed the tattered *Owner's Manual* for my aged Anglia – the kind of manual with a three page fold-out of the car all pulled apart, and little arrows pointing to where the individual parts and their attaching nuts and bolts are supposed to fit. Diagrams in hand I went to visit my friend Roger, who also knew absolutely nothing about fixing cars – he didn't even drive. Gentleman to the core, Roger was more that willing to help and off we went to the raw cider bar, to decipher the hieroglyphic *Operating Manual* and to ask after the local automobile graveyard. "Organization Last!" should have been our battle cry, as the drunken duo from Ciderville took on the Ford Motor Company's team of mechanical engineers.

At the wrecking yard, we located a substitute axle assembly hooked to the rear-end of a smashed up similar model car, and with help from the crazed geezer who ran the place, we tore the thing out. Following a hair-raising ride through the hedgerows, we managed to get back to the Allsop's, who looked aghast at us from their front window as Roger and I came barreling down the drive in a battered 1940s lorry driven by the graveyard geezer. Kenneth and Betty, who didn't like Roger's Hull-tinged voice or odd mannerisms in the first place, were equally distraught when they learned what we were doing. "Not to worry!" we told them, after lying through our teeth about our previous fix-it-up experiences. Roger and I then retreated to the cottage, my hashish pile and the *Operating Manual*. We were like a pair of neo-Beat archaeologists with burning sand under our feet as we set about initiating our rather mad-cap and almost certain to fail fix-it attack on the Anglia.

Our first significant road block came within minutes, when we saw how little space there was between the garage wall and the skewed dimensions of the injured auto. Now we sat there like two dyslexic scientists, contemplating how to safely lift the Anglican rear-end using only one wobbly car jack and an old screwdriver. "Bring on the bricks!" shouted an increasingly enthusiastic Roger, who began to gather usable samples of ancient stone from the Allsop's inner courtyard. An hour or so later we had the car up on its rocks, using the actual car jack as a pry tool.

We got our work lamps to shine by plugging into a series of extension cords leading across the yard to the cottage window, and crawled beneath the frame. To our dismay, everything was covered with Dorset mud, making it impossible to compare the undercarriage with the *Operating Manual* diagrams. Undaunted, we decided to use the "similar model" replacement axle as a surrogate guide, only to find that the new axle seemed to be missing a number of diagrammatic nuts and bolts, and possessed a few odd little 'doodads' not indicated on our fold out map of Rear Anglia! Using the Allsop's kitchen phone, we rang up the geezer and described our dilemma. He advised us to find the something or other number on the undercarriage and to call him back. With hilarity, Roger and I located the mysterious number, and the graven one was able to determine that we had purchased the wrong axle. "Similar model, eh?" intoned our mechanical guru, who said he would see if the correct axle wasn't buried somewhere in his yard. I gave him the kitchen number, and Roger and I, deciding it must be break time, went back to the hashish for further inspiration.

Two hours later the geezer called the kitchen phone, telling the cook he'd come right-the-way over with the correct axle. The cook, who didn't know what an axle was, asked Kenneth, who then appeared on my doorstep, demanding to know what was going on with his cook, and why was the "yard man" bringing us another axle?

"Nothing to concern yourself with," we assured him and off he limped, not at all pleased with our progress. The lorry came barreling back as before, only now the geezer was off the clock and wanted to help us fix the Anglia.

"First things first," he said, and pulled out a flagon of whiskey, offering Roger and me a "full tilt," which set the scene for the next hour or so – the three of us drinking his whiskey, engrossed with the problems at hand, not the least of which was our lack of proper tools beyond the screwdriver and pry bar jack. Our graveyard guru was also keen to point out before he drunkenly lorried away, the inherent hazards of our precarious jack system. When he was gone, Roger and I again crawled under the car when the bricks started to give way, and the axle housing threatened to crush us under the weight of the car. We carefully crawled from beneath our impending doom and wondered what to do next, when the entire operation came tumbling down, sinking the heavy metal housing into the soft garage floor! Roger and I decided to cover the embarrassing mess with some old blankets to hide it from anyone passing by the garage, and walked toward the cottage. "That's it for today" we chimed in unison, and began revising our progress report for our wives, who were due to arrive at any moment.

When the ladies reappeared, Roger assured them that the work was "moving along famously," and that the Anglia would "soon be running smooth as silk!" Roger and Maggie spent the night, and in the morning we returned to our repairs just as soon as Wendy and Maggie had left for the day. Now that we were sober from the night before, though quite stoned on the morning joint, I began complaining the we were traveling backwards with the axle replacement, and that actual tools had to be acquired before going any further. I couldn't bring myself to ask Kenneth for his tools, so Roger and I put on our rubber 'Wellies' and struck off "o'er the fields" to confer with the retired army major who owned the adjoining estate – I had seen him driving a fancy Jaguar and knew he must have proper tools on hand. The Major, well-aged and handle-bar mustachioed, appeared to be thoroughly charmed that we had sought out his assistance, and led Roger and me "straight-the-way" into his "gare-Raj," which housed the expensive Jaguar and, under a large chamois, his new Bentley sedan. The Major opened his equally grand accessory kit to expose an array of glistening metric tools and began sorting out everything Roger and I might need to replace the axle. As we left, a more than adequate tool kit and a set of sturdy car jacks in hand, the old boy said he would, "pop-round-about tea time" to check on our "progress."

Hours later, when the Major popped by, Roger and I had managed to get the old apparatus off the carriage and were attempting to install its replacement

– not an easy task for two mechanical morons taking frequent refreshment breaks. "Splendid job! Well done lads," spouted our sponsor, when Kenneth, noticing the Major's presence, caned over to see what was transpiring. He was quite surprised by our apparent success and eyed our bank of tools with suspicion, but cheered us on good-heartedly before disappearing into the mill house with the Major in tow. Kenneth came back after seeing the aging imperialist off, and was less than pleased that we had borrowed his expensive tools. Admonishing us to be careful with the Major's metric aids, Kenneth left us to our tomfoolery. At this stage of the game, Roger and I firmly believed that even if we managed to get the damn thing installed, the Anglia would never roll toward the White Cliffs of Dover. We worked long into the night, pushing, pulling and forcing things into place and finally got the rear end positioned, although we were left with a box full of springs, 'gizmos' and the odd rubber gasket.

The next day we returned the Major's undamaged tools before we even tried to move the car, convinced that the entire repair job, was as Roger put it, "a right bollix," and that Wendy and I would have to abandon the Anglia at the Allsop's, getting to Holland under our own steam – though we assured the complimenting Major that the operation was a complete success – "Couldn't have done it without you!" With the wives anxious to see the new axle in operation, Roger suggested we take the Anglia out for a trial run, and to our astonishment, it ran! The real wheels made a funny sound but the car appeared to be functional for the moment. We celebrated the success of our repair job with our friends in The Yokel Publican, drinks all around and units of savory steak and kidney pie.

Our last days in West Milton were filled with a mixture of elation and impending separation anxiety from our beatific surroundings, and on the day of our departure we shed copious tears into the babbling brook behind the cottage. We set off for London, where I stopped by the *Time Out* office to thank Bickerton for his semi-lucid patronage, paid a bon voyage visit to Hoppy and the Arts Lab, closed our bank accounts and headed for Dover. On the way we stopped for a bite to eat in a cafe, and as I was paying for the meal, I discovered that our London bank manager had neglected to ask me to return our "Fast Bank Card," which allowed us to withdraw up to thirty pounds, no questions or balance checks necessary, at any bank in England. I pointed out this 'slight of bank' to Wendy who astutely asked, "Well, does it still work?" Not knowing the answer we walked into the nearest bank and presented our card to the smiling teller.

PART FOUR – AMSTERDAM

Woonschip Alcina

Wendy and I ground our way across Flanders toward Holland, taking the overly stuffed Anglia to the brink of auto-destructum. Arriving in Amsterdam we checked in to the Brouwer Hotel as before, and then headed for a reunion with Kees. True to his word, our friend helped us find accommodation on one of the many illegal houseboats (woonschips) harbored within the literally hundreds of islands created by the inner city's intricate system of canals. The first thing he did was to teach us to how to say "Hello," "Thank you," and "Excuse me (Mr. or my lady), do you know of a canal boat for rent?" in Dutch. Then he gave us a city map and a huge bag of his binnenlander "veed."

With our new language tools in mind, "Vendy" and I walked the length and breadth of Amsterdam waterway for three days before we found the ninety foot woonschip (living boat) Alcina on De Wittenkade. The wide flat-topped canal boat was moored across the street from a family-owned birdseed store. Floating quietly on the outskirts of the historic Jordaan District, the Alcina and her very reasonable $100 per month rent suited our purposes to a tee. Our boat lord was a congenial man a little older than I named Tim, who kindly introduced us to the birdseed family and to the adjacent groups of alien-friendly woon-schippers. Noticing that we didn't have any furniture, Tim showed me the fundamentals to the art of kraaking, or as we say in English, "breaking and entering."

Tim and I walked along de Wittenkade until we came to a boarded up, strut supported three-story house. "Ah!" exclaimed Tim, as he proceeded to kick in the front door. The place was dark, dank, dusty and incredibly full of initially indeterminate stuff. Tim began rummaging through the detritus and before long he was pulling out useful items such as an old hat-rack, a sack full of moldy clothing, rat nibbled books, scads of mismatched dinnerware, and an antique mousetrap big enough to catch a small cat. Upstairs there was more dusty stuff, much of it useless: old magazines, dry cat and rat shit, a broken floor lamp, piles of urine-soaked foam rubber, more moldy clothing and a perfectly good table with two matching chairs. Tim said the unclaimed wonderment was for the taking, and in the attic he inexplicably found a neatly rolled twelve by twelve Persian knock-off in near pristine condition! It all fit perfectly into our main salon, and over time I would become something of an expert in the kraaking trade.

Now that the Alcina was liveable, I drove over to the Rapenburger District to pick up Kees and show him the fruit of our labors. When I arrived, he and a guy with blonde shoulder-length hair were attaching lines to a raft full of canal debris and plant life, moored next to the boat. I offered to help them, but Kees told me to go below deck and make tea while they finished tying their water-logged raft to the port bow. When I got downstairs, I was greeted by about a thousand potted marijuana starts, neatly stacked in pallets – they were everywhere. I tried to negotiate the butane stove, as Kees and friend appeared and I was relieved of marijungle duty.

While Kees prepared the tea, the handsome stranger and I started rolling joints from the tray full of binnenlander buds on Kees' desk. Kees began talking about me in Dutch to his silent friend, who would only look questioningly at me and grunt, as if sizing me up. Henep tea service in hand, Kees sat down at his desk, rolled his own joint, and finally introduced me to his cohort, Jasper.

Robert Jasper Grootveld is an infinitely creative shaman, a brujo of psychedelic mystery, and a metamorphic shape shifter. Jasper's solo activities in Amsterdam provided the initial construct for his later Happenings and the magico-radical, sociopolitical grouping now known as Provo. He would float around the inner city canals, reading his morning paper and smoking a joint aboard a tiny raft complete with table, chair and oars, whilst conducting his bold, unrelenting graffiti war against the nation's cigarette machines (not the companies or their in-bulk nicotine products, just their pre-rolled cigarette machines!).

Jasper and his marijuana-friendly compatriots applied their creative genius and prolific visions for the existing social order to the theater of protest

– putting on original Happenings, and unexplained manifestations for change they called acts of "Descundalow" – after the magical activities of their national leprechaun-prankster, het Lefertie. These and many of Jasper's proto-Provo events such as the well-documented "Smoke Temple" occurred every Friday night at midnight near the small bronze statue of the impish sprite, on the Spui plaza, near what is now Amsterdam University. Jasper's well-attended Happenings stirred up a major hornet's nest of trouble and dissent, resulting in much skull-smash and fire hose treatment of the onlookers, after which there was a great public outcry. Second-hand reportage, harsh criticism and unyielding support for the spontaneous Provo's filled the editorial pages of the nation's media. Things in Amsterdam were about to change.

To a much greater degree than San Francisco's altruistic Diggers, Provo was a quasi-nomadic group of radically artistic characters, cryptically mystical in their sociopolitical philosophy and ultra-secretive with their legendary operations. They were relentlessly, however ineffectually, investigated by the police. The then conservative power alliance staunchly, and via the riot squad, physically resisted Provo's numerous demands – but in the end, their persistent mysticism brought the Politi and the local government to their knees. After obtaining a seat for themselves in Parliament, they then officially disbanded themselves! Before disappearing from the obvious scene altogether, they installed a figurehead they referred to as the Kabouter (jester) to oversee their quasi-Socialistic programs for innovative reform, such as the famous "White Bicycle and White Chicken" programs, and then loudly proclaimed to the media that Provo had never existed! This seriously madcap attack on the ruling class by the elusive Provo and their virtual army of ardent Descundalow supporters opened the way for the general tolerance of the unusual that Amsterdamers have become famous for.

Jasper Grootvelt's absorbing story is a long and complicated tale, not without mystery and hilarity, that deserves a lengthy book. My friendship with both he and Kees Hoekert has now spanned three decades and their influence on my life has been significant.

At the time of our meeting on Kees' boat however, I didn't have a clue as to who Jasper was or what he had come to represent in the scheme of Dutch counterculture. To me, Jasper was the comically suspicious and charismatic first mate to Kees aboard the Lowland Weed Company, who initially, and until I got to know him better, didn't have much to say, at least in English. Both he and Kees encouraged me to learn as much Dutch as possible, and would purposely force me to figure out what they were saying even though they both spoke perfectly good English. Over the thirty-odd years that I have known him,

I have come to admire and respect Jasper as a great friend and mentor – a co-conspirator. He is a conundrum of such great proportion that I can only hope that these abbreviated passages will shed some additional and well-deserved light on his enigmatic life.

Using Kees as interpreter, Jasper asked me what I wanted from the Netherlands. I told him that I wanted to continue writing and painting, living as anonymously as possible away from official scrutiny, smoke a lot of binnenlander weed, and to help with the operation of the Lowland Weed Company. He and Kees continued to converse in Dutch, routinely passing me the continuously hash-supplemented joint, until Kees announced that it was time to have a look at the Alcina. The three of us piled into the Anglia, and as we neared Central Station the police pulled us over. Kees wasn't at all pleased with this turn of events, and in English he firmly instructed Jasper to stay in the car and to let him do all the talking. I was to stand at the ready, to supply my driver's license and passport if needed. Kees and I got out of the car and the cops instantly recognized Kees, addressing him by name. Before I could decide if this was good or bad, the Politi began pointing at the Anglia's tired rear-end and then frowning whenever they looked at me. Kees explained to me in English that because of the rear-end list, the Politi thought my car might be defective. They also thought it had too much body rust, a big no-no in Holland, and they were considering confiscation of the Anglia.

Kees told the cops that I was leaving the Netherlands that afternoon for England, where the British government didn't care about body rust. The cops conferred with each other and then told Kees that I should get the car off the street as soon as possible or it would probably be taken away by other, less understanding, Politi. Before they allowed us to be on our way, the cops wanted to take the right-hand drive auto around the block – just for fun! Kees couldn't dissuade them and the pair gleefully jumped into the Anglia with Jasper still sitting quietly in the back seat. Kees whispered to me that this could mean real trouble. The cops couldn't drive the Anglia ten feet without stalling the alien thing. They turned on the blinkers and the windshield wipers, when suddenly they both spun around in their seats to find Jasper sitting behind them. The cops immediately got out of the car, chattering in unison at Kees before they jumped into their little Politi wagon and quickly sped away.

Back in the car, Kees and Jasper started cracking up and told me that when the cops saw Jasper sitting behind them they absolutely freaked out. Not knowing anything about Jasper at this point, I asked why. All Kees would say was that Jasper was the (aforementioned) "shamanic friend" who had helped him escape further torment from the former Politi captain in the Rapenburger

District. Jasper sneered and tersely added that he thought the Politi were afraid of his magic. We made it back to Wendy and the Anglia, where Kees and Jasper approved of our find, and pulled out a sack full of woonschip warming gifts. After they left, I told Wendy about the car hassle and suggested we get rid of the Anglia. We couldn't get any money for the untrustworthy car because of the body rust, so I just parked the car on the opposite side of the canal from the Alcina, signed the pink slip, and with a note taped to the steering wheel declared the Anglia a "free car." I left the key in the ignition, and walking across the bridge, I tore my driving license into little pieces and didn't drive again for many years. On the third day, the Anglia disappeared.

Wendy and I settled into our new abode, exploring the neighborhood and its open-air markets, getting familiar with the courteous and friendly inhabitants of the Jordaan, while mapping out the off-board necessities of woonschip life, such as where the closest public bath house was located. Our floating home was without the convenience of plumbing beyond gravity-fed drinking water and a chemical toilet, which, like all the other woonschip commodes, dumped its contents directly into the canal. One of the prime Amsterdam directives was: "Never fall into the canal," and local rumor had it that full immersion would require the same number of painful injections as a rabid animal bite. Amsterdam's canals are second only to Venice for the fetid quality of inner city waterway, and Wendy and I came to enjoy with an increasingly dark sense of humor the parade of ridiculous jetsam that would float by the Alcina on a daily basis. Nothing was too sacred or absurd for canal disposal. Everything from bags of near luminous garbage to complete bedroom sets made their way down de Wittenkade toward the Amstel river. As a canal-fill prevention measure, the government would send the noisy glopita-glopita machines around every few weeks to dredge the canal bottom of its odoriferous sludge. Deposited in the open holds of flat-bottomed barges, the bottom-globula was then towed out to the glopita dumping grounds. I never inquired where this anti-sacrificial place was, hoping only that it was far, far from De Wittenkade.

The Stedelijk

Away from my Lowland friends, Kees and Jasper, I continued with writing and studio work in private. But as I toured the city's many galleries and museums it became apparent that my reclusive stance needed some expansion if I was going to participate in the pleasantly interactive artistic subculture thriving in Amsterdam, as the well-documented and -attended doings of local artists were prolific. This was due in large part to the municipally funded Artist's Union, and to the art-friendly politics dominant at the time. Numerous clubs, theaters, galleries and art collectives were officially and otherwise created, in an effort to better facilitate the government funded apprenticeship program known as the Contraprestatie. The program was open to Dutch artists of all form and muse, and, along with free studio space and a monthly stipend, this very generous program (initially run by the artists themselves) also provided for its membership through significant art material discounts from a central distribution center known as Atelier 99, and the Ministry of Culture's practice of routinely purchasing their works and related documenta. This ever multiplying collection of art work was given archival storage or exhibited in libraries, schools, day-care centers, hospitals, retirement homes and all government buildings throughout the country on a rotating basis.

The idea was that if the government fully supported emerging artists, they could more easily and quickly reach a level of professional success where the program would no longer be necessary, thus perpetuating and, ideally improving the creative milieu and the level of artistic output in the Netherlands. The system as it originally existed also owed a great deal to the generosity of Queen Wilhelmina, at that time considered to be the richest woman in the world, who would annually donate generously to the program. While it lasted, the forgiving, and ultimately vulnerable Contraprestatie guaranteed Dutch artists and a few tenacious foreigners a bohemian's paradise. Among the many benefits of membership was a private bar/clubhouse, that looked out over the popular Leidseplein entertainment area known as "De Kring". There was also an unusual welfare fund from which the membership could draw in case of an emergency. Obviously, this type of program screamed to be abused, and over time it was, largely due to artistic ennui and the fraudulent acts of unscrupulous characters.

Like most artists, I wanted to sell my work, but I was hampered in this by my stubborn insistence that I and my art remain outside of groups or any other collective identity structure. This standoff-ish and somewhat naive philosophy dictated that if my work wasn't strong enough to stand on its own, it wasn't worth showing in the first place. I also had a complete disdain for the cult of personality that was prolific in the art world of the late 1960s and beyond, where the idea that who you are, what you say, or how you define your art or yourself is equally as important as what you may or may not produce. This has always seemed a patently idiotic idea to me, and a decidedly un-painterly approach. It was largely the result of the commercial success surrounding Pop artists and the increasingly huge commissions being paid to gallery owners – which has only served to inflate the presumed worth of a particular piece of artistic something-or-other, bolstering and inflating the elitist look-at-me egos of all concerned. This scene had little to offer an artist like myself, who rarely thought about the commercial value of his work, hadn't gone to Art School, didn't hustle the set with character routines and who adamantly refused to attend his own rare exhibitions. I was of the mind that if I couldn't honestly join them (whoever "they" were), I should avoid them. This back-door modus operandi of mine offered me a large degree of personal and creative freedom, but it also served to keep my work out of a number of salons that might have otherwise exhibited my paintings. I really was a pill in those days, and my emergent reputation for being an "artistically difficult" specimen began making the rounds.

At one of my first showings in Amsterdam, the canal-front gallery owner was adamant that I be in attendance at "her" opening. Considering that the exhibition was essentially for the cocaine-friendly work (all the pieces on display somehow unfolded or screwed themselves into some form of precious metal snort paraphernalia) of a Scottish jewelry artist, I felt that my topographic canvas work was more of a backdrop for his unique adornments, and that my presence was completely unnecessary. The angry proprietress finally threatened to take my work off the walls if I persisted with my obstinacy and I reluctantly agreed to go. Before the opening, Wendy implored me to behave myself, but true to form, I didn't. Minutes after our arrival, and already higher than the proverbial kite on Kees' binnenlander "veed," I grabbed one of the not-so-inexpensive wine bottles from the patron's buffet and secretly ensconced myself in the gallery's broom closet.

Some time and quite a lot of Cabernet later, I heard voices, including Wendy's and that of the hostess, outside my janitorial redoubt. Apparently someone had spilled something on the gallery's hardwood floor, and in the process of cleaning up the mess I was about to be exposed. The closet door flew open, and as I was about to say something perfectly stupid, my knee bumped the mop handle, which then rudely smacked the astonished gallery owner squarely in the face! I got to my feet in a futile attempt to salvage the unmanageable situation, and in doing so, spilled the remaining Cabernet all over myself. Wendy quickly retrieved our coats and scuttled us out of the place. The reviews the next day were embarrassingly comic, decidedly mixed, and needless to say, I was not invited back.

Though it has rarely helped my pocketbook, I have always taken it as a great compliment that other artists have appreciated my work far more than gallery owners, and as a result of my headstrong attitudes, I would for some time steer clear of the art broker's collective altogether. What I was seeking instead was a creative salon: an unconditional forum of pedagogic exchange and creative mentorship, away from the commercial and singular cultism that I associated with the then definitive milieu surrounding Contemporary Style and the Personus Artisticus.

Through some newly acquired Dutch friends I was introduced to the late Jan Martinet, at that time the curator for Painting and Sculpture at the Stedelijk Museum. When we eventually met in his office, he was intrigued by the fact that I hadn't brought along any of my paintings, presenting him instead with my notes for a series of proposed images.

The Stedelijk had (and to a lesser degree still has) a reputation for being open to fresh and unsolicited approaches, so rather than introducing myself as "just another American artist on the make," I offered Jan a conceptual statement about my new environment – one that I hoped would appeal directly to the Dutch people. To have typically pushed my paintings on to him would have been, to my take, a thoroughly inconsiderate gesture. Jan liked me and my idea, and asked that I draft a formal proposal for the project, which he said he would submit to his director, a Mr. E. de Wilde, upon the latter's return from Paris.

"Water Water Everywhere!"

As a nation entirely below sea level, the Netherlands owes its very existence to the nature and control of water. Dikes, windmills, bridges, locks, and a vast array of canal systems divide the Dutch landscape into a complex maze of man-made islands and lowland waterways. A system used for security, transportation, commerce, recreation, and in fact, continental stability. The images for this presentation will be taken directly from these and other local waters. At numerous source/site locations around the country (urban and rural), water samples will be drawn by the artist, placed in vials and then onto glass slides under a powerful microscope, where the water contents (organic and inorganic) will be photographed onto 35 mm film. These color images are to be enlarged (4'x5') in the form of standard blue prints, imprinted on to an archival, water-resistant paper, and then mounted for exhibition without titles beyond numbering. The individual prints are to be accompanied by the bottle containing the remaining source/water sample along with other (as yet to be determined) source/site documentation. Upon entering the museum, visitors will be given a booklet with a description of the project that will contain a small map of the Netherlands. The map will indicate (by number) the water-image source/sample/site location for each of the enlarged prints.

Jan and I met in his office on two other occasions to review the project's design, and to formulate a reasonable budget, which he assured me would be forthcoming once the director returned from his travels. To his credit, Jan Martinet, unlike so many museum personnel I would eventually meet, was a personable, intuitive, articulate and knowledgeable human being with an artist's heart. But I would soon learn that Jan and many of his tenured colleagues at the Stedelijk struggled with the ego-inspired philosophies of their erstwhile and frequently absent director, Mr. E. de Wilde.

My anticipation surrounding the Stedelijk project came to an abrupt halt when I received a mimeographed form letter from the director's office, anonymously addressed to "Dear Artist," stating: "This museum does not care to accept your proposal." Good-bye! The man didn't even want to meet with me. Refusal I can accept, but this impolite slap in the face from the rubber-stamped director "E. de Wilde" was more than I could take. I called the museum and he took my call. I told the pompous director that I was very surprised by his "terse and impersonal note, after such pleasant and professional contact" with his curator, Jan Martinet.

"What's the deal?" I boldly demanded of him.

This caused E. de Wilde to go into histrionics. "Young man, I reject hundreds of artist's proposals every year, and none of them phone me up to ask, why not! Just who do you think you are?"

I replied that I knew perfectly well who I was and suggested that he take some hints from his curators on how to treat artists. Without us, I reminded him, he would soon be out of work, and I hung up on the man. I fumed around the Alcina until I calmed down and called Jan Martinet. Jan was very apologetic about his director's rudeness, and said that he too was surprised by the flat rejection of my proposal. Jan was as up-beat as he could be, and encouraged me to continue with the project on my own (which I didn't). He thoughtfully offered to visit my minuscule studio space aboard the Alcina and after seeing a few of my paintings, Jan suggested I call upon E. de Wilde's predecessor at the Stedelijk, a Dr. Willem Sandberg, who, Jan said, had just had just returned to Amsterdam after serving as first director for the Israel Museum in Jerusalem.

Within a few days, I took Jan's suggestion to heart, and after a brief accounting over the phone of my distressing tale, the aged voice on the other end of the line suggested that I bring samples of my work over his studio on the Brouwersgracht the following day. As I was about to learn, my youthful indignation over E. de Wilde's blunt rejection of my work had led me to the studio of one of the art world's most highly esteemed gentlemen. That day, however, I knew next to nothing about Willem Sandberg, but as fate would have it, I would come to know a great deal about this generous, multi-talented, and heroic man.

Meeting with, and subsequently growing close to Sandberg would finally offer me "the unconditional forum for pedagogic exchange" that I had so stubbornly sought, and over the next three-and-a-half years he would become my benefactor, my collaborator, my mentor, and most importantly, my friend.

Then in his late sixties, Sandberg, with his kind demeanor and stunning mane of silver white hair, ushered me into his pristine studio, and after offering me a snifter of cognac and a small cafe cigar, he questioned me for an hour or more before looking at my portfolio. I spoke to him openly and honestly of my early life, my frustrations with galleries, and my inadequacies. I felt that I had perhaps made a great mistake by not first attending an art school before venturing out on my own. To my great surprise, Sandberg advised me not to bother with galleries. And as far as art schools were concerned, he said they were "fine places if one wanted to learn how to draw a decent hand," adding that he thought they were a complete waste of time for artists like myself, who, he felt, quite rightly followed the beat of their own drums. I told Sandberg I felt that I could put my trust in his knowledgeable opinion. If my work was simply mediocre I wanted to know it, so that I could alter my path to become a plumber or a pie maker – anything but a back door artist. He spent some time looking over my non-objective, vaguely topographic work and then asked if I was familiar with the work of the Dutch artist, Master-Printer, Hendrick Nicholas Werkman, which I was not. Sandberg said that my work had much in common with the late artist's approach of mixing painting, printing and topography into a format he had called, "Warm Printing".

Without further conversation regarding my youthful sense of inadequacy, Sandberg instructed me to go back to the Stedelijk and present myself to the print collection manager, who was a friend of his. He added that due to the somewhat "caustic relationship" he maintained with his successor, E. de Wilde (whom Sandberg did not recommend for the post nor respect), I should go about my studies of Werkman without the current director's knowledge. Sandberg's significant influence within the national art community while withholding his support from the museum director was a significant sore point between them. Sending me into the heart of the museum's extensive Werkman collection for hands-on research under his recommendation, he said, would not sit well with his successor, especially in lieu of my obstreperous contact with the man.

High in the Lowlands

I went back to the Alcina full of artistic courage after my meeting with Sandberg, wanting to share the uplifting experience. To her credit, Wendy enriched our life with domestic tranquility and I relied on her a great deal. Though I am certain she would have preferred a more lucrative position in life, she loved my sense of spontaneity and put up with my non-commercial whims with a comforting ease. She knew that I was for all practical purposes through with working a "real job" for a living, and that I loved the unknown quantity more that the concrete reality of life's mystery. Wendy stuck by me in ways that I, at that time, took completely for granted. The details of our daily life up to that point had seemed to us both, a magical odyssey where most things of import "just happened," and all that was necessary was for us to wake each day and take in the adventure that was simply there. And much like the canal water supporting the buoyancy of the Alcina, our life bond with each other wasn't going to disappear, and I firmly believed that we would always be together. Had I a more pragmatic vision at the time, I might have avoided some of the darker twists of fate that were soon to follow.

Two or three days a week I would go to the Stedelijk, put on a pair of white cotton gloves, and with the aid of Sandberg's friend Hans I explored the voluminous Werkman Collection in the privacy of the print cabinet. This well-lit study room is located behind a door hidden in the wall of one of the museum's stairwell galleries, designed by Sandberg, well away from the prying, self-centric eyes of E. de Wilde. Sandberg and I had agreed to meet in his Brouwersgracht studio every Friday afternoon at four o'clock to discuss life and my studies. During the rest of the week I divided my time between studio hours, canal life with Wendy, and my extracurricular activities with Kees and Jasper over at the Lowland Weed Company.

The Magic Bus Tour of Amsterdam was in full swing and Kees' floating tea service was among the favored stops. The magic bus riders were usually an eclectic consortium of stoned hippies and vacationing drug smugglers, transfer students, botanists, German Psychiatrists or Swedish Neurosurgeons, and the odd smattering of curious folk from places such as Missoula, Phoenix, Katmandu and Kabul. The upper deck of Kees' boat was a grass-matted tea house with a small stage where Kees would entertain the twice daily guests, while I and whoever else was at hand (usually a couple of Jasper's post-Provo industrialists) prepared the tasty cannaboid tea below decks.

Ours was a spontaneous theater. You really had to be there to appreciate our cirque du cannabis routines, such as "Daze of Pot Seed Rain," or "When The Pot Goes Into The Lungs, The Mind Goes Into The Sky," so it goes without description that a hilarious "High Tea" was had by all. Jasper at this point entered into the initial stages of what would become for him a life-long socio-artistic obsession with rafts.

One day the shamanic Jasper and his beautiful, equally powerful and nearly Amazonian wife Thea Keiser were visiting the boat. Jasper, a consummate collector of rare street side detritus, was cradling the remains of a seemingly useless baby carriage in his arms. He went directly to the port side and ceremoniously dumped the crippled pram into the canal. As we all looked over the railing at the semi-submerged carriage, Jasper enthusiastically explained that what we were gawking at was not a baby's carriage at all, but the foundation for a "great raft" that he intended to build from the debris that would float to him from the canal. Once the great raft was completed, he said, the real purpose of his "vision" could unfold. Jasper was disturbed by the level of amphetamine use and rampant juvenile delinquency infecting the youth subculture in Sweden. He said he was going to take it upon himself "as the Ambassador of the Lowland Weed Company," to go to Sweden on the great raft, filled with marijuana plants, and offer them as a gift to the Scandinavians as an alternative.

True to his vision, Jasper stopped helping Kees and crew with the bus tour, and focused his constantly Delphic eye on the flotsam and jetsam that would pass by the boat everyday. He would row out to a potential necessary item in a small inflatable boat to haul his materials back to and against the port side home of the former baby carriage. For the great raft's sizable keel Jasper used the stem of a seven foot henep plant, and when it was complete, the "daffy raft," as I called it was the size of a small tug boat. With huge wing-like things on each side that sort of swam – it was navigated by a quasi-Rube Goldberg apparatus Jasper pedaled from atop the crow's nest. It took him months to build, and in the meantime Kees, myself and the attendant crew potted up the hundreds of marijuana starts that Jasper planned to take with him to Sweden. All things being equal, it is not surprising that word of Jasper's "secret" humanitarian mission leaked out in the newspapers, and the local government was not amused. Just a few years earlier, Jasper and his Provo friends had stirred up the population, significantly altering the local scheme of things with their visions of socio-mystical revolution, and the presiding officials were well aware of just how powerful Jasper could be. They must have cringed at the thought of the reclusive proto-Provo floating into Goteborg Harbor with hundreds of marijuana plants on board. Meetings were quickly held, and in the end the unsupportive government officials, on the basis of some obscure law regarding the private collection of garbage, decided to confiscate the raft.

Jasper didn't go to Sweden, but the government didn't get the raft either. He turned the whole episode back on the government by inviting their agents and the press to a public Happening, during which he would turn over the raft. When the appointed hour of transfer arrived, Jasper pedal-swam his daffy raft, sans marijuana plants, to the bridge where the crowd and media had assembled. Without a word to the wise, Jasper unexpectedly dove from the crow's nest into the murky canal and swam away, leaving the government officials with large plops of proto-Provo egg on their faces.

Over the years Jasper has constructed innumerable rafts of various configurations and materials, and though none of them has ever gone to Sweden, the evolution of the great raft continues to this day in the form of garden rafts. Rather than collecting canal debris, Jasper now wraps enormous Styrofoam rectangles with thick tarps. He fastidiously knots them together to what ever size he desires (the largest is eight by twenty-four meters), and then lays down a thick layer of topsoil. He and Thea then begin the process of planting, tending and watering the raft until it sprouts a lush bed of grass, in which they plant a variety of flowers, shrubs and even a small tree to complete the garden isle.

His method of construction is not unlike the process of building a polder of land area, which Netherlanders have used for centuries to create more land mass for their tiny country. In the event that a major catastrophe were to strike the Netherlands, the North Sea would swallow up most if not all of the country, so, as Jasper says, "It's always best to have a raft at hand." Jasper in all his Magic Amsterdam glory can be seen on one of his 1980 rafts, singing a snippet from the Beatles song "I'm Fixing a Hole" in the documentary of life in the 1960s, *It Was Twenty Years Ago Today*. The oddest and perhaps the saddest aspect of Jasper's current project is that he builds his visionary floating gardens for survival quite near the government sponsored library which houses the Provo archives – yet the archivists have not once gone down the canal to see what Jasper is doing in the present.

Magic Amsterdam

Amsterdam's well-tenured club and cafe societies are a fascinating network of creative meeting places, each one tailored to attract a different type of patron; young, old and in between. At the time, strictly chess, checkers and Go enthusiasts had their own brown bar parlors, as did journalists, gin connoisseurs, stamp collectors, artists and theater crowds. What was needed were more dope-friendly cafes to accommodate the increasing numbers of goggle-eyed wanna-be hash heads filtering into town. The city's under-culture rose to the psychotropic challenge with enthusiasm – creating soft drug-friendly spots such as Fantasia (soon to become Club de Kosmos) near Central Station, and the claustrophobic (though highly favored) Rusland Cafe off the Nes. The clubs themselves didn't actually sell much hash in those days (at least not over the counter) because just about everyone who came into them was a long-haired, Afghani-vested, scale-toting hash dealer. The colorful Hindu Kush vests were highly sought after items of hip couture because of the kilo carrying secret pocket sewn into the inner linings.

Scoring a personal stash was a loosely organized round-robin of baked red-clay chillums, and unlike the current state of hash cafe, as long as you had guilders in hand, free-sampling the available wares was standard practice. The few existing cafes were soft-smoke havens, near-sanctuaries of dopedom, and as long as all the transaction and consumption remained inside the cafe – and if patrons weren't holding more than a Dutch ounce (100 grams) of cannaboid material, the police left you alone. A truly hospitable state of affairs as far as I was concerned, and within the year openly smoke-friendly cafes and clubs began sprouting up like tulips.

On the artistic front, I was encouraged to continue with my literary writh-ings by the small cadre of writers I would come to meet, largely through Jasper and my association with sound poet Michael Gibbs in England. This loosely knit group of scribes included the esteemed Dutch artist/journalist Simon Vinkenoog and poet/self-trepanation advocate Johnny The Self-Kicker – and the lesser known, though equally prolific writers, six foot six and beyond carrot-haired Michael Chapman, who later bicycled alone and crestfallen to Leningrad, and the terminally expatriate performance artist Peter Pussydog. Peter was an especially memorable and eccentric transplant. He suffered from a genetic deformity causing him to stoop like a rapidly aging troll, loved heroin cocktails, favored extremely young prostitutes, and looked like a demented ferret with a full beard, coke-bottle glasses and a black beret. His bizarre appearance aside, Peter was also a gentle, well-spoken, and talented, if not entirely original, artist. During his unusual performances he would wear an electric suit of his own design, and after plugging himself into the nearest wall socket, Peter and his coat of many 20 watt light bulbs would blink erratically as he recited his angelic Pussydog prose.

The artistic woodshed not withstanding, working with Barry Guy in London and the spontaneous events happening in Amsterdam rekindled my interest in the ritual formats that Max Crosley and I had experimented with in San Francisco, so I sought out the local jazz community in search of avant accompaniment. There were some really terrific clubs, now gone, that catered to the more experimental Free Jazz element, such as the unforgettable Bohe-mian Club and the original Octopus, where I was able to meet and eventually work with some top-quality improvisers, including Dutch contra-bassist Arjan Gorter and pianist Burton Greene.

The Octopus was a great example of what creative minds could do with the socialist-prone government's money. A few Dutch jazz musicians and their families applied, with success, to the government for funding to create a daycare (kresh) facility for their kids in an otherwise abandoned house in their neighborhood. This was a narrow three-story canal front building, and along with the usual materials needed for kresh construction on the third floor, the industrious group included thick sound-proofing, and lots of wiring supplies for the recording studio they installed on the second floor. With the addition of a billiards table, Heineken kegs, and several bottles of jenever (extremely potent Dutch gin) on the ground floor, the Octopus was born.

Early in their operation as an underground club and recording studio, I secured an evening to perform and convinced the reclusive Jasper to put aside his raft management long enough to join me. On the night of our event, the turnout was sizable. I gave a lengthy recitation of Antoine Artaud's caustically poignant essay: "Van Gogh, the Man Suicided by Society;" and Jasper astonished the diverse crowd with an oration from his visionary post-Provo treatise, "Nederland is Bijna Klaar!" ("Holland is Almost Ready!") With this bit of success under my belt I began performing various pieces in the larger clubs in town. At de Kosmos, I presented my "Breath Poetry and the Amplified Heart," as the opening act for "An Evening With Baba Ram Das". In the Paradiso, I was the barber for a manic skit called "Haircut Concerto and The Mystery Guest," with the late exopthalmic comedian Marty Feldman; and in the Melk Weg (Milky Way), I gave a series of well-received cut-up performances titled "This Works From NowHere."

Working the club circuit put me in contact with a much more public milieu of artists, among them writer/entrepreneur Janette Grainger, who published one of the first underground guides to Magic Amsterdam, and video pioneer, Jack Henry Moore. Janette would in time provide Wendy and me with temporary lodging in the northern village of Medemblijk; Jack had worked along side my friends Hoppy and Miles in London at the Arts Lab. Jack also had a hand in creating the studio effects used by Mick Farren and his widely misunderstood rock group, The Deviants. Much to his credit, Jack was also on the editorial staff, along with expatriate publisher Jim Haynes (founder of the Arts Lab), and Bill Levy, former editor for *IT* (*International Times*) in London, for the prurient above-ground journal, *SUCK* Magazine.

SUCK was an unusually literate porn quarterly, with some very creative writing, including a thoroughly scatological piece by my old friend Martin Mosco in San Francisco. The most memorable and enticing image (for me) published in the cryptic pages of *SUCK* was the full-page nude photo of Germaine Greer, author of *The Female Eunuch*, with her yogic legs wrapped around the back of her head, forcing her lovely pudendum into an audacious anal spread shot. As I sat frozen in place, and uninhibitedly staring into the portal of her rather sensuous-looking pooch, the indulgent image brought to mind my one and only contact with this beautiful and talented revolutionary writer.

An Anal Retentive Flashback

A few years earlier in San Francisco, my friend John Brent from the Committee Theater was making his whimsical run for mayor under the banner of his all-inclusive campaign slogan, "Whatever You Want!" It was a time when Gloria Steinem and Ms. Magazine were making the initial pitch for the liberation of the feminine mystique from the severely outdated, male dominated ethos of the 1950s. In a satirically sincere gesture of solidarity, John and myself, along with actors Bruce Mackey and Del Close (also with The Committee), formed a loosely organized male support group we called "M.A.W.L." – acronymic for Men's Auxiliary for Women's Liberation. We held an impromptu press conference at the Committee Theater to announce M.A.W.L.'s unconditional support for the fledgling Woman's Movement, and ended the hilarious con-ference with our more submissive slogan, "We'll Give Them Whatever They Want!" inspired by John's euphonious campaign mantra. This ahead of our time philosophy obviously took a few years to catch on, but as individuals we tried to uphold the banner and sentiments of M.A.W.L. whenever possible. So, when author Germaine Greer showed up in the City to promote her new book on the state of the female, I took it upon myself as one of M.A.W.L.'s men for women to offer our supportive congratulations for her literary efforts.

Insufferably tenacious, I managed to find out what hotel she was staying in and called her up on the phone. Using my best British accent I told the desk captain that I was Ms. Greer's literary agent and needed to speak with her immediately. He put me through without question, and when Germaine answered the phone I introduced myself as M.A.W.L.'s representative and welcomed her to San Francisco. She laughed throughout the rest of my quasi-philosophic greeting and thought our female-friendly take on the situation was great fun. We spent a good twenty minutes laughing and chatting, until finally Germaine said, "Well, I really ought to get back to this room full of impatient journalists and their under-educated questions about my book!"

Back in Amsterdam, I remember thinking that I would probably never get to meet Ms. Greer in the flesh, and that the erotically charged portrait of her would have to suffice. So, in her honor, I framed the brazen image on my studio wall – "God bless Germaine, wherever you are."

Life in the Jordaan

Concerned that I was spreading myself too thin with activities away from studio work and my continuing research at the Stedelijk, Sandberg suggested that I spend more time with him in his studio on the Brouwersgracht. Early on in our relationship, Wil cautioned me against telling too many people about the increasingly student/mentor relationship we were forming. "Word will get around soon enough," he said. He was concerned that by taking on a relatively unknown American artist as what might well be his last student, there were those within the local community of artists who might feel slighted. Indeed, over time, word of our collaboration did spread, but with discretion, and few feathers, beyond those of a certain E. de Wilde, were significantly ruffled. I was deeply honored by our growing friendship, but I must say that his recommendation was huge a responsibility. A few Dutch artists began referring to me as "the American with the golden arm," with respect to my increasing ability to open almost any door in Amsterdam, "armed" as I was with a word or letter of introduction from Sandberg.

Willem Sandberg's international reputation in the art world is well-documented by his outstanding eighteen-year tenure as director for the Stedelijk Museum, his collaborations with many of modern history's greatest artists, and through his sponsorship of painter Karl Appel and the post-war painters collective known as Group Cobra. His selfless and heroic actions leading the Netherlands Underground during World War II included smuggling thousands of indigenous Jewish people to safety with sets of immaculately-forged identification papers. He was the sole survivor among six daring partisans who literally blew up the Dutch Ministry of Records with dynamite during the first days of Nazi occupation. Among his many insightful projects were his designs for the Amsterdam Historical Society Museum, and just prior to my meeting him, his two-year residency as the first director for the Israel Museum in Jerusalem. In brief, Willem Sandberg was a national hero to most of the Dutch populace and one of the most influential citizens in the Netherlands. He spoke seven languages and the automatic dial on his telephone included the Ministries of Culture and Defense, the Rijksmuseum Director, and David Ben-Gurion's home phone.

Through Wil's trust and his unfailing encouragement of my work, many of my insecurities surrounding artistic ability, expatriotism and my significant fear of abandonment were put to quietly hibernate, and throughout our long friendship I wielded the influential sword he had handed me with a duly focused circumspection. I was very fortunate to have had him as my mentor and to have known him as intimately as I did, and I will always be in his debt – a debt I hope to repay someday by helping a younger artist on his or her way.

As the weeks rolled by I spent a considerable amount of time with Wil in his Zen-like studio, going over my latest work. Over a late-afternoon cafe cigar and cognac, we discussed Werkman's warm printing and Sandberg's own topographic techniques, our dreams, and the art and times of his infinitely interesting life as an exemplary man of letters, topographical design, and museum-man with few equal peers. During his semi-retirement, Wil maintained an astounding level of energy and zest for life. As a rule he regularly fasted on bottled drinking water and only slept about four hours out of twenty-four, working steadily throughout the calming solitude of night on his designs and vast correspondence.

Until his spirit passed on 8 April, 1984, and much like painter Henri Toulouse-Lautrec, Wil sustained himself by living life to the fullest, smoking strong French tobacco taken with a short snifter of cognac, and cat naps throughout the day. Humble to the end, my dear friend Willem Sandberg, at his request, would be buried, without ceremony, in an unmarked pauper's grave outside of Amsterdam.

As I worked alongside Sandberg and less and less with Kees and Jasper, my hashful hiatus from the studio and the summer months were coming to a close, and with the autumn leaves marking the advent of winter, most of the pot-head tourists retreated to their various ports called home. Pleased with the seasonal exodus, Wendy and I returned to a quieter and more focused domestic life on de Wittenkade, where the Alcina became our sanctuary, away from the smoke-distracting set that was seminally referred to as "Magic Amsterdam."

Our quaint, visibly friendly, and due to the adjacent seed store, bird-full neighborhood, had an inherent charm – augmented by second story linens and housefrau gossip. We were serenaded by the passing of a strolling accordion player, the melodic song of the knife and scissor sharpener, the rag-picker's bell, and the hoarse busk of the insistent old woman who pushed an onion and pickle cart through the Jordaan.

Red Lights

In the fall of that year, Wendy's best friend Nancie (soon to become the wife of my friend Bruce Mackey in San Francisco) and her ten year old daughter Kirsten arrived from the States. They had come to Amsterdam to visit with us, and more importantly to reunite Kirsten with her terminally estranged father. Nancie's ex-husband Bob, whom Wendy and I had never met, was according to Nancie, a well-seasoned miscreant and drug smuggler on the hard lam from America. Bob and his merry band of bad-boys she said, were quite successful at their chosen trade, and had recently purchased a used J Class sailboat (built for the America's Cup), then at harbor somewhere off the Spanish coast. Looking forward to their reunion, though with natural apprehension, Kirsten was planning to spend part of her European vacation with her father. His lack of presence not withstanding, Nancie said the group was a fun bunch of guys who occasionally used Amsterdam as a safe haven in between smuggle runs. Arrangements for child transfer were made via telegram, and the two of them settled right in to our laid back lifestyle to await Bob's arrival.

It was great to have familiar faces on board the Alcina, and while I worked in the studio, Wendy and guests took in the museums and cafes, wandered the outdoor markets and browsed for treasure among the piles of second-hand junk in the now destroyed Jewish Quarter's extensive flea market. A week or so later, Kirsten's father, Bob (a balding Archie-like thirty-something with orange handle-bar whiskers) arrived at the Alcina with three of his cohorts: Dennis (who looked much like Alfalfa from the Our Gang comedies); Big Mike (he was six foot three with a pro skin diver's musculature); and "JustPlain" John (who was just that, though boyishly handsome with a pencil-line mustache), all three in their late twenties. A friendly, smiling quartet, they came bearing consumptive gifts that Dennis had recently brought back from war-torn Lebanon. While his friends and I sampled the potent fare, Bob reunited with his ex-wife and daughter, and chatted with Wendy.

Unlike Amsterdam's brand of commonly visible drug dealer, Bob and company looked like well-heeled ivy league tourists in their neatly trimmed hair cuts, button-down collars and v-neck sweaters, not international smugglers with a track record. As Nancie had suggested they were a fun bunch, but first looks as the saying sort of goes, can be extremely deceiving. Soon after psychedelic lift-off from the freshly pressed red Lebanese hash, my intuitive nature declared them to be an elusive group, and that they were trouble in the making. Bob and his daughter seemed to get on well together, and though I thoroughly enjoyed the reunion party favors I was equally pleased to have them leave. Shortly after this, and with some trepidation, the untraveled Bruce made his way across the Atlantic to unexpectedly visit, and more importantly, to collect his future wife and step daughter, fearing that they might fall under the sway of ex-husband Bob, and choose to remain in Europe for some time. To his great misfortune, Bruce has never fared well in marriage, and though his rescue mission to Amsterdam would prove successful, in the end, their marriage faltered and within a few short years they would divorce. His sudden appearance on the scene put Nancie on prenuptial alert, but I got a great kick out of touring my old friend around Amsterdam's lesser known quarters. We had a ball together, continuing our "personal research" into the city's dimly lit brown bars, hash dens, and multi-national red light districts.

Bruce, who to his credit remained red-light abstinent, was completely blown away by the variety of openly available hookers – the creamy-skinned to the beyond ebony – the beautifully sleek to the grossly obese and disgusting. The working girls of Amsterdam offer every conceivable type of sexual adventure, and pro's are not the only ones offering up sexual mystery. Many Dutch housewives (with or without their husband's consent) took to the afternoon skin trade as a perfectly acceptable second income. Pimps are largely unnecessary, because once a woman gets her clean bill of health certificate, she can simply rent a maid-attended room by the hour in one of the cities many windowfront bordellos. The extensive Disneyland-like red light tourist district of world renowned sex clubs, such as the Casa Rosa, has been shown in documentary after documentary. It is certainly the largest such area in Amsterdam, offering perhaps the widest variety of sex play – male and female, from the fabulous quickie to the sternest of dominatrix bondage and secret fetish play, but it is hardly the only red light district in town. It is most certainly not the area to visit if your objective is a leisurely frolic with a seasoned professional. These well-equipped and far less obvious play-pens require some "personal research" to locate, but the delay of sex-act is well worth the effort. Compared to the overly-advertised areas of quasi-sin, where sexual rip-off is the real currency, the harder to find, and much more enticing ladies of the night will treat you like an Adonis or abuse you as desired to your heart's content for a not unreasonable sum.

I took Bruce to the Lowland Weed Company to meet Kees, and on a couple of my second-story kraaking runs to gather forgotten treasure from abandoned buildings. Having never traveled anywhere, Bruce gawked like a wide-eyed child, at the Jordaan locals eating their smoked eel and pickled herring sandwiches with a knife and fork. He marvelled at the open drug use in the cafes, and at the casual nature of the Dutch people regarding the kiddie porn and other scandalous material in the city's extremely hard core sex emporiums. My friend was immediately taken with the congenial Amsterdamers, but unfortunately he was unable, perhaps due to his pre-spousal rescue mission, to let go of his, "I come from America" persona, which in many ways prohibited him from experiencing the Dutch people on their own terms. Bob's transient and slightly unnerving presence on the set seemed to alienate Bruce even further, so it wasn't long before he was making plans to abscond to Paris with Nancie, and unbeknownst to Bob, Bruce's soon to be step daughter, Kirsten.

From the beginning, Bruce had been adamant that going to Spain with a boatload of smugglers was not in his future family's best interests, and did all he could to abort their original plans. Eventually successful with his pleas, the three of them left for Paris under cover of night, leaving Wendy and me to offer Nancie's vague explanations without destination to Kirsten's drug running father. He and his cohorts, Big Mike and "JustPlain" John, took Wendy and me out to a lavish dinner in an expensive restaurant, and though he was disappointed that the proposed reunion with Kirsten was now aborted by Bruce, he and his smuggle mates were generously festive that evening, and soon left for Spain. This (for me) relatively uncomfortable meeting, (which Wendy thoroughly enjoyed), would unfortunately set in motion a series of sub-conscious scenarios far beyond my artistic control, and would, in the months ahead, dramatically alter the course of our tranquil life together in Holland. Before Wendy and I could get over the departure of Bruce, Nancie, and Kirsten, other acquaintances from afar, such as Nigel Pickering (an original member of the folk-rock combo, Spanky and Our Gang) and his family, Michael Gibbs from Dorset, a cocaine smuggling friend from Bolivia, and London jewelry artist Hamish Campbell turned up at the Alcina's gang plank. With all the spontaneous visiting activity and added frivolity, my studio work slacked off again, much to the displeasure of Sandberg, who suggested that in order for me to get back to fully concentrating on my art work I should consider getting out of town for a while.

Medemblijk

I was able to heed Wil's good advice due to the hospitality of my friend, writer Jeanette Granger, who graciously let Wendy and me use the unoccupied farm worker's bunk house she owned on the outskirts of the northern village of Medemblijk (Holland's first city). The predominantly Catholic village and our new digs were located eighteen feet below sea level and quite near the significant dijk that prevents the Netherlands from disappearing under the harsh spume of the unrelenting North Sea. Half a mile out of town and next door to a dairy farm, the bunk house had two large rooms, toilet room with shower stall and an adequate kitchen on the ground floor. Via the ceiling-pull ladder, there was a lovely studio space in the attic with thatched roof and three large bay windows, offering me a picturesque view of the lowland fields. My plan was to paint steadily in the afterglow of my Werkman intensive at the Stedelijk Museum. After which, it was Sandberg's intention that I would exhibit a com-

pliment of my proposed "WerkStudies" in a working museum of antique printing machines in Amsterdam called het Drukhuis, operated by Rene Treumann,
son of the Dutch artist/topographer Otto Treumann.

Medemblijk was at the other end of the social spectrum from "Magic
Amsterdam," and though I was quite taken with the flat countryside, and
would produce a sizable body of work there, the isolation and solitude along
with my long hours up in the attic would prove to be almost unbearable for
Wendy. Admittedly I was preoccupied, and at the time completely unaware
of Wendy's growing discontent. Her role as the devoted domestic partner to
a relatively insecure, moody, anonymous bohemian, and at times, manic artist
who came downstairs three times a day to play house was wearing thin. While
I found solace, tranquility and creative spark in Medemblijk's solitude, Wendy
began to brood, missing the high life in Amsterdam while scraping the daily
cream off the milk we got fresh from the udder at the farm next door. Even a
four-day trip to Paris didn't do much to brighten her fading light, and once
we returned to Medemblijk, I adjourned to the studio, again leaving Wendy
to her own devices.

While we were in Paris visiting friends, we bumped into a jazz world
acquaintance of mine by the name of Raphael Garrett. I had met the avant
bassist and former side-man to the Art Ensemble of Chicago some years earlier
in San Francisco, when Max Crosley and I had briefly hung out with the Mid-
western free jazz composer Rosco Mitchell. He and Raphael stopped in the
City to perform a series of relatively unadvertised gigs with their short-lived
avant-road ensemble, The Music Circus. Raphael was, and perhaps still is, an
innovative multi-intrumentalist, and long-term heroin user, then traveling
with his drug-free paramour, a Swiss cellist named Sousant. In one of those
completely on-the-cuff invitations, I suggested that if they came to the Netherlands they might spend some time with us in Medemblijk, adding that I might
rustle up an impromptu gig for us at The Octopus.

Never imagining that they would jump Paris on my suggestion, Wendy
and I were quite surprised soon thereafter, when we came back to Medemblijk
from a day in Amsterdam to find the two atonal musicians jamming away in
the bunk house for the benefit of our next door farmer's four wide-eyed teenage sons. I'm sure none of them had ever seen a six foot six black man, who
was slamming extraterrestrial riffs from his stand-up bass into their provincial
forebrains, while Sousant produced an entire zoo of exotic sounds with the
collection of odd-ball instruments Raphael had made from antique bamboo
and rubber shower attachments. Raphael could make an instrument of some
sort from just about anything. From the look of their musical luggage (well-

traveled bass, cello and two large duffel bags of instrumental whatever), they intended to stay awhile. Not wanting to insult the pair by going back on my invitation, I offered the unexpected guests our spare room. As if to reassure his hosts and not wanting to draw the heat to our quiet retreat, Raphael assured me that he was clean – jazz-user slang for temporarily off of, and currently not holding any skag (heroin).

In the days that followed, a lively and enthusiastic Raphael and I toured the jazz/hash clubs in Amsterdam and began discussing our options at the Octopus, where I had complimentary access to the recording studio. We agreed on a multi-track (26 to be exact) spontaneous over-dub format of indeterminate length (it finished up at an hour and sixteen minutes) with Raphael and Sousant on strings, toy piano, and bamboo shower tubings, while I added the more percussive metal wastebasket/antique Tibetan gong-bowl reverberation. I would also add my "Component-World Breath Poetry" to the multi-over-dubbed concoction of avant be-thrubs, cello-angs and virtuistic scale-thrizzo's of progressive improvisation. Our first sessions went well, and although our collaboration would soon come to a crashing halt, our textured recording would eventually be broadcast by a free jazz-friendly FM station in St. Louis, Missouri.

A week later and following our fourth all-day session in the studio, Raphael and Sousant opted to stay in Amsterdam overnight while Wendy and I went back to the bunk house. When the pair returned to Medemblijk the next evening Raphael didn't look so good. They retired to the spare room, and once Sousant had tucked the lumbering bassist into bed, she came back to assure Wendy and me that it was "probably just a twenty-four hour bug." She then excused herself for the night. Two minutes later she was screaming for help from the back of the house. Raphael, all six foot six of him, was slumped between the sink and the toilet – a blood filled syringe not so innocently on the floor next to him. Quite obviously, my previously "clean" friend had overdosed on the skag he had picked up, unbeknownst to Sousant, in Amsterdam (where street heroin is much stronger than in Paris). We managed to get him onto his feet, and the three of us walked and talked him back to the land of Medemblijk, working in shifts throughout the night. The next day, Raphael nodded face-down in his oatmeal and would have drowned if I hadn't pulled him out. I gave Raphael twenty bucks, threw the both of them out on their ears, and our recording sessions were over!

Dangerous Liaisons

Much to my chagrin, the only time Wendy would really perk up was when Nancie's ex-husband Bob and his crew of Bobbettes would come by every few weeks to rent our shed, where they would customize a newly rented Mercedes sedan with freshly pressed kilos of red Lebanese hashish bound for the lungs and minds of American GI's stationed in Germany. These periodic moments of aiding and abetting were helpful financially, but unlike Wendy, I was not at all enthralled by their intrigue. The Bobbettes, who in no way resembled typical drug smugglers, were in the game for the rush, the money, and the deep cover anonymity they maintained in Amsterdam. Here, in between cash and hash runs, they could enjoy the three C's: conspiracy, cognac and cocaine, in the privacy of their hideaway near the far end of the Vondel Park. As a group they initially came to trust Wendy and me because of our close friendship with Nancie. Before we moved to Medemblijk, whenever they hit Amsterdam they would invite us to join them in their inconspicuous revelry, something Wendy sorely missed living as we did, in rural-bohemian seclusion.

Thinking the Bobbettes would only show up on rare occasion, I at first went along as a cheerful co-consumer of things beginning with the letter C. But in my heart, and again, unlike Wendy, I wasn't taken in by their over-the-top rationalizations and group-inflated status as "soft drug providers," or their expensive indulgences. For one thing, rather than turning me into an uninhibited motor-mouth with visions of personal or sensual perfection, when I snort topple-over-the-line or bottom quality blow, it does just what it's supposed to do if you stick it up your nose – it anesthetizes everything upto and including my brain. Not exactly my idea of recreational drug fun. Wendy on the other hand, relished sitting up with them late into the dawn, filling her nostrils with Bolivian flake, and her increasingly curious mind with conspiratorial tales of Bobbette lore. I indulged Wendy's participation with a wary eye, but I was completely blind-sided by her first-thing-in-the-morning Medemblijk confession, that in a moment of "coke passion," she had willingly hopped in the sack with one of the Bobbettes, the otherwise generous and friendly (to me) "JustPlain" John.

Before I could react to her statement of transgression, Wendy ad libbed that it was simply a one-time skip in our marital record and would not happen again. In order to "even things out," she suggested that surely I had been attracted to someone in Amsterdam, and if that were so, she advised that I should go to the woman post haste to dip my otherwise untarnished wick into her pot of extramarital honey. At first, I found this to be a preposterous idea. I protested vigorously that, even though there was such a person, to act on her equally adulterous suggestion would be doing a great disservice to the woman in question – not to mention the fact that she was currently the girlfriend of a well-known Amsterdamer. But in the end, Wendy's skewed logic prevailed, and I went into Amsterdam to visit my proposed courtesan. I'll call her Suki.

Denial can momentarily get you just about anywhere, but I felt the ridiculous cuckoldry as I rode the train into town. Suki was a beautiful, henna-haired Dutch woman in her late twenties, who I had met in the club de Kosmos following one of my performances there, and yes, I was indeed enamored by her exotic fashions, her chanteuse-like mannerisms and her slinky body. Suki was also no dummy, so to simplify matters I told her the truth, rather than try to concoct some ill-fated scenario for seduction. This proved to be quite an effective line. At first, Suki thought my "not entirely unexpected approach," and Wendy's sudden infidelity, was the result of my not being able to "get it up." I assured her that wasn't the case at all. We laughed, had some tea, shared a binnenlander joint, and then devoured each other during an hour or two of thoroughly uninhibited, purely-for-the-fun-of-it sex play. Suki actually thanked me (with censored graphic detail) for the erotic interlude, and patted me on the butt as she sent me from her bohemian boudoir back to Medemblijk. I truly enjoyed the sensual tryst and Suki's open affection, but I still felt at odds with the situation at home.

Back at the bunk house, Wendy acted as if she had been absolved from her indiscretion by my balancing the books with Suki, and wanted to drop the matter. I went back to my attic easel (made from an antique wheelbarrow I found algae-floating in a canal), painfully aware that if I wanted to save my marriage I needed to finish up my woodshedding and move us back to Amsterdam as soon as possible. In the meantime, Wendy dutifully stayed downstairs, impatiently embroidering elaborate designs on bleached cotton shirts, just counting the days. When my WerkStudies were nearly complete, we moved temporarily into a small inexpensive room on Amstelveensweg, near the far end of the Vondel Park. The unfortunate aspect of this re-emergence onto the set was that our room was on the third floor of the same building that provided the secluded attic for Bob and his unscrupulous partners. "JustPlain" John made some gesture of amends for having bedded my wife, and undoubtedly the band of free-spirited pirates had heard all about my "equalizing" rendezvous with Suki, so all was supposedly forgiven. Fat chance!

Out of the Woodshed

My time was immediately absorbed by meetings with Sandberg and Rene Treumann at het Drukhuis in preparation for my first solo exhibition, while Wendy
supposedly searched for a more private living accommodation. Due to the lean
months spent in Medemblijk seclusion, our financial situation wasn't much
to speak of, and finding affordable housing proved to be difficult for her. My
exhibit and any potential influx of cash were still some weeks away, so Wendy
and her admiring bunch of Bobbettes came up with a plan to tide us over. Bob
(out of the kindness of his heart, it seemed at the time) offered to have Wendy
ride along with him as female cover during a short-run; i.e., just another pair
of American tourists in a rented Mercedes (carrying thirty-six kilos of hash) on
their way to visit Germany. Or, as Wendy succinctly put it, "We need the cash!
and I can make us a fast thousand bucks (at the time nearly eight thousand
guilders) – I'll be back the day after tomorrow." Without an alternative solution, I regrettably broke my own rule and agreed to their scheme.

Once upon another time in expatriate space, Wendy and I resorted, due to
thinning assets, to a mutually beneficial collaboration with another exporter
of illegal substance. Bob knew the details of this Canadian escapade, and felt
that Wendy would be a solid compliment on the trip to Germany to drop off
product with German John, the active duty arm of the Bobbettes. The trip was
touted as a reasonably safe adventure which would provide for Wendy and me
with the necessary funds to rent an apartment and leave us with a grub stake.
What the Bobbettes forgot to mention was the distinct possibility that the two-
day excursion would irrevocably alter my life with Wendy. I was thoroughly
preoccupied with the preparations for my exhibit, but, had I taken the time to
considered the unlikely consequences of entrusting my wife into the safe-keep-
ing of her best friend's ex-husband, I would most certainly have declined their
(seemingly well-meant) offer.

As predicted, Wendy and Bob safely returned to Amsterdam, and we were
now in a position to move from the chateau Bobbette. I awoke early the following morning, and as I was lacing up my boots, Wendy blurted out the Ham-
mond-shattering news that she wanted to have an affair with Bob! Waves of
panic attack ran through my psyche, and the world around me twisted into the
confusion of a Mobius strip. She rather hesitatingly revealed that she had "slept
with" (insert: deliberately screwed) Bob while in Germany, and her attraction
to the adulterous scenario was more than I could handle. Sobbing, Wendy haltingly confessed to a mounting confusion regarding her strong and independent

feelings toward two very different men. When I encountered their leader later that day, his muscular team of Bobbettes had to forcefully intervene as I fixed my hands around Bob's pathetic throat in a serious attempt to strangle him. Bob and crew beat a hasty retreat to points unknown, and Wendy and I moved into the spacious apartment I had found for us on the Keizersgracht, just three blocks from Sandberg's Brouwersgracht studio. The move was carried out in a state of quiet denial, but I knew that Wendy was at sixes and sevens regarding her temporarily absent paramour. Internally, I was beside myself with anger, humiliation and grief over this second transgression, which offered nothing in the way of support for my up-coming debut.

Something had to give if I was going to stay on track with my career, and at the same time salvage my previously committed marriage. More than anything, I wanted Wendy to come to her senses, but I could tell from her sorry demeanor that ignoring the matter or my having it off with another surrogate was not going to work. Wendy fully realized the strain her infidelities were putting on me, and half-heartedly offered to stop seeing Bob. This was certainly my preference, but to have her do so only because it was hurting me, seemed to be an equally dishonest route without resolution. For my part Wendy needed to add some soul and sincerity to her offer, and I intuitively felt that the only way for us to re-unite was if she knew, beyond any shadow, that our life together was far more important than her desire to have a triadic love life. As difficult a decision as it was for me to make, I told her to follow her extra-marital impulses while I proceeded with my exhibition, which to my great surprise nearly sold out on opening night The uncomfortable compromise I had reached with Wendy made our life together momentarily tolerable, and in the weeks that followed I focused my diminishing enthusiasm on my collaboration with Rene Treumann and his partner, artist Bart Boumanns, who offered me a small work space in het Drukhuis.

Other than than my biased wife, Sandberg was one of the few people with whom I shared my increasing anguish. Having been in a similar situation at one time, he was very supportive, offering me his candid advice along with the name of his personal physician, should I come to need his (pro bono) services. At the time, I declined Wil's generous suggestion for medical intervention, but soon after, as my inner life began to run fully amok, I would come to need professional attention. Wendy and I began setting up our new digs and acquired a speckled cat we named Specula, after the popular Dutch cookies, speculas.

Now that she had my rueful blessing to suss out her feelings for Bob, Wendy started bringing home self-help books for me to read, such as *Be Here Now, The Prophet, Are You Sanpauku?* (I was not, though Bob and Richard Nixon were) and more pointedly, *Open Marriage (A New Life Style for Couples)* by quasi-sexologist authors Nena and George O'Neil. My take after reading this innocent-looking paperback, was that their philosophy of egalitarian partnership, where the very concept of monogamy is seen as the great destroyer of relationships, was little more than cheaply adulterous corn. It had absolutely nothing to offer a struggling young married couple in the way of therapeutic advice. As examples of cultures that eschew monogamy, the authors had to seek out Eskimos, Marquesans, the Lobi in West Africa and the obscure Toda tribe in India. The sexo-philosophical rationalizations and obnoxious pillow talk of the O'Neil's simply didn't have a place in my marital construct.

The only reason I tolerated Wendy's extra-marital behavior was my firm belief that, without active exploration and resolution on her part, I would never be able to trust my partner or believe in our marriage again. I also knew that if I took her up on her half-hearted offers to "just forget about it," all I would have for a partner would be the hollow shell of a previously vital and trustworthy companion. So I took the pain in lieu of spousally enforced abstinence, and suffered through each and every hour that she was away, "shopping," knowing full-well that it was a lie. Wendy was caught up in a sensual vortex, filled with almost bi-monthly occasions of libidinous lust, and there really wasn't much I could do about it. This was an extremely bitter pill for me to swallow, causing me agonizing fits of jealousy and a quickly eroding self-esteem. Unfortunately, I failed to get out from under my own emotional fallout, and as the illicit affair continued to unfold, like Artaud, "I could feel the pain sweating in my bones."

Whenever Bob would surreptitiously come to town, Wendy would "shop," or visit with a "girl friend" all day. I stayed in my studio listening to the internal hiss of my decaying nervous system, and ill-advisedly consulted the Tarot cards about her real activities – much like comedian George Burns did from his private television set to covertly watch the non-adulterous antics of his astutely hare-brained wife Gracie.

This was fast becoming a very unhealthy state of 'affair', and it became increasingly difficult for me to think about anything else. Things came to a head one evening as she was about to leave, dressed for seduction, looking lovelier than I had seen her in months. She looked at me with those beautiful hazel eyes that I had once trusted beyond all others and said, "Don't wait up for me. I might not be home tonight." With those painfully fateful words that no self-respecting husband wants to hear, Wendy finally crushed the fragile hinge that held my psyche together. In the wake of her quick departure, I took a belly-flop into the dark recesses of cuckoldry. I fumed for hours, trying to convince myself that she would see the monumental heartbreak she was causing and return home. Around midnight, realizing that this was not going to happen, I took a taxi over to Bob's hideaway and had the driver wait with his meter running while I climbed the stairs to retrieve my wayward spouse.

I knocked angrily on his attic door, eying a case of empty beer bottles sitting on the hallway floor. Thinking that I should break one of them and slit Bob's throat, I listened to the bed sheets rustle on the other side of the door. At first, Bob refused to open up, but when I told him I would just break the door in because I wasn't leaving without my wife, he relented, though allowing Wendy enough time to get dressed. Latent shame and horror on her face, she appeared in the attic doorway, and we took the taxi home in silence. When we got back to our place on the Keizersgracht I immediately began packing her suitcase. Wendy pleaded with me not to throw her out. She said she realized that things had gone too far – that she wanted to stop the confusing affair and remain with me. This time I accepted her proposal, and told her in no uncertain terms that she could never see Bob or his band of Bobbettes again. She tearfully agreed, and the next day I went back to deliver the news to Bob in person.

Bob tried to offer me an empty apology, but I cut him short. I looked at him as I have never looked at another human being, and flatly told him that if he made any attempt to see Wendy again I would turn him into a rotting corpse, after happily watching him die. I learned through intermediaries that he fled for Spain later that day.

For a number of weeks Wendy was attentive at home. She tried to be enthusiastic about my increasing sales and on-going collaboration with Sandberg, but I could see the distance in her eyes, and knew she was pining away for Bob and their expensive trysts. Finally, I couldn't take the charade any longer. Without telling her of my intentions, I went to one of my collectors, sold him a large canvas at a greatly reduced price, and bought her a one-way ticket to oblivion. I went back to the Keizersgracht, where I presented her with the ticket to Barcelona, and after she packed her suitcase I took her to the Central Station. As I helped her onto the platform, I told her not to bother coming back unless she was finished with Bob. A the train pulled out of the station, my eyes filled with tears possibly tinged with blood, and without looking back, I walked away. With Wendy out of the way I tried to keep up appearances, especially around Sandberg, but soon resorted to diversion in order to keep my inner hounds at bay.

Into the Fire

Amsterdam is a very tolerant city when it comes to the personal at-home use of intoxicants, and as the lonely days progressed I stepped up my substance intake. At first, satisfied with chasers of jenever and copious amounts of opiated Kashmir and Afghani hash, I frequented the late night clubs such as the subterranean Oxoff, but more and more I was locking myself into an indulgent self-pity at home, sending me into a downward spiral.

During the summer the vacant building next door to our place on the Keizersgracht had been liberated by the macrobiotic set, and the temporary inhabitants of the former convent called their brown rice redoubt the East-West Centrum. They advocated long periods of organic brown rice fasting and the Be Hungry Now teachings of Gorges Osawa and his primary adept, Misio Kushi. But with the ebb of summer, the anti-Sampaku crowd moved on, and the penitence cells of the former nunnery began to fill up with transient needle freaks and a far less health conscious menagerie of adepts. They hung a portent un-welcome sign on the former convent's front door that read: "Paranoia Is a Heightened State of Awareness!" My building mates and I had to pass by the Gothic-looking shooting gallery on a regular basis, and though our backyard gardens were separated by a common wall of stone, we gave the increasingly unfriendly neighbors a wide berth – though the one time I dared to ventured into the used-cotton labyrinth, I received a surprise.

One Sunday morning as I was sitting on the garden overhang outside my apartment, I heard the unmistakable voice of Nico singing the Velvet Underground song, "I'll Be Your Mirror." I started to sing along with what I assumed to be a recording, when half way through the song, the atonal voice stopped, and then began again with an acoustic version of "All Tomorrow's Parties." Curious, I went into the courtyard next door to find the proto-Gothic Nico herself (real name, Christa Paffgen), dressed in layers of beyond ebony and seated next to a small harmonium, strumming away on a beat-up guitar. Without disturbing her, I sat down next to a pillar as the formerly beautiful co-star of Fellini's *La Dolce Vita*, and Andy Warhol's Exploding Plastic Inevitable unwittingly gave me a private concert of Underground samples. When she finally noticed me, I introduced myself from afar and thanked her. She smiled and invited me over – her long ash and once blonde hair was like castle gossamer – her album-cover eyes were now dark sockets of imminent doom, and I could see that the underground chanteuse was well into an on-going demise from heroin addiction. We chatted for a minute or two, but when she found out I wasn't interested in junk, she went back to singing ("Sunday Morning") and completely ignored me.

Coincidentally in the same time frame, the poet Simon Vinkenoog introduced me his old friend – the infinitely mysterious artist Vali Meyers – "The Witch of Positano, Italy," and object of an earnest Hemingway diva-desire in late 1950s Paris. The colorfully exotic and facially tattooed (by Maori needle) artist arrived in Amsterdam to open a showing of her self-portraits drawn in India Ink mixed with swashes of her own menstrual blood!

I began taking long walks in the Vondel Park, still vibrating from the nomads of summer. Amsterdam's municipal park is a lovely quarter mile expanse of sculpture, manicured lawns, white gazebos, and a man-made lake, edged by trees, dense plant life and a network of hidden pathways with a notorious reputation for quick and anonymous sex play. It wasn't uncommon (or particularly illegal) to find men with men, and women, tucked back among the semi-exotic shrubbery having it off with each other. On one of my mournful strolls, I encountered a young blonde – a German woman with a shapely figure and flared skirt, who invited me into the bush for some friendly foreplay. This led to a heated passion, and we unabashedly stripped from the waist like a pair of exhibitionists as the passing voyeurs watched us giving each other simultaneous oral sex amid the foliage of our blatant interlude. It was all quite civil really, and when we were done licking and sucking each others groin, we simply dressed, pecked each other on the cheek, and went our separate ways (smiling for a change!).

Among the few friends who knew about Wendy's slight of marriage was the Dutch artist/set designer Nils Hamel and his American wife, Jeannie. Our friends lived on Prinzen Island near the Jordaan District, and one evening as I was about to leave their art studio/home, Nils suggested that Jeannie take me to "the scream tunnel," as a means of releasing some of my pent-up anger and frustration. Agreeing with Nils, Jeannie led me through the Prinzen darkness to a railroad trestle with a small tunnel running underneath. We stood there shivering in the night air as Jeannie explained that we needed to wait until a train passed, and when the sound of a commuter engine approached, Jeannie told me to get ready to scream at the top of my lungs while the train roared over our heads. With the thundering sound of the train above us, I screamed louder and longer than I thought possible. The train faded from earshot, and though I did feel a therapeutic release from the primal exercise, the brittle psychosphere surrounding my grief continued to expand for the worse.

I lied to friends and to Sandberg, telling them I was going out of town for a while, and instead, furthered the course of my spousal deprivation and diversion, by visiting and briefly participating in the S&M bordello scene. Here I had myself flogged with a cat-o-nine tails by a dominant, though essentially beautiful transvestite, and then shamelessly ventured into the ill-lit parks and tea rooms around town, where varying styles of anonymous male to male sex could be had, but I soon grew tired of the nocturnal and (for me) completely unnatural kink activity. It has been suggested that you can't oppose something intellectually that is over powering you emotionally, and under the strain of my loss I began haunting the shadowy Zeedijk and the subterranean mah-jongg parlors along the Binnen Bantammerstrat, in search of the oblivion offered by red tar opium. After scoring the dreamy substance, I would spend the dazed afternoons in a narcotic fugue, wandering my apartment and despair like an inarticulate Rimbaud, consumed by my own angst-ridden season in hell.

My growing sense of purgatorial decay was supported by a monstrous denial and the daily doses of addictive drugs I continued to consume with an increasing hunger. Alone and distraught, and largely without hope for the future, I locked myself away from the world in our Keizersgracht home.

To occupy my faltering mind I began torturing my fragile psyche with imaginative visions of the adulterous Wendy in the arms of her lover. As a result of these hallucinatory portents, I cut my own arms with a shard from an empty gin-bottle – smearing the blood onto the surrogate-canvas of my own endless eternity. I went out only at night, like a vampire, to purchase narcosic supplies, and would wake each day a mess, hung over and fully clothed, thinking that I must be working again because of the chaotic Rorschach blots of blood forming on my studio wall.

When my stool took on the color of the La Brea Tar Pits, I gathered my wits and went to see Sandberg's doctor, who informed me that I had developed an acutely bleeding gastric ulcer. The kind and compassionate physician wanted to hospitalize me immediately. When I adamantly refused, he sternly ordered that if personal survival was my goal, I had to cease and desist with my hash, gin and opium fast, and to get religious with his proscribed regime. When I agreed to the self-treatment program, he gave me some medication to stop the bleeding in my stomach, and put me on a strict diet of cultured yogurt, yogurt and more cultured yogurt, with little in between except bottled water and bed rest. At home, I washed my coagulated paintings from the walls of the apartment, bought most of the cultured yogurt in the neighborhood, and was well on my way toward recovery, though still emaciated and withdrawn, when Wendy, having tired of her Majorcan frolic and without having resolved much of anything, unexpectedly returned home. Shocked by my deterioration, she tended to my physical and psychic wounds, and for the moment, largely to accommodate my doctor's orders, she returned to a semblance of her formerly devoted self. Further discussion concerning her infidelities and the nature of our future together was put on hold.

The Inferno (revisited)

The weeks, along with the majority of my stressful preoccupation, passed, and my health returned to a relatively normal condition. I began to work at the easel again, and resumed my weekly meetings with Sandberg. To bring in some money I made a number of original manuscripts, now loosely referred to as "artist books," consisting of twenty or more original images, and then bound as individual works, which my small bevy of collectors thankfully snapped up at very reasonable prices. The best of these was a series of collage renderings of industrial parts mixed with random Arabic and Hebrew alphabets, titled, *The Machine Fires Itself*, and a collection of my Fluxus-like work, *The Original Was a Reproduction*, which Sandberg purchased. For the time being, and without mention of Bob, life on the Keizersgracht with Wendy seemed almost normal, that is until our quiet building became the target of a persistent arsonist.

The first, and nearly successful attempt, came one night when almost everyone in our building was away, attending a Rolling Stones concert at the Rai auditorium. Wendy and I were upstairs visiting our through-the-ceiling neighbor when I smelled something like rubber burning. When I went into the hallway, I found the stairwell engulfed by noxious smoke, and proceeded to run through the building, shouting, "Fire! Fire! – Get Out Now!" Downstairs, dense smoke was pouring from under the door to our apartment, and without thinking, I broke the door's fire seal and was hit hard in the face by a toxic blast. I put a wet rag over my mouth and crawled under the smoke to find our cat Specula, who had taken refuge under a step leading to the back window of the apartment. Flames shot up the wall from the basement below as I grabbed up the terrified Specula, our passports, cash on hand and overcoats before crawling back to Wendy in the relative safety of the street. Fire trucks assembled and the flames, which were fortunately contained in the basement, were quickly extinguished. According to the fire marshal, the significant blaze had been intentionally set by someone familiar with the building's wiring system. To our relief, other than destroying the communal kitchen downstairs, the damage to our building was largely smoke-related.

The second attempt came a few days later, and again, I discovered the fire. This time it was less serious, in that the source of the limited although noxious smoke came from a burning roll of plastic hidden in a hall closet on the second floor, which I managed to extinguish without the aid of the local fire brigade.

As a household, we held smoke-tinged meetings, blamed the insufferable army of speed freaks next door for the arson and established a fire watch.

All was quiet for a week or so, but the minute we let our guard down the arsonist struck again. This time the fire was on the ground floor near the main stairwell, fueled by an alcohol-soaked mattress. When the fire crew arrived to put out the flaming staircase, I went into the smoke-filled hallway with them. None of us was prepared for the Dante-esque tableau awaiting us inside. Sitting in a lounge chair near his doorway at the top of the landing, just above the threatening flames, was our duly elected maintenance man. Through the smoke and flames, he looked like one of Poe's apparitions and was wearing a pair of dark-lens motorcycle goggles! Mahler blared from his stereo system as the flames leaped before him and he laughed maniacally. When the fire was put out, an ambulance was called to "take him away, Ho-Ho!" and the arson came to a halt. Later we learned that our confused fix-it man, prior to becoming a fire-bug, had unbeknownst to any of his friends or house mates, volunteered for a government-supported study of a new and as it turned out chemically flawed form of synthetic opium, which apparently rearranged his neural connections. When he came down from the presumably pain killing concocti he was released in what the opiate scientists deemed to be a recovered state of normalcy. Two days later, the fires started.

The Alpbach Forum

Though my general health had returned, my brushes and personal demeanor were largely influenced by the previous sorrow, and time spent at the easel helped to fill the on-going void, regardless of Wendy's tenuous presence. Unbeknownst to me, my dear friend and mentor Willem Sandberg had submitted my name and a sample of my work, along with that of two Dutch painters, as possible candidates for the Alpbach Forum. This is a very prestigious art symposium held every ten years in the Tyrolian village of Alpbach, high in the Austrian Alps, where twenty European countries are invited to send one artist to represent their respective nations.

Sandberg unexpectedly summoned me to his studio one afternoon and asked me if I would like to go to Austria in three weeks to represent the Netherlands at the well-publicized event.

"But I'm not Dutch!" I exclaimed in surprise.

Wil looked at me with an incredibly piercing expression and said, "I think the Ministry of Culture is well aware of your ancestry, but they left the final choice to me, and I want you to go."

I told Wil that I was truly honored by his recommendation, but that I found my nomination to be just a little embarrassing. After all, aside from not being a Dutch artist, I was an illegal alien! Nonetheless, we set about planning for the trip by selecting pieces that I would take with me, as each artist would be allowed five works of art which were to be exhibited in the Forum's main salon for the duration of the two week Symposium. The Cardinal of Austria was to give the opening address, and members of the Austrian royal family would be in attendance.

I was to travel to Innsbruk overland by train, receive red-carpet accommodations with my own chalet, and all of my expenses, including Wendy's, would be paid for by the Dutch Ministry of Culture. Over the next couple of weeks I worked with a renewed passion, in order to present fresh oil, and to put some much-needed artistic integrity between me and my tepid marital situation at home. Wendy was complementary and happy for my success but uncertain about going along. She said that she felt her presence would only be a distraction for me. I tried to assure her that this was not the case – I honestly wanted her to be with me. Round and round we went, back and forth, regarding her increasing unwillingness to go to Austria. Finally, the night-light in my heartbroken soul clicked on and I realized that what she really wanted was to cavort with Bob, while I received honors in Alpbach! Needless to say, I was deeply hurt by her desire to again fly off to join the Bobbettes on their amoral sailboat, instead of being with me. Going to the Alpbach Forum was to become my greatest moment as an artist up to that time, and I would have to experience it alone.

My artistic dreams were merging with reality, and my persistence in the studio was resulting in recognition and sales. I was at my creative peak, and at the same time my emotional nadir, and I knew that if I was to be successful in Alpbach, I needed to be free of Wendy and her betrayals. Persistent to a fault, I convinced her to at least join me on the thirteen hour train ride to Innsbruk, where, hoping against hope, I might also convince her to see the folly of her decision. I failed, and as I climbed aboard the private ride to Alpbach, Wendy caught a public taxi to the Innsbruk airport and her flight (at Bobbette expense) into the arms of her lover. When she had gone, I vowed to myself that I would put her out of my mind.

Spring was bringing out the best of Tyrollean flora, and the Alpine snow was still in place high above the beautiful landscape surrounding Alpbach. Lovely time-polished chalets festooned with flower-filled terraces faced the valley, and the flags of the many attending nations lined the main street. My private mini-ride stopped in front of a large building with a grand facade of carved lattice work where I was greeted by the symposium hostess. She told me that I needed to register and that my bags would be sent directly to my chalet, where I could freshen up after my long journey. My paintings, along with the work of the other nineteen artists, had been sent ahead and were already on display in the main salon. I signed in at the desk, and made my way down the row of flags to my chalet, with its soft eiderdown, freshly-cut flowers, and stunningly romantic view of the fertile valley below. Once inside, I sat down on the spacious four-poster bed and began to weep uncontrollably, longing to share my good fortune with my now thoroughly estranged wife.

This symposium marked one of the most prestigious moments of my artistic life, and rather viciously, Wendy didn't want anything to do with it. I fell into a deep sleep, and some time later I was awakened by a knock on my door. It was the attractive hostess, who invited me to a private meeting with the other artists and the Forum chancellor at five o'clock. I assured her that I would be there, and took a hot shower before again walking the row of flags leading to the chancellors' office. Once we were all seated, the chancellor greeted us and asked that we stand, one at a time, to introduce ourselves by name and country. When I introduced myself as representing the Netherlands, the chancellor remarked that Guthrie was an unusual name for a Dutchman. Flushing a bit, I explained that I was actually a Californian, but thought of myself more as a citizen of the planet residing in Holland. He thanked me for my participation at the Forum and went on to the next artist. After the meeting, I walked out, and to my astonishment, next to the Dutch flag, in its first and only appearance at the Alpbach Forum, flew the Stars and Stripes! I was honored beyond belief as I followed my peers into the opulent main dining room for our first meal together.

The tables were covered with crisp linens, the glassware was hand blown, and the place settings were a fine bone china decorated with Tyrolian heraldry. I was seated with French artist, Jean-Luc Septier, nominated by the Louvre, and his lovely wife Maya. We were quick to embrace each other as comrades and would remain so throughout the days to come. Our waiter appeared and offered the menu du jour but I demurred, explaining that I was on specialized diet, and presented him with a letter of cuisine from my doctor in Amsterdam, detailing my dietary restrictions. The waiter assured me that this would not be a problem, and suggested that I leave my meals to the expertise of the chef. While the others received a delicious yet standardized fare, I alone was presented with a delectable serving of freshly caught trout with young potatoes, fruit compote and a semi-baked yogurt Alaska for dessert. From that first meal, I was more than happy to leave my gastrointestinal safety in the hands of the

Forum's culinary staff, though the pampered treatment made some of my peers politely jealous.

The two weeks spent in Alpbach were very good for my self-esteem. Individually, myself and the other artists presented workshops and generally enjoyed the cultured attention and press we all received. The only glitch in the proceedings came when the Austrian artist (whose name I've forgotten), unveiled his quasi-pornographic and distinctly anti-government canvases following the opening address by the Cardinal of Austria. The Cardinal, along with the Forum's chancellor were duly embarrassed by the crudely rendered works and demanded that they be censored from the exhibition. This was not to be, because as a group, the other artists and I threatened to turn our paintings to the wall in protest, and the matter was grudgingly dropped.

I was honored by the Forum's purchase of two of my works, one of which went into the collection of the University Museum in Innsbruck, and my workshops were well attended. My new friend Jean-Luc and I were further recognized by the Forum's invitation to conduct seminar presentations to an international group of psychiatrists who would be convening the following year in Vienna. At the conclusion of the Forum, I returned to Amsterdam emotionally refreshed, and with no one to greet me but our cat Specula. Wendy remained in Spain. In my absence, Sandberg had kept abreast of the symposium and was quite pleased with my performance and significant acclaim. With his recommendation I secured an apprentice position in the studio of master printer Piet Clement – cleaning and polishing heavy, time-worn lithography stones. Along with my studio work, I kept myself busy: visiting with Kees and Jasper, strolling the Vondel Park, taking long dry saunas at de Kosmos, and working in het Drukhuis along side Rene Treumann and Bart Boumanns.

In-laws and Outlaws

Just as I was getting used to life without Wendy, I received a telegram from her parents, with the disturbing news of their imminent arrival in Amsterdam. This totally unwanted turn of events was complicated by their long-standing hostility toward me, and by the fact that I really had no idea where Wendy was. I cleaned the house, and two days later they arrived at my doorstep bearing gifts for their wayward daughter. I lamely explained that Wendy was "away with friends in Spain," and they immediately wanted to know, "Where in Spain? What friends? When would she be coming back?" and "Why wasn't I with her?" I told the travel-weary pair "not to worry," that their daughter was "floating happily off the Spanish coast on a J Class sail boat!" (cue the applause) while I had gone to the symposium in Austria. I reassured them with a lie, that we would be hearing from her any day, and while they rented a room nearby, I sent a red alerto-gram to the only Bobbette Port of Call I knew, telling Wendy the unsettling news of their arrival. In the meantime, my quasi-fabricated explanations mollified her parents for about thirty-six hours. They had traveled halfway around the world to see Wendy, and in their increasing dismay over her absence they began to seriously doubt my attempts to reassure them.

Another day passed, and her father finally accused me of not knowing where Wendy was and threatened to call the American Consulate in Barcelona. Thankfully, before he could call out la garda civil to search for the vacationing smugglers, Wendy and the Bobbettes arrived at the Port of Call, and after reading my cable, Wendy sent one of her own announcing her immediate departure. Much to my abandoned-husband relief she was headed home, but for reasons known only to Wendy it took her another two days to get back to Amsterdam. "Mom & Dad" had already overstayed their trip, and by the time the roving Wendy appeared, bearing Spanish curios as reunion gifts, her parents had only twenty-four hours left. They were quite ready to shoot both us, and after an anticlimactic gift exchange (with nothing for me) and a tense night out on the town, the disgruntled in-laws left for home while Wendy and I tried to act the happily reunited couple.

As much as I was pleased to have Wendy home again, having her there, filled as she was with resentment over her early exodus from Spain, as well as the shock of seeing her parents under such unsettling circumstances, did not bode well for us. For advice I turned to Sandberg, who suggested a hasty retreat to Paris. There, with his recommendation, he said I might study with an old friend of his, the internationally famous and aging Dadaist, Man Ray. I was stunned by his suggestion but jumped at the opportunity. Man Ray was one of my most revered agents of influence, and the very thought of meeting the great artist much less studying under him renewed the sense of artistic hope engendered in Alpbach. I contacted my friends Jean-Luc and Maya Septier in Paris, who offered to lend me their studio on the Rue du Faubourg St. Antoine near the Place Bastille while they were away in Switzerland visiting Maya's parents.

Sandberg gave me letters of introduction to both Man Ray and the noted designer and former gallery partner (circa 1939) of Leo Castelli, Monsieur Rene Drouin. A few days later I left for Paris at midnight, riding shotgun for the French driver who delivered the newspaper *Le Monde* to Amsterdam. I had used this pocketbook-friendly method of transportation in the past, where, for the price of his breakfast on the outskirts of Paris, the driver would carve out a niche for me among the stacks of Dutch and Belgian newspapers bound for France on his return trip. Traveling in this manner was much cheaper and certainly faster than taking the train, although the train was undoubtedly safer – it also accommodated smuggling my significant stash of (non-opiated) Kashmir hash and binnenlander "veed" into France.

The driver, who was usually wired up on something, drove his newspaper laden Citroen station wagon in a high speed race against time for the French border. Traveling unlit back country roads, and occasionally using fog lights, we would arrive on the outer edge of Paris in just under four hours, compared to six on the train. Once I glanced over at the speedometer, and we were hurtling along at one hundred and eighty-five kilometers (115 miles) per hour! Noticing my alarm, the driver tossed a full pack of Gauloises over the dial and asked, "Ca va?" I nodded with nervous approval and tried to sleep for the rest of the trip. This alternative method of travel was discontinued after an accident in which the French driver and his undoubtedly terrified passenger were killed.

I arrived at Jean-Luc and Maya's hidden courtyard, third-level studio filled with enthusiasm and immediately called Man Ray. Madame Ray answered the phone, and once she determined who I was informed me that her husband was ill and that until his health returned he would be unable to receive me. Disappointed but not deflated, I called Rene Drouin. He too had heard of my impending arrival from Sandberg, and after getting the number at Jean-Luc's studio, he suggested that, when he returned to Paris after meeting with the director of the Louisiana Museum in Denmark, we meet for lunch at the Les Deux Magots to review my work and discuss the possibilities for me in the French capitol. With time on my hands, I set up my traveling easel, smoked a fat joint, and began exploring the maze of Napollioneric streets surrounding the monument to the former state prison home of Voltaire and Fouquet. Cafe Tabac, news kiosks, small shops and other casual haunts were plentiful, and the near-by open air street market more than satisfied my culinary needs. Oddly shaped loaves of freshly baked bread, local cheese and recently cultured yogurts, warm hen house eggs and savory roast coffees filled the bins. In contrast to the trendy area it has since become, my immediate neighborhood was then home to a quiet warren of fully entrenched bohemians and elderly Parisians – a late-night bar called Le Domino Club, and a steady influx of arabic-tongued expatriates pursuing French sanctuary.

Over the next ten days, apart from studio work and getting high, I visited the Centre American des Artistes on the Blouevard Raspail to see a performance by avant-trumpter Don Cherry. I visited the Louvre, the Jeu du Pomme, the contemporary galleries and curb-side raree of the St. Michele district, and peacefully strolled the now demolished quay along the Left Bank. Surveying a

Metro route indicator I was humorously reminded of Kerouac's naive awe over the advanced push-button technology when confronted with a similar device in the late 1950s.

When I tired of the more typical sight-seeing, I quietly meditated (joint in hand!) in the enclosed courtyard of Delacroix's former studio. I also spent hours browsing the offbeat stacks at Shakespeare & Co., located near Notre Dame, and thoroughly enjoyed the resourceful and anecdotal company of the well-established bookstores late owner, George Whitman. Nearer to my redoubt in Jean-Luc's studio, I conversed over bottles of cheap wine and smoke with a gaggle of local closhards, who explained to me the small tinsel bows, placed in the branches of trees by indigent-friendly shopkeepers in honor of their subterranean crowd. At night I rode the Metro all over Paris, venturing into the back-alley joints of Pigalle, and, like so many artists before me, I attended a few afternoon quick-sketch classes in the salon of the esteemed Academie de la Grand Chaumier.

Rene Drouin finally returned to Paris, and in the company of his charming daughter we met for lunch in the well-documented artist's cafe off the Boulevard St. Germaine des Pres. Drouin (now deceased) was an impressive but humble gentleman, then in his early seventies, with an astonishing reputation in the art world. Among his innumerable artistic associates, he was a close friend to Picasso, and sponsored Wassily Kandinsky's first exhibition in the City of Light. I must have glowed in the daylight when he enthusiastically praised my work, and, after some thought, he generously offered to make an appointment for me with Madame Ilena Sonnabend, owner of the prestigious Sonnabend Galleries and the former spouse to the equally famous art dealer, Leo Castelli. After lunch, Rene presented me with his card for me to give to Madame Sonnabend, and we agreed to meet again once I had met with the illustrious gallery owner. Electricity running through my veins, I left Rene and his daughter sitting in the famed artist's cafe. I was stunned by the realization that my back-door approach, along with the notable recommendations I was receiving had placed me on the verge of success! Filled with emotion and artistic pride, I celebrated my triumph at La Jullien – then a simple working-class restaurant with antique screens for table dividers, butcher-paper table cloths, sawdust on the floor, and scads of museum quality Art Nouveau murals painted on the walls. Unlike today, the eatery was then a raucous place, with a daily hand-written menu from which you could actually order something to eat for less than a franc (90 centimes for the sauteed mushrooms). The buxom waitresses strolled the aisles with wicker baskets, offering irregularly torn hunks of fresh bread and ribald joviality to the low-end customers. It was a great evening for me, but underneath the celebratory mood, I missed my wife's previously supportive company more than ever.

The next day I contacted Madame Sonnabend with great expectation, but was disappointed to learn that she was preparing to leave Paris for a two-week holiday. With Rene Drouin's recommendation in hand she requested that I leave my portfolio with the gallery, and that upon her return to Paris she would consider the work, and I agreed. In the days that followed I worked in the studio, drank white wine over hard-boiled eggs with Kenny, the expatriate owner of Le Domino Club, and again contacted Madame Ray. She was openly supportive of my stay in Paris, and encouraged me to call again, but due to his failing health, my dream of meeting with her husband was put on hold indefinitely. Regrettably, the artist would not recover, and some months later quietly passed away in his sleep.

I had originally planned to remain in Paris for another month or perhaps longer, but soon after leaving my portfolio with Madame Sonnabend, I began experiencing a dull pain in my stomach. Thinking it was my ulcer acting up, I started consuming cultured yogurt and cut out the wine, but the persistent pain only grew more severe. When finally the discomfort became debilitating, I sent a telegram to Wendy letting her know that I was returning early. The following day, I left Paris by train for Amsterdam.

The Art of Denial

Stretched out in my compartment and feeling like a dying mongrel, I weathered the unpleasant six-hour trip racked with spasmodic nausea, severe pain and nearly delirious. Noticeably wan and feverish, I arrived at Central Station, but Wendy wasn't there to meet me, so I managed with my bags and the painful taxi ride home. With increasing discomfort and apprehension, I stumbled through the door of our canal-front apartment to find Specula the cat, and my unopened telegram lying on the floor. I must have passed out, because when I awoke it was dark outside. Later that evening and quite unexpectedly, Wendy arrived with her overnight case in hand. During my absence, Bob had whisked her away to London for a few days of extramarital tryst. I was too ill to respond to her liaison. Fearing the worst, Wendy called my doctor, who thankfully lived nearby and agreed to see me immediately. He took one look at my sorry self, called an ambulance and put me in the hospital for supportive bed rest and blood tests. It was quickly determined that my discomfort wasn't caused by the previously bleeding ulcer: my appendix was about to explode and I was rushed into surgery.

During my convalescence, Wendy dutifully visited me everyday, but her rather vague demeanor, and the appearance of Katie, another smuggler's moll, told me that the Bobbettes were most likely in town. I felt even more alone and adrift, and in my confusion began to blame myself for Wendy's indiscretions. I felt that my life as a struggling artist with strictly bohemian tendencies had pushed her dreams aside, and in a moment of monumental stupidity, I vowed to abandon the only God-given talent I possessed, and strive to save my marriage.

When at last I was released from the hospital, I went directly to Sandberg's studio and told him of my decision to suspend painting and writing. He knew perfectly well how tortured I had been these past months, but my words took him by surprise. After a silence that seemed to last forever, he asked me if I was certain this was what I wanted to do. I told him that for the time being it was all I could do, and though we continued to visit often, my previous goals were not discussed. With his participation, I wrote letters of thanks, apology and resignation to Madame Sonnabend, Man Ray, Rene Drouin, Jean-Luc and the university in Vienna. In retrospect, I wish that I had been strong enough to have left Wendy and returned to Paris with my career and sanity in tact. Instead, I cast my fate to the wind. (Much like asking a carnival huckster to hold your passport and all of your money while you go the the toilet.)

Just two short weeks earlier my creative juices ran like beads of mercury across warm glass, and now I was terrified of what might emerge if I continued to paint, and of what I might say if I continued to write. A suicidal ideology and some of my chemical habits returned, but thanks to Sandberg, they faded quickly when he told me about his own brush with self-destruction. In the midst of confusion and self-loathing, Wil had once thought of all the possible ways and means before finally deciding to kill himself. When I asked him what happened next, he answered that he "took up chain-smoking French cigarettes, because it seemed to be the least painful method!" Wil's unconditional support and his unfailing regard for me saved my life.

The weeks continued, and though I had resigned myself from all things personally artistic, I did stay in touch with friends. One afternoon, fellow writer Simon Vinkenoog informed me that Allen Ginsberg had arrived in the city for a reading with Imamu Amiri Baraka (formerly Leroi Jones) at the Melkweg (formerly a milk factory). When the esteemed poet reportedly asked (the equally esteemed) Simon who was in town my name was mentioned. Allen said that he knew me from San Francisco and encouraged Simon to invite me to read with them. This was such an honor that I momentarily forgot all abut my self-imposed exile, enthusiastically agreed, and lit off with Simon to reunite with Allen.

Simon's place was one of those ultimate bohemian pads, where books, posters, records and scads of east African obscura dominate every available space. Clouds of swirling hash smoke filled the air, and young acolytes clamored for recognition from the visiting Beat ambassador. Allen was very cordial, although laid up on crutches and a short leg cast from "slipping on a banana peel in the Village." As he and I caught up on old and new friends, Simon lay waste to our minds with his never ending stash of binnenlander cannabinalia and intriguing discourse.

Late in the afternoon on the day of our performance, I decided to take a short nap with Wendy. When we awoke it was well past the time I was to have joined the others at Simon's house, and we ran to the Melkweg, where a rather drunken Simon, was acting as the evening's host, and the neo-Beat proceedings were just getting underway. Not at all impressed with my late arrival, Allen peered at me wryly from under the rim of his reading glasses and Amiri Baraka ignored me altogether. Being the rookie in our impromptu trio, I was to go on first and was overjoyed to be reading alongside these great authors. Just as I was asking Allen something about his work, Simon, much to my dismay, introduced me to the sizable crowd as a "young Jack Kerouac!" Ginsberg thought it was funny, but I was beside myself with indignation over the patently undeserved acclaim. When I got up to the microphone I denounced Simon's remark, but the damage had been done, and the crowd expected prodigy in action. I retaliated by beginning the recitation with some of my weakest material. This negative tactic actually worked in my favor, because once I got the uninhibited hollering at me to "get the fuck off the stage," I finished my set with what was then my best piece of prose/poetry – written in tribute to Kerouac. I call the poem, "Treatise On The Bum," and it begins: *Word-shedding the sloe-freight crucifix upon Ole Lady Midnight's trax-back the Great Divide – afore and afterall asea this endless eternity – Where dawn-age tenements harbor an ashen twelve-step Now! Outside this broken window pains the permanently sunset aire – agrounding in demise this-lexic-sailors-sad-satoric-song."*

My lengthy abstract thankfully brought the terminally stoned house to their shoes in appreciation, and thus salvaging what was left of my nascent literary reputation. Simon read from his most recently published work, Amri then gave an impassioned reading of Amiri-African Blues. Ginsberg closed the set by mesmerizing the hashful crowd with his Neo-Blakean word-songs. A memorable evening to be sure, but it would mark the end of my public performances for some time to come.

PART FIVE – TANGIER

Unexpected Reality

The past year had been thoroughly draining and I was exhausted. Due to my self-prescribed penance I was now empty of artistic dreams, and suffered from an unrelenting depressive remorse which I had accepted as due punishment for my imagined marital neglect. It took a great deal of effort to consciously drive my ambition for studio work into a never-again-world, which eventually stifled my muse – giving me the time to act the forgiving husband. This state of fictitious grace came screeching to a halt one afternoon, as I was boiling up a codfish for our quasi-feral cat, Specula.

The knock on the door came from the clenched fist of Dennis, the level-headed point man for Bob's gang of adulterous miscreants. Dennis carried out the contractual leg-work for Bob and his Bobbettes, and while moving around Europe like an unremarkable diplomat, he managed theaters of illicit hashish operations that included Oslo, Istanbul, North Africa, war-torn Lebanon, and US military installations in Germany. Hat in hand, Dennis stood there with an expression of post traumatic doom on his Alfalfa-like mug, and I knew that our tenuous life in Amsterdam was about to change. Wendy and I had agreed to a mutual silence surrounding her past transgressions, and the unannounced and for me completely unwanted appearance of Dennis could only spell disaster for the co-emergent charade that my roving wife and I had spent weeks constructing. Wendy, on the other hand, was overjoyed to see anyone connected to Bob and ushered the worried-looking smuggler inside, where his usually calm demeanor rapidly began to unravel.Bob and crew had been arrested and imprisoned in Morocco. The adulterous smuggler and his equally nefarious mates had been caught red-handed along with a bribed Moroccan policeman while endeavoring to load a metric ton of "Class A" Moroccan hashish aboard an unregistered trawler. To compound their misfortune, their capture occurred on the same day that an attempt was made on the life of the country's monarch, and as the Bobbettes hopped around the deserted beach in black nylon wet suits, they were incorrectly presumed to be part of the ill-fated assassination squad. In shackles they were taken to a less than accommodating prison in the city of Tetouan near the Alboran Sea, where the Bobbettes were reportedly thrown naked as jay birds into a dank cell.

According to Dennis, the head guard (quite correctly) singled out Bob as the weakest link in their conspiratorial chain and took him alone into the prison's courtyard, where his previously bribed policeman hung unmercifully upside-down from a Brazilian parrot's perch by his knees. Electrodes running from an old car battery were attached to his testicles and a urine soaked towel had been wrapped around his face to muffle his screaming. The guard reportedly told Bob that unless he immediately confessed, he and his comrades would suffer greatly from the same ordeal. Bob quickly admitted to everything hash-related, but denied having anything to do with an assassination squad. His confession was accepted and the Bobbettes were spared from being tortured. Their arrest had drawn a lot of fire from the media by being incorrectly associated with the failed attempt on the life of Hassan V, and was subsequently featured in a defamatory article denouncing international drug smugglers. With kangaroo-like speed the Bobbettes received individual sentences of sixty years of incarceration, and were unceremoniously transferred to the infamous Malabata Prison in Tangier, where according to the high court's decree they were to remain until they reached a median age of about eighty-six.

I won't deny being somewhat elated by Bob's misfortune and very glad that Wendy had not been involved. Dennis described in detail the considerable list of illicit duties he had to perform in order to arrange funding for their hopeful release, and was calling in favors from all over the globe to keep their operations afloat while his compatriots languished. To further complicate matters, Dennis couldn't go to North Africa for any length of time because of some previous nefarity and, with the hubbub, feared his own arrest. He just couldn't do everything alone, and needed our help, he said, because we were the only people he could trust who didn't have active Interpol files! He implored me to put aside the reality of my past complications with Bob, and asked Wendy and

I to fly to Tangier with a fifteen-thousand dollar start-up fund, and see what we could do about obtaining their release.

I was appalled by his request, and at first felt that Bob and his Bobbettes should stay right where they were and rot. But one look at Wendy, undoubtedly imagining the worst for her ex-paramour's safety, turned me around. Though I savored her discomfort in many ways, I also felt that if I were to reject Dennis's plea for help she would never forgive me. I knew in my heart that our tepid situation in Amsterdam was getting us nowhere, and that without some serious diversion I would soon begin to resent giving up my artistic life and perhaps treat Wendy like the serial adulteress she had become. I also feared that if I didn't agree to Dennis with his plan, Wendy might go to North Africa without me, and this was something my fragile psyche could not withstand, so I agreed to go to Tangier.

Interzoned

In no time at all we packed up the apartment on the Keizersgracht, offering it as a sublet to friends of friends, stored most of our belongs and my studio materials with Sandberg, and prepared to leave for North Africa. This humanitarian mission was an extremely acrid pill for me to swallow, but I had accepted the job and resigned myself to the adventures that surely lay ahead.

We flew to Madrid where, despite Wendy's impatience, I insisted we take the opportunity to visit the Prado. While she blindly paced the dim, naturally-lit galleries, I immersed myself in the colorful masterpieces of El Greco, Goya, Valazquez, Bruegal, and Titian – spending nearly an hour engrossed by the increasingly familiar scenes depicted in Hieronymous Bosch's bad-trip trip-tych "The Garden of Earthly Delights." As we left the truly grand museum, I remembered a quote from an interview with the painter Salvador Dali. When asked what he would save if the Prado was on fire, he replied, "I would save the flames!"

Traveling overland to the southern port of Algeciras, I tried to ignore the ever-present la Guardia Civil in their patent leather uniforms, stationed on every street corner and aboard all forms of public transportation. During Generalismo Franco's repressive regime even uttering his name in public was considered a punishable offense, and his fascistic mentality cast a demented shadow over all of Spain. I was sincerely relieved when our ferry to Tangier passed Gibraltar, and I could wonder about the historic rock's curious Barbary Ape colony instead of the heartless stares of Franco's henchmen. Stoically posed and heavily armed, they appeared to observe the world around them through the opaque eyes of the recently deceased.

As we disembarked the ferry at the Port of Tangier, Wendy and I were greeted by a torrential downpour and the grim faces of Moroccan soldiers with machine guns slung across their chests. Following a thorough search of our luggage, undoubtedly looking for a copy of *Playboy* or some other heathen contraband, the agent du jour marked our bags with slashes of pink chalk and allowed us entry into one of the world's great dens of iniquity.

No longer an international haven of indulgence without rules, Tangier had been well-tempered by independence and the ever present cloak of Islamic fundamentalism. But the city still maintained some of the "Interzone" quality so aptly described in *Naked Lunch* by William Burroughs as "the composite city, where all human potentials are spread out in a vast marketplace." We took one of the thousand and one mini-cabs into the modernized Arab Quarter to the Boulevard Ferdinand to meet up with Janice, the attractive blonde-haired girlfriend of David, one of our imprisoned charges. Janice had arrived a week earlier, and had secured a two bedroom apartment just across the Boulevard from the Roxy Cinema as our operative headquarters. As Wendy and I unpacked, Janice filled us in on the dreary situation confronting Bob and his Bobbettes: David, "JustPlain" John, German John (no longer on active duty), and Big Mike.

Coupled with the responsibility of finding a sympathetic lawyer was the more immediate problem of feeding them. Without daily nutritional support from family members on the outside, the prisoners of Malabata were reduced to eating a watery gruel-like substance issued twice a day, hardly a sufficient diet for five strapping drug smugglers accustomed to a much finer cuisine. Acting as our point-woman, Janice had checked with the local authorities and found that in order to visit the prison we needed an official pass issued once a week by the Tangier tribunal. This was a laborious procedure, requiring grave discussions with unswerving civil servants who appeared to take great pride in their purely bureaucratic roles.

It was glaringly apparent to me that to these crumpled-suit and inappropriate tie Moroccans, acting as poorly paid servants of the court was far superior to owning their own shop, driving a mini-cab or tending to a flock of goats. Those occupations had a more lucrative return but lacked the notion of superiority that seemed to bolster these insipid little men. They all smelled like rancid hair tonic, and openly exhibited an arrogant delight in forcing us to wait for other anonymous under-departmental heads who, in turn, sent us from one officious dolt to the next with forms lacking the proper signatures, for which we would, of course, have to wait. When we finally obtained our officially crumpled purple strip of odd smelling paper, stamped five or six times by said dolts, we had to take a long taxi ride out to the prison, incongruously located near a Club Med installation.

Tangier's municipal prison is a good example of a really bad correctional facility, and looked more like a huge chicken coop constructed of white-washed concrete, surrounded by intimidating machine gun turrets. The unfriendly guard behind a peep-hole in the prison's enormous wooden gate refused to honor our tribunal pass, muttering, "Flous, m'bizzef flous!" which our taxi driver translated for us as a request for money.

Once inside the walls, as we walked up the dirt path toward the visiting area I was intercepted by a hard-looking prison trustee who introduced himself in French as Michele. Given that the Bobbettes were the only captive foreigners, Michele knew exactly who we had come to see, and informed me in whispered pidgin English that if I wanted to "send in cigarettes, books, money or drugs," he could be of service. However, we had to give Michele his due, and for every carton of smokes sent to the Bobbettes, he expected one as well. As for drugs and money, he said he would simply and honestly take twenty percent off the top. I handed the rather impressive prisoner about twenty dollars worth of dirham as a measure of good faith, and asked him to look after the Bobbette's welfare whenever possible. Michele was noticeably pleased, and commented that he could see that I was "a man of understanding," and that he would see me again with some news on our way out. My dealings with Michele (who looked much like and was about the same age as Henri Charrier, author of the best-selling novel *Papillon*) would become a regular part of our visiting schedule. Later we learned that Michele had been a notorious male brothel owner and was serving a lengthy sentence for castrating his boy lover when the later had become unfaithful.

The visiting area was located in a long narrow building connected to the side of Malabata proper, with a parallel aisle screened off by layers of thick chicken wire. The cramped and packed earthen space was then divided by a wider third aisle of poorly set concrete, along which two armed guards strolled menacingly back and forth giving us the evil eye with each passing. There were perhaps thirty or more of us crammed into the sweltering visitors' section, eve-ryone but us laden with bags of supplies and chirping away like claustrophobic sparrows, clamoring for the best position against the wire barrier as the expect-ant prisoners filed in to their side of the stifling room.

Janice's boyfriend David and "JustPlain" John appeared amid the captured throng and shouted out to us above the din that only two of them would be allowed out per visit, and that they had won at straws for the privilege. John looked rather gaunt from malnutrition but said they were all holding up well enough, although from David's report we could tell that conditions inside were wretched. He said the five of them shared a small windowless cubicle with twenty other prisoners, and everyone slept head-to-toe on filthy grass mats. The toilet was a disgusting hole in the corner of their cell with a rust-stained water tap to use in lieu of toilet paper, large carnivorous bugs called 'moohsks' ran rampant over the gritty walls of their vile sounding containment and they all reportedly had body lice. "JustPlain" John added that they were allowed out of the claustrophobic cell for only twenty minutes a day for some exercise, and that an obnoxious bare light bulb burned out of reach, twenty hours each day.

Before we could respond to their unenviable predicament, the pair launched into a long list of supplies they wanted us to bring the following day: "salt tablets, Vitamin C tablets, tea bags, half a kilo of sugar, 10 pairs of underwear and socks, five hand towels, thong slippers, toothbrushes and paste, deodorant soap, one roll of toilet paper (all that was allowed at one time!), a box of large Band-Aids, two 4" ace wraps, an economy size can of foot powder, plastic tweezers, antibiotic cream, DDT for the lice, five thick books, two cartons of French Gitanes, some money, bottled water, immediate Freedom! and food. Lots of food. They ordered next-day delivery of emergency kilos of citrus fruit, cooked brown rice and vegetables in plastic containers, two rounds of goat cheese, a pound of butter and five loaves of fresh bread, "just for starters" – and further adding that they would have "a more comprehensive list" for us tomorrow! When the chattering pair finally got around to asking us how we were managing on the outside and if we had found them a lawyer, visiting time was over.

On our way out the door another ominous and mustachioed guard demanded some "m'bizzef flous" of his own by rubbing his thumb and index finger together as he blocked our passage. I was quickly growing accustomed to this routine, so without protest I just handed over some more flous. In silence, Wendy, Janice, and I stood there a moment as David and "JustPlain" John were herded back toward their cell along with the other gaunt and dusty convicts. Outside, I found Michele waiting. He said that conditions inside were indeed bad for our friends, but noted that they were strong, and as a group of five they wouldn't be bothered by strong-arm tactics or rape. He advised me to always bring in extra cigarettes for them to barter among their cell mates for things such as better cell space and extra blankets. When we reached the main gate, the same guard who let us in demanded more "m'bizzef flous" before he would let us out! Blatant graft seemed to be the only language these guards spoke, and on the ride back into Tangier our driver (Ahmed) confided to us that "nearly all of the bad things about Tangier" were covertly controlled by the director of the prison. We tipped Ahmed heavily and made arrangements with him to be picked up at a given time Monday through Friday (no weekend visits were allowed) for our trips out to Malabata. Ahmed also agreed to act as our advisor regarding matters of "m'bizzef flous" so that at least we could be assured of being ripped off fairly instead of arbitrarily.

We shopped daily for our charges at the market stalls in the main 'souk' (marketplace) and in the many international shops along the Boulevard Pasteur. At the apartment we cooked and tupper-packaged fresh rations for five in plastic containers before meeting Ahmed to take the ride out to Malabata. Once there we would again pay the guard to let us in and out, even though we had our weekly (mandatory) strip of odd smelling purple paper. Inside the gate I would then make the not-so-subtle hand off to Michele. This rather humorous routine could occur only because, via Michele, we were m'bizzef flousing two guards to look the other way while he and I made the seemingly unnoticed transfer of contraband.

Every Monday, Janice volunteered to go down to the tribunal for the by-now standard civil service harassment before getting us a new pass for the week, and she became none too shy about offering a bribe or shot of breast cleavage to speed up the process. With all the non-stop activity surrounding the daily welfare of the Bobbettes, a week or two had passed before we could actually take stock of our circumstances, surrounded as we were by inept bureaucrats and corrupt prison officials on the one hand, and on the other by the mystifying yet increasingly friendly 'tanjawis' (locals) living in our (their) neighborhood.

Beyond the daily prison routine we needed to open a bank account to hold the incoming operational cash, which thanks to Dennis had grown considerably; employ a trustworthy lawyer, and connect with the black market trade in the Zoco Chico district. All of which made our initial attempts at keeping a low profile just a little ridiculous. At the end of our exhausting days we would usually repair to a seedy little place called The Ranch Bar, run by an exopthalmic expatriate Australian. This quasi-tropical and dimly-lit after hours hang-out catered to an eclectic mix, served stiff drinks, taped rock'n'roll, and offered us a degree of much desired anonymity – nothing stays a "secret" for long in Tangier.

Shortly after our arrival, we had a brief meeting with the representatives of what remained of the American Legation, and their unsympathetic demeanors quickly indicated to us that any official intervention concerning the Bobbettes would not be forthcoming. This unfortunate complication was due, the men in blue seersucker suits said, "to a lack of adequate staffing". As our diplomatic advisors rather undiplomatically reminded us, the Bobbettes had "caused a major stink in the national press – they were guilty as sin of engaging in a major drug smuggling operation – and had furthermore embarrassed the United States Government by promoting the corruption of at least one municipal police officer." (Said as if the trade was exempt from graft!). The officials then added that being friends of the prisoners didn't exactly put us in a good light. The steely-eyed ones from America didn't want anything to do with us, wouldn't give us the name of a reputable lawyer, and told us in no uncertain terms not to come back.

Janice was nominated to spearhead the search for a lawyer and to continue her increasingly successful dealings with weekly tribunal matters, while Wendy explored the warren of 'hanootz' (produce stalls) filling the central souk for food supplies and initiate banking the Bobbette's money. I was to take care of the necessary pharmaceuticals, diverse sundries, "thick" literature, and other matters best left to the man in the house, and I took to my delegated tasks with glee.

The Medina

Unlike Wendy and Janice, whose combined knowledge of North Africa was limited to an outdated Fodor's manual, I had been reading about the seamier sides of Morocco for years. Here I was brought into physical and psychic proximity to the impregnated word-hoards of William Burroughs, Paul Bowles, Jean Genet, Mrabet and Yakoubi, and as I strolled the extrinsic environment, latent imagery taken from the transcriptions of their (at times) depraved exploits accompanied me on my treks through the Medina (the main square of old Tangier), and along the notorious foot pads in the Petite Socco – the terminal cafe, alternative drug, and black market sector.

In order for me to become relatively invisible while going about my chores, the first thing for me to do was to practice the ancient art of imperceptible movement. By combining Burroughs instruction, the lung gomchen (spirit walker) teachings of Lama Govinda, and coupled with my admittedly limited knowledge of Tai Chi, I was able to approximate the subtle legerdemain. However, the esoteric techniques were of little value when it came to dealing with the insistent packs of greasy little street urchins who encircled every passing foreigner. Endeavoring to rid myself of these poly-lingual extortionists, I discovered the sugar cube trick.

To test my theory, I began carrying a cache of wrapped sugar cubes in my pockets. Whenever the undaunted crews of professional beggars would turn in my direction I would simply toss a few cubes some distance away from me, and the little pests would then divert themselves and the immediate crowd's attention by diving for the sweets as I passed by, largely unnoticed. It worked every time, because the sorry little brats, all afflicted with varying degrees of rickets and strabismic deformities, didn't care what I gave them as long as I gave them something.

In these shaded environs one needs to dress down and attempt to see through things. Otherwise you will become utterly disoriented by the chaotic sound/imagery and alien cries of the many glass bead merchants, leather tanners, snake charmers, herbalists, cafe hustlers, and the muezzin (priests) calling the faithful to prayer from ancient minarets towering above the Medina floor. All around them, brass-belled water bearers hawked their wares astride sand-blown donkeys, braying in competition with scores of honking mini-cabs. These were interrupted by the sudden appearance of exotic Berber tribesmen, clattering their 7-up and Cola-can tambourines to accompany the enticing gyrations of pubescent Berber boys, cross-dressed for Chelula dancing, gathered near the portal leading to the higher depths of the mountain-top Kasbah (living quarter).

In short, this is truly an enigmatic zone, where it's best to say as little as possible and hug the the ancient walls. Rhythmically swinging ones arms, with a steady pace and a politely hidden agenda one can comb the disorienting layers of everyday Petite Socco life – well-hidden from tourist stare behind a maze of stone archways, loom-gossamered curtains and inexplicable dead-ends. I found the near-daily exercise an invigorating challenge and took to the milieu like a fish let loose in a foreign sea of mystery and intrigue.

During her search for a trustworthy advocate, Janice was befriended by a street-wise young Moroccan named Mohammed (all first-born sons are named Mohammed) who quickly became an invaluable member of our little team. Through his kind recommendation I was able to establish a discreet black market connection with a barbaric-looking contrabandista by the name of Mustafa, who operated out of a sprawling villa near the historic Marshan district. Being introduced to Mustafa was a great burden lifted from my shoulders, as our circumstances quite obviously demanded that the three of us remain undeniably covert when it came to doing anything illegal. Under Mustafa's guidance, and within the quiet confines of his black market storehouse, we were able to procure not only a better exchange rate for our Bobbette dollars, but an on-going supply line for illicit rations.

Our shopping cart on first meeting with the Johnny Walker, opium-friendly black marketeer, contained: a sizable block of first-rate hasheesh from the village of Ketama in the Atlas mountains, commonly known as "Double Zero;" half a kilo of unchopped KIF (weak pot); a two-ounce bottle of freshly pressed hash oil of mind-boggling potency; an unregistered case of American cigarettes in flip-top boxes (many of which which we would dip into our small vat of hash oil for the Bobbettes to get off on); a box of rolling papers and a quart of decent whiskey. Now all we needed was a good lawyer.

Our new compatriot Mohammed fast became our staunchest supporter, and with the help of his large family of friends, we were able to obtain the services of an inscrutably rotund, fez-topped barrister we called "Monsieur Avocado." At first, we were wary of the Peter Lorre-like character, whose opening gambit was a request for "m'bizzef flous" to begin the process of grafting his way through the country's antiquated judicial system. Mohammed assured us that the obese lawyer could be trusted, and we retained him with a pocketful of Bobbette dollars. Monsieur Avocado quickly hustled himself off, as he put it, "to seek out the heart of things," and advised us to "pray to Allah for guidance." Not being Muslims ourselves, we nevertheless looked toward Mecca once or twice a day, and now that we had the Avocado on their case, we had a degree of hope to offer the imprisoned five.

A few days later, the lawyer reported back to inform us that in order to proceed with any degree of success we would have to bribe an entire tribunal of 6 judges to the tune of about ten thousand dollars, plus his legal fees, which, not surprisingly had yet to be determined. The money was well within the boundaries of our growing release fund, so we readily agreed to his plan of action. With great flourish, M. Avocado requested more "m'bizzef flous," and announced that his next mission would take him "first to Fez and then on to Rabat!" where he would actually approach the row of magistrates on our behalf. He said that his trip might take him as long as three weeks to a month, and that in the mean time we "should continue our daily offerings to Allah." It was hard for us to contain our laughter, as our fat, fez-topped barrister stood there inscrutably stuffing packets of "m'bizzef flous" into the leviathan inner pocket of his silk smoking jacket.

Wisely, Bob had remained absent from the daily visiting-area chaos, and knowing that this was more the result of his trepidation regarding me than to his poor luck at straw drawing, I was prepared when Wendy asked if she and Janice could go to the prison one day a week without me. This was ostensibly to facilitate some anxiety-free contact with the outside world for the Bobbette leader, but it went without saying that the adulterous scofflaw also wanted to play goo-goo eyes across the chicken wire with my wife. Moroccans have an age-honored out when they don't have time for something that phonetically come across as: Svie-doffs-sabah, and correctly translates as "the best thing to do is resist," so, rather than upset our little rescue ark with added hostility, I enthusiastically agreed to take Fridays off.

Zoco Chico

Prior to taking on this benevolent escapade, Wendy and I had agreed that we would not address our marital status, and that we would act as "independent agents" while caring for the Bobbettes. That was agreeable to me in the main, but on my days off I certainly didn't want to examine too closely my rather embarrassing position as care provider for my wife's ex-lover and his wayward partners. So in order to divert my increasingly candid thoughts surrounding cuckoldry and revenge, and to make Fridays more interesting, I began exploring the deeper recesses of the ancient city, higher than the proverbial kite on 'majoun.'

First thing Friday mornings, I would go into the Zoco Chico district to a terminal cafe – one where I could easily purchase and openly consume majoun (melted hash and honey/herbs) without officious scrutiny. Or I would then sip a tall glass of scalding 'atay nanna' (heavily sugared mint tea), and peruse the back pages of the *International Herald Tribune*, while I awaited the hallucinatory psyche-sphere that routinely manifests from ingesting a well-prepared dose of majoun.

Aimlessly wandering the lower Medina and amongst the clamor of the tanjawi populace, I could easily sense Tangier's previously hedonistic life without boundaries. From within the ocher-infused walls of the Kasbah, sitting remarkably high above the harbor, under The Gate of Rest (the Bab ar-Raha), I would become as close to one with my surroundings as possible. My approach was to politely crouch and lean against a secluded wall, clad unobtrusively, where I could most fully absorb the immediacy of the moment while inhaling sea breeze, antimony and kohl, and the aromatically fused scent of human toil, animal dung, and kif.

Along with the full beard I maintained in those days, I routinely wore a traditional Berber scarf around my neck, a plain cotton shirt, light cotton trousers and a pair of Moroccan sandals to help disguise my western appearance. With a bit of courage and naivete, I endeavored not to interface with my immediate environment by extending myself onto the alien set, but by quietly "laying out," much like a jazz musician might, to momentarily experience whatever was happening around him as if he wasn't there. Unlike Burroughs, who apparently had little use for the local inhabitants, I was infinitely intrigued by their puzzling culture. As I became braver in my subtle penetrations into the enigmatic zones of Tangier, and more proficient with my Arabic phrasing, I approached and was subsequently befriended by a small atay nanna-clatch of Berber spice merchants who frequented one of the area's strictly non-tourist kif cafes. Following a nearly subliminal introduction from one of the traders, the Ali Baba-like owner of the place approved of my presence in his micro-establishment by offering me a freshly loaded 'sebsi' (a double-joined, long-stemmed, clay-bowled pipe traditionally used for smoking a mixture of finely chopped kif and harsh black tobacco). Once his gift had been fully consumed my new friends and I were able to openly converse and laugh heartily with one another in a polyglot of tongues – Arabic, Spanish, French, German and pigeon English.

These weekly get-high togethers became wonderfully enlightening for me – and I was quick to learn that what is not said is, in many ways, what most intrigues the tanjawi spice merchant. Within this exotic sensoria I could at times edge myself outside the strict confines of my body, and enter into a state not unlike a Zazen satori – described by the late philosopher Alan Watts in his book *Cloud Hidden Whereabouts Unknown* as a state where "The individual becomes an aperture through which the entire Universe becomes aware of itself."

Visiting with my new friends opened my mind considerably, and introduced me to the confusing mysteries surrounding Mohammed's ebony-colored box in Mecca. I truly relished the education I was receiving, and time spent within the confines of the shadowy, lantern-lit cafe, sitting on well-worn pillows stuffed with camel hair, puffing sebsi fulls of high-grade kif while discussing the spice of life and the rudiments of North African mysticism was invaluable to me as a resident stranger. As a result of these pilgrimages, I began to understand the Mogrebi (the indigenous tribe) mind-set, which was decidedly complex. Yet my Berber friends were almost child-like in their camaraderie, and would introduce me to their cafe mates as, "Bearbah (bearded one), the European with two wives."

Wendy and Janice weren't exactly thrilled with my increasingly frequent majoun excursions. But when I began exploring the strictly indigenous groups of people living in the Bidonville district, named after the discarded canteens of the invading French soldiers, and accepted invitations to dine in the ramshackle homes of my spice trading friends in the Beni Makada, (a sprawling tin shack and cardboard slum positioned at the lowest level of Tangier society), they demanded that I refocus my attentions back to the less majoun-oriented business at hand.

Three weeks had passed without a word from Monsieur Avocado and our spirits (and those of the imprisoned Bobbettes) were beginning to flag. Impatience was starting to get the better of us, and for diversion we sought the numbing effects of alcohol in the Ranch Bar. On one such evening, the exopthalmic bartender brought a round of unordered drinks to our table and said that "some gentlemen at the back would like to have a drink and a few words with you." I looked into the dim recess and saw two handsomely-dressed Moroccans who appeared to be their late twenties, sitting at a table with their attractive dates. As I approached to thank them for the drinks, the two (unveiled) women got up from the table and quietly left. The men invited me to sit down, and after the bartender had brought them fresh drinks my hosts politely introduced themselves in near Oxford English. They were both named Mohammed. Mohammed #1 asked me if I was the "European with two wives taking care of the five smugglers in Malabata." I said that I was, and he inquired how things were going. Thinking I had nothing to lose, I told the pair exactly how difficult and expensive our situation was. Mohammed #2 asked if the Bobbettes were "gangsters or good boys," and I assured him that they were certainly not gangsters. Mohammed #1 offered that they lived in Casablanca, but came to Tangier frequently on business, and that they had been following the well-publicized case in the newspapers. I sensed that our little meeting was over when they both stood up, offered me their right hands, and thanked me for being so candid with them. I went back to my table to tell "my wives" about the bewildering episode, and later that evening as the Brothers Mohammed and their dates left the Ranch, Mohammed #2 pointed our table out to the bartender, and drinks were served.

A day or so later, on our daily excursion to feed the Bobbettes of Malabata, the extortionistic peep-hole guard didn't ask for any "m'bizzef flous," and when I offered him our stinky purple paper for inspection he flatly informed our driver Ahmed that we no longer needed the weekly pass. As Wendy, Janice and I tried to absorb the guard's change in attitude, Michele came running up to say that we should hurry to the visiting area because "the boys" were already there, waiting for us. To our amazement this was to be a private visit, and for the first time since arriving in Tangier all five of the Bobbettes stood with their noses pressed against the heavy chicken wire barrier. The head guard, an uncommonly tall and fierce looking man, stood in the middle aisle casually smoking a cigar butt, and as we entered he looked directly at me with the coldest eyes I have ever seen and said, "Fifteen Minutes No More!" He then turned on his glossy heels and marched out of the area frantically puffing on his well-chewed stogie.

Cooing like a covey of captured sparrows, the Bobbettes wanted to know what had happened on the outside. They suddenly had more out-of-cell time than the other prisoners, and Michele had told them that "things were going to be much easier from now on." It didn't occur to us that these unexpected changes had something to do with the Brothers Mohammed, so we didn't mention my encounter with them at the Ranch Bar. We mistakenly thought that Monsieur Avocado must have made some headway with our intended bribery of the magistrates in Rabat.

To celebrate our sudden release from the weekly crumple of odoriferous paper and other flous related harassment, we took our friend Mohammed out to dinner at the Parade, followed by drinks at the Ranch Bar. As we were enjoying the evening, the Brothers Mohammed, who we never expected to see again, came by our table and asked if "things" were getting any easier out at Malabata. I told them that "things" were surprisingly better and that we had had our first decent visit with our charges that very day. The Brothers Mohammed smiled knowingly, adding that if we had "any further problems" we should just tell the bartender, and our well-heeled benefactors moved to the bar.

I looked over at our own Mohammed and his jaw dropped. Astonished by the brief encounter, he asked where on earth we had met these two other Mohammeds, and I related the story from the previous evening. Our friend smiled broadly and said this certainly explained why "things" were getting so much better out at the prison. The Brothers Mohammed, he said, were the favorite sons of the man who controlled most of the private gambling tables in Tangier and all of the black market activity in Casablanca. Mohammed jubilantly proclaimed that this was surely a sign from Bou Arrakia, the Patron Saint of Tangier, and that our "heathen mutterings to Allah" had been worthwhile after all!

With all the shopping, cooking, pack-ratting and running around for the Bobbettes, we were in no mood to cook for ourselves (or eat left-over brown rice and vegetable dishes), so at the end of our busy days we began frequenting the walled patio of the well-documented Parade Bar. Originally under the ownership of 'tangerinos' (resident foreigners) Jay Hasselwood and Ira Belline (the favorite niece of composer Igor Stravinsky), the Parade offered a rich and at times salacious fare for Tangier's 'le beau monde'. Visiting literati and the cliques of affluent pederasts flocked to Tangier in the late 40s and throughout the 1950s, and their gossipy cocktail lounge served as a respectable alternative to the more infamous Dean's Bar, which by the early 1970s had become a forgettable shadow of its former self. The Parade, was at the time owned and operated by Lilly Wickman. It was an alluring garden affair, hosting a fine cuisine with an aura of exquisite mystery. As the late painter, poet, and restaurateur Brion Gysin aptly described the set, "In Tangier, all things begin and end at the Parade."

On first dining there, Wendy, Janice and I were seated in the patio awaiting our dinner and the wine we had just ordered, when the liveried wine steward appeared to make an elaborate fuss over the bottle and cork before dribbling a sample into my glass for approval. To match his emotive stride, I knowingly inhaled the wine's bouquet before swilling its savory body around in my mouth. The overly proud wine steward had neglected to bring me a 'crachoir' (wine spittoon), so I spat the vintage grape onto the patio's Italian white marble floor. The silk-vested steward was appalled by my abrupt action and began scolding me in Arabic before bolting off in the direction of the kitchen. My "wives" and I were having an embarrassed laugh when the aged proprietress came toward our table with the now-subdued wine steward in tow. Lilly, then in her seventies, moved with an elegant stride, and her eyes sparkled with an ageless wisdom, almost lost within the crevass-like lines of her face. Arriving at our table she introduced herself, and remarked that I was perfectly correct to have spat out the wine. She hoped that her waiter's ignorance had not caused us any embarrassment and insisted that she pick up our dinner tab!

As time went on, I would regularly stop in at the Parade for an afternoon tipple, and Lilly would regale me with ribald anecdotes about playwright Tennessee Williams, Woolworth heiress Barbara Hutton, author Jane Bowles, and cut/up originator Brion Gysin, whose calligraphic work hung on the wall behind the bar alongside the famous embroidered slipper of Tallulah Bankhead's sister Eugenia. Rarely paying for these afternoon drinks, I was a rapt audience for Lilly's bawdy tales of having been one of Tangier's most respectable bordello madams, and of acting as the daredevil in a "Wall of Fire" motorcycle act. I also bought rashers of sliced bacon (no easy feat in a Moslem country) from the resourceful, eloquent septuagenarian, who smuggled in a fresh supply of porcine product from Spain every week. Lilly Wickman passed away some years later, and with her demise the Parade Bar, one of the world's truly great watering holes, closed its wrought-iron patio gates forever.

Ramadan

Ramadan was nearly upon us when we received word from the office of M. Avocado. Via the lackluster voice of his secretary, our Casablanca bound lawyer informed us that it was customary for the king to reduce the sentences of long-term prisoners during the Islamic holiday, and that the "delicate matter" of tribunal bribery would have to be postponed until after the month-long period of fasting. His secretary assured us that "Good News!" would surely be forthcoming and that "with the blessing of Allah," our prayers would "soon be answered."

Now that they were under the distinctly protective arm of the Brothers Mohammed, the Bobbettes began acclimating to prison life, and their status inside Malabata improved dramatically. Wendy, Janice and I were no longer bothered by the irrelevant and time-consuming demands of the fanatical 'moqadams' (government officials). Due to the benevolent patronage of our mysterious benefactors from Casablanca, we attained a "strictly hands off" status around Tangier, where quite literally no-one (including most of the street urchins) asked us for any more illogical or unwarranted "m'bizzef flous." Our purposefully entrenched residency in the Arab Quarter was now genuinely accepted by our neighbors, which enabled my "wives" and I to go about our chores for the Bobbettes with a sociable ease that allowed us to begin experiencing day-to-day Tangier in a manner that is not casually extended to transient foreigners. Our continuing presence in the neighborhood merged with the tanjawi's innate sensitivity to all things 'mektoub' ("it is written"), and outside the banging glass and wrought iron door of our apartment building, "my wives" were now greeted openly by the Mogrebi women, and thus Wendy and Janice began to learn bits and pieces of domestic tradition and feminine no-no. In the local cafes, over glasses of unremittingly hot atay nanna and sebsi bowl, the men would try to reassure me that our fates, and those of the Bobbettes, had already been determined.

Our travel-weary lawyer returned from points unknown, (my "wives" and I suspected he maintained a covertly ensconced second family living in Fez) and invited us to dine with him at the Parade, where he would give us "the good news, and the not-so-good-news." Seated inside the patio gate, and once we had all ordered dinner and an expensive bottle of vintage French wine, M. Avocado began his much anticipated report thusly:

"In a benevolent gesture of mercy, his Majesty Hassan V has ordered that the prisoners sentence be reduced to just forty years of incarceration!"

Assuming that this was the "not-so-good news," we awaited his next words with great anticipation.

"Alas," he began, "the delicate matter regarding the magistrates was only a partial success."

Our hearts sank as he gently informed us that the tribunal judges had balked after the case had come to the attention of their king. Although they "fully accepted our generous offering, the (thoroughly bent and decidedly unbenevolent) magistrates would only further reduce the prisoners sentence to twenty-five years of servitude." Squirming in his patio chair, Monsieur Avocado gave us his sympathies along with an extensive bill for services rendered, and advised that, "until further developments," we could not expect to obtain the release of our charges. As our well-fed lawyer beat a hasty retreat, leaving us with the dinner tab, we contemplated how to go about explaining the concept of "until further developments" to the Bobbettes.

After spending nearly fifteen thousand of their perfectly ill-gotten dollars in tribute to guards, magistrates, lawyers and utterly useless government officials, the Bobbettes were still rotting away in Malabata with no end in sight. Most importantly to "my wives" and I, the Release Fund was now severely depleted. We sent an overnight (stop) – "emergency words" – (stop) telegram to Dennis requesting more operating capital. "Lots More!"

The Kasbah

Dennis, now busier and more paranoid than ever, wired additional funds to a variety of American Express offices in Ceuta (a Spanish protectorate), La Linea (a neutral zone), and to Gibraltar (British territory). Due to the sums involved and because it was forbidden to send international currencies directly to our bank in Tangier. He wasn't about to bring a suitcase full of questionably-earned dollars into North Africa, so Wendy and Janice went on ferryabout to pick up the fresh deposits of operational cash.

While the "wives" were away, Barbara Hutton flew into town with a large entourage to throw one of her last ostentatious galas for her army of Hut-tontot wanna-be's, to be held in the Woolworth heiress's lavish Kasbah retreat, known locally as Sidi Hosni. In order to enjoy the festivities myself, I repaired to a dimly-lit keif cafe just above the gown and tux-clad celebrants, where, high on majoun, smoking my sebsi and drinking atay nanna, I could covertly observe the elite cacophony going on below. It was an elegant, elaborate affair – the high-brow version of Hassan i Sabbah's ancient hasheesh sect of assas-sins, where "everything was permitted and nothing was forbidden." From my hillside vantage, Barbara's over-the-top party appeared to be exquisitely catered by liveried servants, with guests attended to by thinly veiled women; and the flute and drum of musings of Berber musicians, with the occasional roar of thoroughly exotic-sounding, and most probably species-endangered animals hung in the air.

Later that night I wandered high and alone through the corridors of the moonlit Kasbah, filled with an ethereal sense of well-being that seemed at odds with my claustrophobic surroundings. The pronounced echo of celebrants, Pan's music from Jajouka, and the curious Gerrahhk! of wild beast uncom-monly mixed with faint, unidentifiable sounds that drifted upward from the harbor and into the stone fortress. The only artificial illumination in the predawn hours came from the sporadic low-wattage light bulb, covered with antediluvian dust, gently swinging in the near-silent salt sea breeze. I waited there for what felt like eons, unalterably lost in the long moment, until the sun came up on the horizon, and I was able to watch the majoun Kasbah morning come alive.

A few days after we delivered the disappointing report from Rabat to the Bobbettes, and as I was leaving the visiting area, I heard the unmistakable voice of "JustPlain" John calling my name. I looked over to see his head sticking out of a little side window of the prison, with a look of grave concern on his face. "JustPlain" John informed me that Bob was unquestionably losing it inside. He went on to say that the fallout from their leader's continuous panic attacks and neurotic filibusters of obnoxious yammering were driving everyone crazy. John demanded that I "do what ever it takes" to get Bob out of there, if only temporarily. "This is serious," he exclaimed, and added that he and the rest of the Bobbettes feared one of the other prisoners might strangle Bob in his sleep, to shut him up. I thought this was a marvelous solution to their problem, but after tossing other ideas around with Wendy and Janice, we decided to flous the prison's doctor into putting the panic-stricken smuggler in the hospital. The parsimonious doctor agreed to our bribe, and scheduled some "tests" which required "isolating the prisoner in a private room in Benchimal Hospital." This costly intervention served to significantly reduce the level of tension in Malabata, and to quell Bob's panic attacks, but in doing so, we had also complicated our Bobbette feeding schedule. The hospital was on the other side of Tangier and had its own maddening set of protocols and visitation times. While Janice went to Malabata with Ahmed and the regular fare du jour, Wendy and I went to deliver sustenance to the privately bedridden Bob.

Panic free and tucked away in his latrine-green room with a young prison guard who sat on a grass mat at the bedside smoking kif, Bob soon started asking for extras, such as his own kif pipe, imported cheese instead of the usual goat, and a six-pack of cold beer. Wendy and Janice thought it was a good idea to fatten him up with this special menu, but his namby-pamby routine quickly got old and I was about to blow a fuse when Wendy short-circuited my neurons entirely. Wife #1 wanted to visit with her former paramour alone! I was ready to murder her on the spot, but somehow I resisted the urge to commit spousicide, and took advantage of that infinitesimal moment between action and reaction where there exits a degree of freedom, and instead, I told her "that would be just fine." I never mentioned this to Wendy or any of the others, but later that day I made an unscheduled flous withdrawal from the bank and paid the prison doctor to have Bob returned to Malabata immediately. "His tests have come back negative," I told the confused physician, and within the hour, the Bobbettes were reunited with their miraculously cured leader.

The Sirocco (a hot easterly Saharan wind) began to dominate each passing day. Weary of our daily routine, the women and I felt oppressed by the fatigue that results from carrying dead weight across your shoulders for any length of time. Tangier had lost much of its initial intrigue for us, and the Bobbettes were now a sullen crew, facing what must have seemed like an eternity of incarceration, and our daily treks out to the prison did little to cheer them, or us up to any noticeable degree. Along with futile and thoroughly unrealistic plans for escape, their increasing demands for better this and more of that, at first endearing, became intolerable. Something had to give.

On our way back in to Tangier after one of these discouraging visits, we discussed our limited options for what could be considered a "next step" with our faithful driver Ahmed, who had by now become a trusted ally. Ahmed offered that he had an idea for moving the Bobbettes to another prison, located in the coastal village of Asilah. There, he was certain, "the boys" would at the least receive far better accommodation with more out-of-cell activities. He said that his brother-in-law was the assistant director of a "transit prison" situated on the outskirts of the small fishing village. Getting "the boys" transferred there would however, be somewhat problematic he said, as the comparatively quiet and relaxed prison served primarily as a stop-over for convicts being transported to other lock-ups and did not house long-term prisoners in its regular population. Ahmed suggested that he contact his brother-in-law on our behalf and see what could be done about changing that statistic. As far as the three of us were concerned, getting out of Tangier sounded like a great idea, and, after all, what did the Bobbettes have to lose? Two days later Ahmed returned with an invitation for us to eat lunch in Asilah the following day with his brother-in-law and the director of the prison. It went without saying that we needed to bring "m'bizzef flous" along if we were going to carry the day, and unwilling to offer the Bobbettes a false sense of hope, we did not mention our new plan of action to them.

Ahmed drove us the 46 kilometers south to Asilah, all the while making suggestions as how best to deal with the director of the prison. If we openly offered him money he would take it as an insult, so we needed to be "very discreet," Ahmed warned us. He said that the director was a "devoted Muslim," as opposed to a devout worshiper, but one who "on occasion," our astute advisor quipped, "likes to have a glass of good whiskey."

Ahmed further advised that, "in order to keep the conversation in the proper perspective," I would need to do all the talking.

"Your wives," he added jokingly, "should remain quiet during the discussions."

This was of course a direct challenge to Wendy and Janice, who behaved like harlots at the meeting. After we were all seated at a large cafe table, "my wives" proceeded to preen themselves shamelessly in front of the director and Ahmed's brother-in-law, who squirmed uncomfortably in his chair, playing almost idiotically with his significant mustache. Meanwhile the director, Ahmed (acting as our translator), and I discussed the Bobbettes over drinking water glasses of cheap whiskey. We dined on chipped mismatched dinner plates heaped with green salad, herb and vinegar soaked 'pulpo' (octopus), and deep fried sardines with their crispy little heads still attached. As I described our five bad-boy smugglers in glowing terms with promises of good behavior to the sternly faced director, Wendy would occasionally stretch the top of her breasts into view, and Janice actually played footsy with the horny assistant director under the table! Fortunately their blatant feminine high jinx did not scotch the business at hand.

Via Ahmed, the director began reeling off a list of the many required procedures, the vast amount of paperwork involved, the added stress on himself and his assistant, and how terribly difficult the discreet transfer of five highly-profiled drug smugglers would be.

"It will not be an easy thing for me to accomplish," he said, and with that in mind, we finished our tapas meal and whiskey in relative silence.

Any worries I had dissolved during the post-prandial handshake with Ahmed's brother-in-law, when I slipped him five one-hundred dollar bills as a down payment toward future "m'bizzef flous." I thanked the smiling official for arranging the lunch with his director, and again assured them both that the Bobbettes would not become a problem for their prison.

I assured him that I fully understood just how difficult the process would be, adding that, "I would be more than happy to pay for any and all expenses involved with the transfer of our charges."

The director replied that he would "consider the situation in private," and that Ahmed would be hearing from his brother-in-law by the end of the week with his decision.

Three days later, Ahmed said that he had spoken with his relative in Asilah, and that the decision to move "the boys" had been made. In a nutshell, it would cost the Bobbettes another five grand for the director to "confuse the paperwork in Rabat" which would transfer the boys to Asilah, without question. They could then hopefully outlive their twenty-five year sentences in a perpetual state of transit, because the "confused" paperwork would not list a final destination beyond the seaside transit prison. Ahmed said there would of course be an "extra fee of another twenty-five hundred dollars" for his brother-in-law's cooperation in the scheme. Ahmed himself refused to be compensated for his efforts. Added to the seventy-five hundred dollar bribe was our continuing expense for Bobbette supplies, and now, with the need to rent a new operational headquarters in Asilah, our transition budget was adding up. When we combined this amount with what we had given the Avocado, and then added in our travel expenses and cost of living in Tangier, it put the Bobbette financial loss (not including the value of their confiscated ton of hash!) somewhere in the neighborhood of twenty-eight thousand dollars to date.

When we first told our sullen charges about the intended move, they balked at the expense and refused to "authorize" our plan. We told them in no uncertain terms that if they wanted to stay in Tangier they could, but they could do so "without us." We had had it up to our ears with Malabata and that was that. Grudgingly, they accepted our proposal and we made arrangements with Ahmed to deliver the discretionary bag of "m'bizzef flous" to the director and his brother-in-law, and hopefully get Morocco's antiquated spinning wheel of justice turning in our favor for a change.

PART SIX – ASILAH

Life in Asilah

Settled in the 8th century by Phoenicians, and repeatedly fought over by Carthaginians, Romans, and Iberians, Asilah played a significant role in the formation of Morocco. It was at one time the stronghold of the notorious Rifian bandit 'er Raissouli'. But in the early 1970s Asilah was a marauderless fishing village, with little in the way of amenity for foreign visitors – though playwright Tennessee Williams found Asilah so alluring he used it as the model setting for his play, *Suddenly Last Summer*.

With Ahmed's help we contacted what passed for a village real estate agent (i.e. just another rotund, djelaba-clad hustler with, in his case, a string-attached monocle and a tasseled fez looking for his share of the Bobbette relocation fund), who explained to me the additional "delicacies" of our situation. He said that, other than some archaic tourist facilities in little cement cones (Camp Safari) located near the beach, there really wasn't much available for us in the way of accommodations.

"But," he emotively added, "due to the uniqueness of your situation, I have made some discreet inquiries on your behalf in the Kasbah and had found a house for you to rent."

Our estate agent (yet another first son, named Mohammed) led us along a dirt path adjacent to an ancient Portuguese sea wall and beyond the centralized Medina into the strictly non-tourist Kasbah. Hordes of chirping villagers shopped at the many hanootz that lined the area's cleanly swept earthen thoroughfare.

While Wendy, Janice and I trooped along in a respectable row (i.e., "wives" at the rear) behind Ahmed and Mohammed, literally everyone in the street stopped whatever it was they were doing as we passed by. When I asked Mohammed if our presence was disturbing the locals, he laughed out loud, and went on to admit that everyone in Asilah knew about our arrival. Apparently they were all very curious about "the bearded European with two wives who was going to take care of the five American drug smugglers!" It was glaringly apparent that any chance of keeping a low profile in Asilah was going to be impossible. Down another swept dirt path leading from the main artery of the Kasbah we came to a Moorish-looking cinder block house, (much like all the other white-washed Moorish-looking cinder-block abodes in the Kasbah). Here the proud owner of the sun-bleached cube, a turbaned man in his early-fifties, his veiled wife and their three adolescent children, stood beside their front door to greet us.

Via Mohammed and Ahmed, I conferred with the man of the house about the rent, while "my wives" were taken inside by the homeowners family. Mohammed explained (without actually giving me a reason) that the man was unable to work, and that he would happily rent his house to me as long as he and his family, their dog, and a few chickens could live on the roof! I tried to hide my surprise at this sudden turn, as Mohammed went on to assure me that as there was a small room on the flat turreted roof with a staircase from outside, affording the family of five and their menagerie a private to and fro. The fundamentalist owner of our prospective operational headquarters actually apologized when he quoted me a monthly rent of $75 plus the cost of electricity.

The decor inside the house was characteristic of Moroccan living, with decorative arches, ornately tiled floors, brassware on the low tables, cloth covered wall benches for sitting and a number of camel hair 'poofs' (pillows) laying about. Sheer cotton cloth adorned with glass beads served as doorway separations and each of the bedrooms had a funny little window looking out onto the main living room. The polite and rather charming homeowners offered their antique brass, four-poster bed frame and mattress to Wendy (wife #1) and me, and Janice (wife #2) would have a room to herself. The butane-supported kitchen was plumbed, but the room also contained a deep well with a bucket attached to a rope for drawing the wash water. The house toilet was a hole in the floor with elevated concrete footpads next to the shower drain and a faucet (to be used in lieu of toilet paper). How could we resist! I paid the homeowner four months advance rent, tipped our agent appropriately, and "my wives" and I returned to Tangier with Ahmed.

In no time we closed up our redoubt across from the Roxy cinema and made what we hoped would be our final visit to Malabata. The Bobbettes were now charged up and enthusiastic about the move and asked me to "take good care of Michele" for them, which I did with generous compensation for his help. After which, we filled up our illicit shopping cart at Mustapha's, and treated our good friend Mohammed to a tailored suit, before heading back to Asilah with our faithful driver Ahmed (who "with all due respect," refused to take a dime of appreciation from us, and asked us not to offer). Here we impatiently awaited the extralegal transfer of the still-anxious Bob and his prison-weary Bobbettes. We segued smoothly into our new digs, which looked out onto a hard-packed empty lot, and beyond which sat the local 'hammam' (public bath house). The family on the roof seemed to be taking their new habitat in stride, and the six egg-laying hens, now aloft, clucked away as if nothing had changed.

The main artery through our neighborhood was rife with street-side hanootz and their ware-hawking owners who offered up for purchase everything unimaginable – well supplied granaries, sugar blocked by the kilo, colorful textile bins the size of a postage stamp, and any number of match-box cafes. There was one industrious hanootz merchant whose clapboard shelves held just one candle and one box of wooden matches – nothing more. Every evening, the old man would sit patiently in his minuscule hanootz in front of the after-glow from a low-wattage light bulb, swatting at the persistent bluebottle flies. I felt sorry for the old man and one evening I bought his candle and matchbox, but later that night, when I again passed his hanootz, there he sat, swatting at the flies, with another candle and box of matches on display!

The village dentist was another example of the color permeating our immediate neighborhood. Two days a week, this iron-age orthodontist would set up shop near our house by spreading out a large sheet of newsprint in front of an old metal chair where he would sit most of the afternoon. Potential customers always knew when he was open for business because he would uncover a rather large pile of previously pulled teeth (still encrusted with tissue and blood) as advertising. This was an open-air office ordeal, and if his patients needed an anesthetic, they brought along a friend to hold them down in the dentist's chair. It really was unnerving to hear the screams of another one of his satisfied patients from our living room.

Closer to the center of town was the fish market, which supported much of the local economy. The centerpiece for this lively trade was a rustic fountain where I would on occasion stop to take in the sociable fish-chop milieu. Quite often I shared the rim of the fountain with an elderly Berber who had developed a set of rather misshapen hips from riding too many nomadic camels into the desert. He was a turbaned, humble man, with facial scars that would frighten away most strangers, and to ease his considerable discomfort he sat on triple layers of folded cardboard molded to his behind and tied with rough twine. He was a knowledgeable, well-traveled old man and over time we spoke animatedly with each other in a near-gibberish of Arabo-Joycean tongues.

One day as I was about to sit down next to him, he moved his cardboard cushion to my spot and gestured for me to sit down. At first, not wanting him to be uncomfortable, I politely refused. My companion became very angry with me, and with the aide of a nearby fishmonger, and a lot of hopping up and down on his bad hips, I came to understand that my fountain buddy wanted to give me something, and his folded bits of cardboard were all he had to offer. My acute embarrassment seemed to let my nomadic companion know that I was truly touched by his gift, and from then on, whenever I came to the fish market fountain, he would insist that I rest for awhile on his sole possession. Unlike Tangier, where indigent berserkers might run amok at the drop of hat, Asilah was a gentle environment, largely free of vice and corruption, excluding our recent bribery of the local prison officials. Compared to Tangier, our new environment was an oasis where the fundamental omnipotence of Allah held sway over most of the population.

The Bobbettes were transferred from Malabata without complications in the sweltering confines of a windowless armored carrier. At the prison in Asilah they were met by the assistant director, who personally installed them in a clean cell with actual lice-free beds to themselves, although the flesh eating moohsks were still a DDT manageable problem. Soon after arrival, and to their great delight, the Bobbettes were each given work assignments to occupy their hearts and minds for the long months, and potentially, years to follow. In order to keep our significant presence at the prison in as low a profile as possible, the director allowed us to visit with the Bobbettes (through two barriers of chicken-wire-enhanced steel bars) away from the other visiting families. This afforded the eight of us with twenty minutes uninterrupted visiting time without the hysterics of wailing women and children. All in all, the move to Asilah was a win/win situation for everyone. With some inscrutable goading from M. Avocado, along with additional deposits of "m'bizzef flous" to the bent magistrates in Rabat, we managed to have the Bobbette sentence reduced to fourteen years, and our charges were in much better spirits.

On the visitless weekends, the ladies and I would taxi into Tangier and stay in a balconied hotel near the Parade Bar, where we could catch up on the night life with our friend Mohammed and drink mid-afternoon gin & tonics at Robinson's beach. We basked like landed seals under the unrelenting sun near the Pillar of Hecules, and refilled our illicit shopping cart at Mustapha's with items largely unobtainable in Asilah. On one of our impromptu visits to the black-marketeer's, in what we assumed would be an appropriate gesture of our gratitude, we bought a quart of good whiskey for the prison director – a purchase we would soon come to regret.

With Ahmed's earlier comment in mind, and in the confines of his office, we presented the director with our tribute, and unanimously thought we had done the right thing. When we arrived at the prison gate the following day with supplies, however, the usually friendly guard behind the requisite prison peep-hole flatly informed us that "his director" had cut off our visiting privileges! The apologetic guard hesitantly accepted the bags of food we had brought with an expression on his face that said: "I don't know what's gotten in to my director." Hoping that he would reconsider, we waited two days before going back, but again we were refused entrance to the prison. We asked to see the director personally, but the flustered guard told us his "director didn't want to see us anymore!" Ahmed's brother-in-law agreed to meet with us but offered little in the way of explanation. He said the director was "at home, taken seriously ill," couldn't be bothered, and sternly added that he had no idea why our privileges had been lifted. We were persistent and he advised us to come back the next day.

When we reappeared in his office the following morning, Ahmed's brother-in-law was furious with us, and shouted at us.

"What in the name of Allah possessed you to give the director an enormous bottle of whiskey?!?"

We said we thought the director liked whiskey and that we had only wanted to please him.

Our frazzled go-between shook his head with frustration and disbelief. "Yes, yes," he said, "the director likes the occasional drink, but when he has a bottle of whiskey he gets drunk – and," he added ominously, "when the director gets good and drunk, he quickly becomes mean and nasty!"

The assistant director looked at us like we were a trio of complete idiots and said he would instruct the guards to accept the daily rations, but as for our visiting rights, we would "have to wait until the director decides to sober up."

The week went by without change, and we began to fear the worst, but on Friday evening, as we walked toward the fish market fountain, Ahmed's brother-in-law came from one of the cafes and invited us to have a glass of atay nanna with him and the director – who was now oddly overjoyed to see us. He asked us where "we" had been! Before we could respond to his absurd question, the director assured us that he was "feeling much better now," that his "sudden illness" had passed, and to our surprise, he added that we should "come by the prison tomorrow (a Saturday!) and have a nice long visit with the prisoners." To our great relief, nothing more was said regarding the ill-fated bottle of Johnny Walker Red, and our visiting privileges were restored.

Souks and Sparrows

Our anomalous presence in the Kasbah was politely tolerated but we were still the neighborhood curiosity, and beyond the subtle nod in acknowledgment, or the infrequent and not so subtle cat-call and whistle directed toward my "wives" from out one of the cafes, our veiled and cautious neighbors gave us a wide berth as we went about our hanootz shopping. The bulk of our weekly food hoard for eight came from the large open-air souk Asilah would host every Thursday for the neighboring villages, adjacent to the ancient, rust-colored Portuguese sea wall. Offering colorful entertainment and a wide variety of organic vegetable, mineral/spice, and desert goat product, this gathering of the tribes was not a simple affair. With the influx of nomadic traders and families bringing in wares to market, Asilah's transient donkey population would increase tenfold. Traditionally dim-witted beasts of burden, donkeys when penned together for any length of time become profligate sybarites, and their makeshift containment often produced a glaring spectacle of donk-frenzy. Twenty or more jacks, braying in chorus, would be raised up on their haunches, thrusting their two-and-a-half foot prongs of sub-equine lust in and out one bucking jennet pouch to the next, waywardly spewing copious donk-jism en route. This moving tableau of seasonal donkey hunger was always a good warm-up for the souk itself, which had its own diverse collection of primitive eccentricities.

On souk day the general population of Asilah dressed in traditional finery and preened themselves to mix and shop among neighboring friends, family and honored merchant guests – the nomadic descendants of Berber warriors, the 'al-Mulathamin' (Veiled Ones), cliques of unusually tall Tuareg tribesmen, and Blue People from Goulimine dressed in their traditional indigo robes. Entering this infinitely fascinating arena, Wendy, Janice and I usually encountered one of two 'jilala' ritualists (desert sooth sayers) working the crowd from opposite ends of the souk. Our end of the market was the quasi-delphic territory of the White Practitioner. This bare-chested oracle would wander in a semi-trance with his blood-shot eyes rolled back into their sockets – a rusty tin can hanging from a shoe lace tied around his neck, and a writhing snake held in each hand. From his forehead, which he would periodically slash with a hidden shard of glass, narrow rivulets of sun-dried blood ran down his mesmerizing face. As he moved about the entrance to the souk his pet reptiles would dart in and out of his mouth, and for a few coins dropped into the tin can, he would issue forth with messages of snake prophesy to his ogle-eyed patrons.

The souk itself was an enormous, multi-aisled grass-mat of people and produce from one end to the other. Our normal routine was to hire two or sometimes three children to carry the kilos of fruit and vegetables needed to feed ourselves and the Bobbettes for the week. The Berber women, who virtually ran the souk while their husbands hung out in the cafes smoking kif, would engage Wendy and Janice with a mixture of gentle suspicion and child-like curiosity, while saying little if anything to me. My presence at the largely female event was seen as just another anomaly surrounding "Bearbah, the (bearded) European with two wives."

At the far end of the souk the "wives" and I would customarily rest for a while under a shady tree near a white-washed dome-on-the-dirt, known as a 'koubba' (holy hut), where an aged 'Mara-bout' (priest/storyteller) dressed in high turban and a flowing robe of white cotton would hold forth, pointing at the images on one of his many hand-woven pictographic carpets spread out before him. This was also the prophesy spot for the souk's other jilala specialist, the Black Practitioner.

Sitting squat-legged on the ground, black-turbaned and clothed in greasy-looking rags of ebony-tinged cloth, and with a wooden bowl full of sticky black seeds in front of him, the oracle served as the human link in a gruesome chain, otherwise comprised of the rotting, bottlefly-covered bodies of seven decapi-tated ravens. In the center of his circle of dead bird magick hopped a squawk-ingly alive, though inexplicably wingless raven, with the shackled talons of one leg tethered by a chain to a rusty railroad spike set in the ground. Whenever an overly-curious passer-by would toss a few coins at the deformed creature, his greasiness would whack the seven lifeless bodies with a long crooked stick, swill some of the putrid-looking seeds around in his mouth before spitting them and a mouthful of ill-smelling oracle ooze into the circle of decay. From this unsightly mess the wingless raven on the chain would pick at the unappetizing seeds, thus charting the direction and content of the jilala reading. Some time later I learned that this was the very spot where the noted surrealist, author Alfred Chester (*Behold Goliath* and *The Exquisite Corpse*), then in residence, had himself tied to a tree by the villagers of Asilah in a vain attempt to conquer his significantly paranoid delusions.

One one particular Thursday, I left my "wives" to the weekly souk-gabble and wandered the outer edge of the sea wall, high on a dose of majoun. On my return to the souk I passed through a small sea wall archway and came upon two young boys selling sparrows, which are eaten as a bony appetizer in North Africa, from hand-made cages. I picked up one of the cages, and seeing that there were five of the imprisoned avians, I offered to buy the birds. As the boys and I haggled over the price I noticed an uncommon tittering about the souk, where the Berber sales-women and their customers seemed to be getting a great kick out of "the European with two wives" who apparently like to eat sparrows. After purchasing the chirping little birds, I named each of them after one of the caged Bobbettes and with a flourish, released them into the souk. The young sparrow merchants were astounded by my abrupt and unexpected action and began sing-songing around me in a circle of joy – "He let the sparrows go! – He let the sparrows go!" – and the over-all souk mind was blown.

In the aftermath of my sparrow release, I became a small part of the village lore, gaining a new status among the superstitious mystically-minded villagers, who relied heavily upon one-way-or-another omens from Haruspex divination (oracle readings taken from bloody goat entrails poured onto the sand). The previously snide and distant men of the Kasbah now looked me directly in the third eye, openly greeted me in the street, and occasionally invited me to join them for sebsi, atay nanna and the music of Pan. Even the Kasbah's rotund baker got in on the act. Now when I went to his subterranean bakery/oven to pick up our numerous loaves of fresh bread, he would give me two extra little pastries and say: "Here, Bearbah, these are for your wives!"

Weeks passed in our tranquil setting where the seemingly everlasting light of day would abruptly sink in to the Atlantic, leaving behind a darkness you could almost taste, and I could well understand Tennessee Williams' attraction to the place. Oddly enough, on one of my infrequent trips into Tangier alone, I bumped into the aging playwright. Curious and adventurous as usual, I went for an early afternoon tipple at the notorious beach-front cafe, The Windmill. At the time, this was an elder-gays "take me I'm yours" arena where the infamous tangerino George Greaves held a daily Gin-boy and tonic court. Remarkably, sitting on a barstool next to the obese pederast was the great writer himself. Unfortunately for me, Williams was so drunk he couldn't say his own name. I wanted to ask him about his time in Asilah, but when I made the futile attempt to introduce myself, all I could illicit from the dramatist was an unflattering belch! I left the rapidly aging bar-flies to themselves, and I remember thinking as I left the place, that fame was perhaps the worst of all vices.

In my absence, my "wives" had somehow managed to offend the woman-head of the family living on our roof, and when I arrived home there was a standoff in place. Whatever the cause, I needed to intervene immediately if our peaceful home was to remain that way, but before heading upstairs I went to one of the hanootz in our area and purchased a confrontation-warming gift for the devoutly Islamic woman. When I went up to see her I acted as if nothing was amiss, and told her instead that while I was away in Tangier I had purchased the colorful rendering of central Mecca for her. She gushed and tittered with pride, rendering to me an openly friendly smile that exposed her full set of solid gold of teeth. After she had explained to me the nature and purpose of some of the religious shrines depicted in the drawing, she offered me some atay nanna, and the real purpose of my visit could take shape. I asked her how she was getting along with my "wives," and she humbly admitted to a misunderstanding. I told her not to worry, that I would smooth things out with Wendy and Janice, who dutifully baked the family upstairs two dozen chocolate chip cookies, and the differences in between were quickly forgotten.

Tea du Quincy

Living in Asilah, I missed the weekly majoun cabal with my merchant friends in Tangier, and now that I was becoming more accepted by the villagers I made it a point to befriend the local spice trader. He took an immediate liking to me and we visited often in his hanootz, where we shared sebsi and personal anecdotes such as the finer points of majoun preparation, while sitting under an old card table amid his pharmacopoeia of dried goods – all stored away in countless little gunny sacks. One afternoon, I innocently pointed out some bundles of dried pod hanging from the ceiling of his tiny shop, and without batting an eye, my friend wrapped the pods in newspaper and gave them to me along with his instructions for brewing up a batch of dry opium/citrus tea.

Narcosium in hand, I arrived home to find that we had houseguests from Tangier. Peter (then in his early thirties) and his slightly older, white-haired wife Carol, were a pair of hardy expatriates, most recently released from a drug-related prison stint in Sardinia. In Tangier, the industrious pair supported themselves by hustling their own line of one-piece, bleached cotton apparel, without buttons or zippers (which they would eventually display in the windows of Bloomingdale's), and just about anything else they could find that would turn one dollar into ten. While Wendy and Janice caught up with our friends, I repaired to the kitchen with my bundles of pod. It was early evening by the time my concoction of citrus juices, spiced honey and opium dust was ready for consumption. I had no idea how much essence of narcosia was actually in my "tea du Quincy", but I suggested that we drink three or four cups each, and wait for the distinguishing warmth of the opium to take effect.

Two hours later everyone eyed me suspiciously as nothing continued to happen. Seasoned consumers all, we smoked some hash, drank more tea and resumed waiting. By eleven o'clock everyone had declared my sweet concoction a dismal failure, and after a final cup (just to make sure) we all retired for the night. The next morning I woke up with a vertiginous earthquake going off in my skull, accompanied by a sickening moaning and retching coming from the direction of the kitchen. I made a lumbering attempt to get up to see what was happening, and found that during the night the earth's gravity had tripled! I struggled vainly to get off of mattress when Wendy came back to the bedroom, looking like a plate full of mashed lima beans, and she fell onto the four-poster bed, groaning. Finally I managed to get myself up and into the living room where I found Peter and Carol, equally distressed, rolling on the floor with cramped bowel syndrome and headaches to match my own. Poor Janice, who like myself, had consumed more tea than the rest, was purging herself into dehydration through the hole in the painted cement floor we called the toilet. It was distressingly clear that my near-lethal elixir took a lot longer to have an effect than I had anticipated, and now we were all paying for the indulgence. Knowing that everyone (quite rightly) would blame me for their discomfort, I decided to avoid the issue altogether. Without a word of apology, I got dressed, muttered a sheepish farewell to the suffering mass in my house, and took a well-paid express taxi (46 km.) into Tangier. When the nauseating ride was over, (I think I paid the driver twice!), I installed myself at a sidewalk table at the Cafe du Paris on the Place du France. They served a mean cup of coffee with a cognac back at the well-known cafe, but most importantly, the lavatory staff maintained one of the cleanest rows of real toilet stalls in all of North Africa.

Following a triple shot of everything, two tranquilizers, and my own set of discomforting eruptions, I was pleasantly distress free – and, much to my delight, intensely stoned. At one with my cafe chair, I nodded in and out, basically immobilized by the persistent and smooth opiate-tea fog, observing the infinitely more mobile world passing in front of my table. When I had recovered somewhat, I recognized Paul Bowles, the noted writer and composer, sitting quietly in the back of the cafe wrapped in an overcoat under a large fedora. To my great disappointment, I was unable (due to obvious reasons) to converse with him. Through his writings, particularly *The Sheltering Sky*, he had become a guiding influence for me in Morocco, and I wanted to thank him. My condition prevented me from introducing myself with any decorum and, regrettably, I would not get a second opportunity to meet the great writer.

Late in the afternoon, Wendy and Janice, well on the way to recovery, dropped Peter and Carol at their hotel and found me, still in my cafe chair, sipping cognac and holding forth in their native tongue with a discouraged quartet of Dutch tourists who had been ripped off while trying to negotiate the Petite Socco. Not surprisingly, my "wives" were not interested in my learned discourse, and remained stoic all the way back to Asilah, where my opiate miscalculation was soon forgiven.

Too Much!

Asilah didn't have a Parade Bar at hand, and as the ladies and I were still unwilling to dine more than twice a week on Bobbette leftovers, we ate our rather inexpensive dinners al fresco at one of the wrought iron and glass-topped tables, over-looking the Atlantic, at a congenial bar and restaurant called Pepe's. It was a jovial, family affair where we could enjoy honest drinks, a spectacular view of the setting sun, and a savory rice 'paella' crammed full of fresh prawns, mussels, and clams brewed in a spicy tomato sauce at the end of our day. Aside from the restaurant's delicious fare and scenic ambiance, dining at Pepe's was also an endless source of comic relief for us, due to the generous and hilarious hospitality we received at the Spanish-run establishment from our regular waiter – an urban Berber descendant we lovingly referred to as, "Too Much!"

On first dining at Pepe's, Too Much! (who spoke almost no English beyond the obvious) was our server and (by his proclamation to the rest of the staff) would remain so throughout our residency in Asilah, so we got to know him rather well. We gave him his well-deserved moniker because every time he would arrive at our table, grinning and slapping himself like a crazy hyena in stitches, he would exclaim, "Too Much!" in response to his having discovered the five reasons for our noteworthy presence in Asilah. As soon as we sat down at our table, Too Much! would go into his act by appearing at our table with a serviette over his wrist and three icy gin & tonics at the ready – "Too Much!" and would be gone. Even if we had out-of-village guests for the evening, Too Much! patently refused to offer us the menu du jour – but then he knew we came for the paella.

Our "over-joy-to-seen-you-todays" waiter would then begin delivering an endless series of little serving plates, filled with an interesting and delicious 'tapas' (appetizers), such as raw oysters on the half-shell, octopus vin-aigrette with tentacles, roasted sardines with their roasted little eye-balls staring at us, piles of deep-fried squid rings, "Eat, Eat – Too Much!", wine soaked olives and mushrooms, shrimp cocktails, fresh drinks, more sardines (they were fabulous), small loaves of freshly baked bread, dinner salads, more drinks, "Eat, Eat – Too Much!" and finally our paella (large enough to feed an industrious party of six), fresh drinks, more octopus, and on and on, "Eat, Eat – Too Much!" for as long as we sat at the table – and with each new plate or bowl arrival with a table cleaning, he would unabashedly laugh, shake his head in amazement and exclaim, "Too Much!" before disappearing into the kitchen, undoubtedly to look for more tapas to bring to us. This highly entertaining and overly-filling fare came at a small price to us, because not only did we not order any of the appetizers, none of it ever appeared on our bill except for our first round of drinks and the paella at the end of the evening! "Too Much!"

The Hammam

Tired of struggling with the lukewarm shower head protruding from the wall of the same cinder block space as the foot pad toilet hole, I decided to join the other men in the village and bathe at the hammam – a large quonset hut-like structure just across the dirt lot from our house. I didn't know this until after my "bath," but the innocous-looking building was designed in the complex manner of a Neo-Roman nymphaeum (bathing palace), featuring, a (cold) fridgidarium, a (lukewarm) tepidarium, and a (swelteringly hot) caldarium. Entering the enclosed public service house, I found a welcoming group of djelaba-clad men (a hooded wool burnoose) sitting on a slightly elevated plat-form covered in grass mats. They enthusiastically waved me over to sit with them by offering me a fresh hubble-bubble (econo-sized water pipe) full of excellent hasheesh, mixed with powdered kif.

As "Bearbah, the European with two wives," was by now a welcome face wherever I went in the village, the men were very sociable with me. When it was somehow determined that I had smoked enough hash, the hammam-keeper handed me a pair of red wool bathing trunks and pointed to a shelf where I was to store my clothing. I put on the itchy, ill-fitting garment with extra-long draw-strings, and after yet another hubble-bubble and some scald-ing atay nanna, a similarly-clad young man appeared and took me by the hand.

He led me into a cold, glare-lit room, where he enthusiastically gestured for me to sit on the cold stone floor, and without preamble produced a five-gallon bucket and doused me head-to-toe with icy water. Sputtering, I tried to protest, as my amused attendant stood me up and led me down the cold concrete hallway into a warmer, dimly-lit space with a low ceiling. My escort deposited me on the polished stone floor in one of six open concrete stalls with a common drain pit in the center, and he disappeared. Shivering in warmth, I felt somewhat on display while sitting there with my head sticking out above the concrete stall divider. My eyes adjusted to the rust-colored light and I could discern the dark outlines of other "bathers" leaning up against the back wall of the hammam. Ten minutes later my bath buddy returned, carrying two more of his five-gallon buckets, and poured the warm contents of one of them on my head. Now I had detergent-sized soap suds all over me, coming out my ears and into my nose – my scrupulous attendant proceeded to work me over with a wash rag in one hand and a large sponge in the other. When he was satisfied that "I had never been so clean before," he rinsed me off with the five gallons of near-scalding water from his other bucket, and again disappeared.

When my skin finally started to cool down, he led me by the hot-hand outside the cubicle and sat me down on the equally polished stone floor of the main room, which was noticeably hot. Now I really was center stage, though none of my fellow "bathers," who all had blank stares on their faces, seemed to notice. The room had a musky odor, and the only light seemed to come from a hidden portal somewhere in the hammam's roof. I had begun to sweat after the immediate effects of the cold-water/hot-soap treatment had worn off when my fastidious attendant stretched me out on the hot floor, and began to vigorously scrub every inch of me with a fist-sized pumice stone! This was an intense session, and I vowed silently that, like a young warrior about to enter manhood, I would not cry out during the uncomfortable depilatory ritual of hammam passage. When I thought he had finished with me, he sat me upright and began dancing around me, softly but precisely kicking me about the arms and back with the terminally macerated toes and heels of his stubby little feet. Finally, satisfied with his work, the young man splashed cool water over my head, handed me a dry rag, and led me to the rear of the hammam, where he leaned me against the wall. In a hammic daze, I understood why my silent companions all had blank stares on their faces. They had just undergone the same ordeal! I quietly simmered for an hour or so. When I at last exited the steamy caldarium my smiling attendant was at the ready with a well-laundered towel for me to dry myself off. I got dressed, but before I could leave, the hammam crew leaders, still getting loaded in their makeshift lobby, insisted that I have a final blast from the office-sized hubble-bubble.

When finally I got out of the place, I had decided that the predictably lukewarm shower at home wasn't so bad, compared to the wild hammage I had just undergone. Walking back across the dirt lot to tell "my wives" about our neighborhood bath, the kids who lived on the roof came running from behind our house, chasing one of the chickens who now had a rope tied around its neck. When one of the chirping pursuers caught up to their frightened prey, they grabbed the rope, swung the chicken around their heads three times, tossed the disoriented bird into the air, and the squawking chase was on again. As I entered the house their mother yelled at them from the turreted roof-top to, "hurry up and kill the bird," because she wanted to begin preparing dinner! It really was becoming difficult to accurately distinguish everyday reality from its weirder coefficients.

Too Much! invited us to dine with him, for a home-cooked meal. Ever the excessive host, Too Much! poured relentlessly from an ice-tea pitcher filled with what he called, "Moroccan cognac" – "Drink, Drink, Too Much!" – a thoroughly hideous tasting combination of cheap burgundy wine and warm Coca-Cola. When my "wives" and I finally couldn't stomach anymore of the alcoholic sludge, his wife and four daughters, (unseen until now) served the four of us dinner in the dining area – while his mother, wife, and their seemingly-mute daughters ate in the kitchen. The entree that night, a gargantuan pile of cous-cous with boiled goat meat and a gooey-looking potato-pea-carrot sauce on top, was ceremoniously presented to the table on one enormous brass serving tray along with four kitchen table spoons and a pile of paper napkins. "Eat, Eat, Too Much!" cried our gregarious host, and the four of us dug into our private sides of the common pyramid of gamy tasting cous-cous, with Too Much! at the ready with his never-ending supply of "Moroccan Cognac." Regardless of how much Wendy, Janice and I ate, Too Much! felt we hadn't eaten "Too Much! enough," and sent us home with a gamy care-package of cous-cous, which we unceremoniously served to the equally unimpressed Bob-bettes (sans the Coliac brew) the following day.

The Brief Escape

Though Asilah's quiet, laid back atmosphere afforded us plenty of free time to relax, it also gave me more and more time to think about my ill-defined relationship with wife #1, and in the weeks that followed I became increasingly withdrawn from the daily routine, leaving Wendy and Janice to feed the Bobbettes. I was experiencing a psychic storm of ill-defined proportions, and according to my "wives," it was becoming increasingly difficult to be around me. To temper my growing discontent, and to give Wendy and Janice a respite from my darkened mood, it was decided that I should take a therapeutic pilgrimage back to Amsterdam and check on the status of our sub-let canal house. Wanting to turn my vacation into a profitable venture, I bought a large quantity of locally-made cotton, and six, four by four squares of handsome tweed, which I planned to sell in Paris. With just the essentials in a back-pack,

I stuffed the cumbersome fabrics into three well-traveled, double-large leather suitcases, and took the ferry to Cadiz, where I unthinkingly boarded the ill-titled "Express Unlimited" (which took twice as long as the "Direct Train") for Madrid.

At each change of train and border crossing, I needed to come up with a fresh excuse for having so much fabric with me and so little else. The Port of Tangier was the easiest to negotiate. When the stony-faced agent opened the presenting suitcase (and this would have been the case no matter which of the three cases he had opened first), he was respectfully greeted by a right-palmed, tricolor tribute to Fatima (all first daughters are named Fatima). Without inspecting the folds of material, the man smiled and devoutly muttered, "Alam-ham-doola" (Thanks being to God), shut the case, and passed my bags along with out question.

Entering Spain, I glowingly told the seemingly heartless La Guardia inspectors that the bolts and squares of hand-woven cloth were for my beautiful and very pregnant fiancee in Holland, who was going to make us a set of curtains and a "macho-grande" bed spread, "wink-wink, nod-nod, know what I mean?"

When I finally arrived in Paris, I toted my naive, unannounced self and the three-piece set of well-tattered luggage to the main offices of *Vogue* Magazine, where I unpacked the attractive material and politely asked to see the buyer. By the time the lovely purchasing agent came down to the lobby, I had nothing left to show her, because the agency secretaries (hard French currency in hand) had purchased all of my wares (including the three suitcases) for six hundred times what I had paid for them! Following a superb lunch near the Arc du Triomphe (now the Place de Gaulle), and nearly a thousand dollars in the black, I headed for Central Station.

Our lovely house on the Keizersgracht had been well kept and Specula had survived our absence, but the current residents were not the people we had sub-let to. The youthful pair described themselves as "the friends of the friends of the friends" we had left in charge. They were nice enough looking, and everything appeared to be in order, so I didn't protest, and to accommodate my sudden appearance they offered to stay somewhere else while I was in town. Over the next couple of days I settled affairs, visited with Kees and Jasper, and dined with Sandberg.

The evening before my early-morning departure for Morocco, I folded my traveling money and the profits from the fabric sale into my wallet, tucked it under my pillow, fed the cat and went to bed. When I awoke the next day, the cat was still there, my wallet and pillow were still there, but the money, all of it, was gone! The only rational explanation was that the "nice-looking couple," had quietly slipped in during the night like rats to pick my pillow. If indeed this was the case, I wondered why they had bothered to leave the empty wallet? – but more to the point, what was I going to do next? I still had my return ticket but no cash on hand to show solvency at border crossings, and my non-refundable train was due to leave Central Station in just a few hours. In a frenzied mix of humiliation and unexplained mystery, I borrowed a sum of money from Lucas and Ellen, Dutch friends I hadn't seen in months, and in their debt I sheepishly headed for North Africa.

Tangier Returns

When I got to Tangier, I found Wendy and Janice having dinner in the patio of the Parade with Mohammed, our white-cotton friends Peter and Carol, and the elusive Dennis. They welcomed me back, but as I sat down next to Wendy I felt the air around me thicken, and the mood of the previously happy group became subdued. I imagined that somehow they all knew of my fabric misadventure, but when I told my sorry tale they were all aghast. Wendy went so far as to suggest that I was fabricating my tale, and that I "must have squandered the money in Paris!" The carnival mood at the table had evaporated, and Wendy and I went back to her hotel room.

I had just completed a tedious overland journey of more than twenty-six hundred miles in less than four and a half days – I was exhausted, humiliated, mystified and in debt. All I wanted was a decent night's sleep and a little encouragement from Wendy, but this was not to be. As we lay there in the dark she told me why the mood at the Parade had changed. While I was away playing Marco Polo, my nomadic wife had bedded yet another paramour – a mutual acquaintance, the handsome young son of a real estate baroness on the island of Ibiza.

"It was just a moment of passion," she said, as if that were enough to reassure me of anything!

Alone and distraught, pacing the time until dawn, the painful reality began to sink in that the sacrifices I had made in Amsterdam had been in vain. I had let go of everything – my career and budding success, my studies with Sandberg, all of my hopes and dreams – to be with this once-trusted woman, turned serially-promiscuous, who had promised (apparently without enduring sincerity) to unconditionally stand by me. Wendy was simply not going to come to her senses. Quite the contrary, she was becoming consumed by them, and I knew that our life together was all but over. However, knowing something to be true and accepting it are altogether different animals, and with firm denial in lieu of happiness in my drying heart, I returned with my "wives' to Asilah to continue nourishing the Bobbettes.

Our lives outside the transit prison were mutating on a near daily basis, but for the incarcerated five everything remained in a sun-bleached stasis, and it was becoming increasingly difficult to blend the two separate realities with any real sense of optimism (or spousal decorum). Wendy and I were completely at odds over my "unwillingness to be open and free" – she and wife #2 bonded together at the hips, and I was left to my majoun and heartbreak.

After a few weeks of this estranged camaraderie we decided to go for broke. We offered the director, via Ahmed's brother-in-law, whatever he wanted in the way of "m'bizzef flous" to release the Bobbettes from their captivity. A week later we were called into the director's office where without the usual polite preamble he told us that it would cost the Bobbettes fifteen thousand dollars to be "misplaced" long enough for the eight of us to get out of the country and on to foreign soil. Without conferring with our charges we taxied into Tangier, closed the sizable bank account, got back to the prison, and handed the substantial bribe to the director before he went home for the night. He advised us to start packing. Two days after this, Ahmed's brother-in-law called us into his office and told us to wait. In her excitement, Janice, noticing the prison's official seal on his desk, picked it up and stamped the soft inside of her thighs with it! After about fifteen minutes the door opened, and there stood the five bewildered Bobbettes with disbelief on their faces and their innocent-looking passports gripped firmly in their unrepentant drug-smuggling hands.

The assistant director said that his taxi-driving brother-in-law, Ahmed, was waiting for us at the prison gate, and that "with the protection of Allah," we "should be out of my country within thirty-six hours!" In less than twenty-four we were safely aboard a Spanish tourist-liner, headed for the sanctuary of the Bobbette's J Class sailboat, long at harbor in the Canary Islands.

PART SIX – Amsterdam (Reprise)

Home Sweet Shooting Gallery

I should never have agreed to go along on this final leg of the Bobbette's journey, knowing as I did that it could only end in disaster. When we arrived in Las Palmas the Bobbettes went on a frenzied post-containment buying spree, and by the time we climbed aboard their demasted sail boat, Bob and crew had spent a kilo of pesetas on exotic foods, sun glasses, hash, booze, stereo equipment, island apparel and scuba gear. Their plan was to motor the disabled yacht to one of the smaller islands nearby and party for a few days. The Bobbettes were of course overjoyed to be free again and naturally enough wanted to stretch their wings. I, however, was consumed by physio-spiritual exhaustion which was quickly separating me from the free-spirited group. My ominous feelings of an impending doom were only increased the following day when I was eighteen feet below the surface of the bay, scrubbing barnacles off of the boat's substantial J Class keel with a wire brush. Unlike most of the Bobbettes I have never been a certified diver, and by trusting in their expertise I nearly drowned.

The "full tank" of air Big Mike had given me began to run dry after about fifteen minutes. Knowing enough not to panic, I tried to swim to the surface but my weight belt and tank held me relatively in place. Suddenly I was without air altogether. I dropped the belt, instinctively blew out my remaining breath, and shot toward the surface with my lungs feeling as if they had already collapsed. In true last-second-panic, I ripped off my face mask and useless respirator gasping for air, and as I caught my breath, I looked up to see Bob standing on deck, glaring at me (perhaps in disappointment over my survival!). I crawled aboard like a recently harpooned flounder, and everyone, including Bob, seemed to be sympathetic. But in the end it was agreed that, uninstructed novice or not, I should have checked my own gear.

Later that day, when I was certain that Wendy and Bob had made plans for an island tryst, my withered psyche imploded. I shaved off my full beard, packed my belongings, and demanded from the unscrupulous Dennis that he cough up my airfare back to Amsterdam with ample compensation. When the diplomat of the group unsuccessfully tried to calm me down, I told him that he and the Bobbettes were "a bunch of self-indulgent, ungrateful shits" – and bluntly added that they could go fuck themselves to death. I headed directly for the skiff to row my nearly uncompensated self to the pier when Wendy came from below decks, to see what the fuss was about. I told her I was leaving. She protested, and I told her to join her friends. When she saw how serious I was she asked me to wait long enough for her to pack her bags, declaring that she wanted to "stay together long enough to sort things out," and would return to Amsterdam with me. With deep reservation, and after securing our return fares from Dennis along with "compensation," (I accepted whatever it was he had in his wallet at the time) Wendy and I – following nearly fourteen months of North African misadventure, boarded the good ship Nausea for the Spanish mainland and the remains of our life in Amsterdam – where Wendy would remain fixated by the concept of triads – (subcultural arrangements considered to be a more enlightened way of loving one another), and I was without philosophy at all together.

Thinking that we still had a house to come home to, we went directly to the Keizersgracht. I unlocked the door and, to our horror, our once-lovely abode had become a shooting gallery! Our spacious and previously well-lit living room had compressed itself into a gray bunker, strewn with blood stained mattresses, fast-food wrappers, scorched tablespoons, used cottons, and the other addict detritus that collects in the wake of terminal geezing. Following our unexpected arrival, the stuporous group began to stir. Everyone of them was pretty much oblivious to our presence until one of the narcosic creatures stopped tormenting his anticubital space long enough to realize we were not there to score heroin. He began mumbling that everything was "cool man, very, cool, okay?" Wendy and I stood there with our mouths hanging open, thanking our lucky stars that the bulk of our possessions were in storage with Sandberg.

Recovering from my dismay, I told the rapidly fading junkie that we were the nice people who had lived in the place before it became a dope den, and that we were just back from Morocco. "Of course, everything is cool, very cool, okay?" I inquired if anyone had seen our cat, and in fact one of the untouchables had seen Specula earlier that morning nosing around the back window. I told them to keep the cat inside when it came back, and that I would return in a day or so to pick it up. They all nodded (out!), and Wendy and I blankly strolled with little more than our fading memories toward an inexpensive room in the Brouwer Hotel, without direction or much in the way of funds, and for the moment, homeless.

In a matter of days we rescued the indignant Specula from the Keizersgracht hovel, and with the help of good friends we secured a temporary roof over our heads. Wendy had become stronger and certainly more independent during our sojourn in North Africa, and though I had had my own share of personal awakenings in Morocco, back in Amsterdam I was confused and adrift. Irretrievably estranged from Wendy, nearly penniless, and physically exhausted, I was now a sad, overly-burdened replicant of my former self – and I desperately needed some time away from my "wife's" conflicting loyalties and the nowhere dialogue surrounding our questionable future together.

Norwegian Woodshed

As chance would have it, my friend Wes came to town looking for a "mast and spar guy" to fill out the complement he had assembled in Norway to rebuild a Colin Archer designed fishing (sail) boat. He told me that his "rather bohemian crew" and the stripped-down Archer were anchored six miles off the Norwegian coast on a tiny blip of an island called Skudneshaven. Shamelessly and with calmly presented abandon, I lied through my bleeding gums and told my old friend that by the oddest of coincidence I had single-handedly crafted the teak masts and rigging spars for my father's quite real sixty-foot ketch, the EPOCA. Wes hired me on the spot, and a day or so later I left Wendy what little money we had, advised her to "Think long and hard about everything," and took to the high seas with Wes – heading blindly toward my own personal slice of "Norwegian Wood."

Wes is another one of my beyond-the-fringe acquaintances who I'm certain would prefer I didn't say anything at all about his adventurous and colorful past – so, beyond the necessary comment, I'll just say that Wes was a self-made entrepreneur and Tai Chi aficionado who was devoted to his charming wife Camille and their cherubic son Sebastian – and who had enough "free floating" capital to do pretty much do what ever he wanted.

Having survived the cold, nauseating car ferry ride across the North Sea to Stavanger, Wes and I made our way overland to the port of Bergen. There we left Wes' van and caught a taxi-boat, taking us six miles out across the North Atlantic into a naturally-formed rock harbor on the tiny isle of Skudneshaven. To ensure our isolation from prying eyes, Wes and Camille had rented a four bedroom farm house on the otherwise unoccupied side of the island, facing the cold North Atlantic sea-ward wind. Our closest neighbors were an unsociable flock of Norwegian sheep, and once a day their mute-like Shepherd would come by to tend to his ewes. Other-wise, unless we were in the village, straddling the bare-bones of the Colin Archer, we didn't see a soul. Stark anonymic-privacy was my captain's middle name. I settled in easily with the Hammond-friendly crew (all of whom have led colorful and preferably unchronicled lives), and we soon went to work rebuilding the Norwegian sailing vessel. Wes and the boys had stripped the classic, single-masted ship down to the ballast (some of which Wes actually replaced – just because!). In stark contrast to the inclement weather and working conditions outside, I was warmly and dryly tucked away with my forty-foot Norwegian pine tree in a Norwegian welder's shop, abutting the pier. I took to the task of shaping the mast like a seasoned hand – making a platen from the spar support on deck, and began scraping the rough bark off the future mast with a draw-blade, and hand-planed the remainder into a manageable form.

Not one to be easily fooled, Wes came up to me on the third day to evaluate my progress. He appreciated my efforts, but recognized that I really didn't know what I was doing and said as much. When I started to protest, he laid his hand on my shoulder and said that he new how stressful things had been for me over the past year and a half. He didn't blame me a bit for my subterfuge, adding that he was glad to have me on the crew, and knew that if I set myself to the task I would make him a fine mast. Without another word, I broke down in tears and he held me like a brother until I had recovered. Much to his credit as a skipper, and to my great relief, Wes never said a word about my ruse to the rest of the infinitely more experienced crew.

The increasingly dark and sub-arctic weeks passed with long hours of hard work, Camille's tasteful cuisine, thickly smoked joints and the usually hilarious after-hours camaraderie and guitar pluck. Back at the shop the next day, I tapered the Norwegian pine with blade-draw, sandpaper, and unswerving attention (for me a meditation) – finally laying on more than sixty coats of cloth-smoothed oil as sealer before my "tree" fit the deck's support housing, and became a usable spar.

Following a sudden ice storm, I was about to take on other Archer duties when Wendy called the shop phone. After which, in unison, and to the great bewilderment of the resident Norwegian welders, Wes and my eavesdropping crew mates started singing the Box Tops' anthem, "The Letter." Within days I was safely aboard an aeroplane to Amsterdam, and the uncertain presentense with Wendy.

Ending The Beginning

Wendy was "house-sitting" near the Rembrandtplein, in the antique-filled home of yet another drug smuggler. (Nameless) skippered a rather successful twenty-mule team operation in the Atlas Mountains of North Africa, and to say the least, I wasn't thrilled with her temporary digs, but being with her again was a great relief to my Norwegian-weary self – for about three days. Wendy's separate-reality had grown even stronger while I was away, and bursting with her new independence, she told me that she wanted to return to California – but not together. Her unalterable plan was to "fly to Venezuela and stay for two weeks with Bob (at his expense) on his father's strawberry farm." She said we would then "reunite" at the home of Bruce and Nancie (Bob's ex-wife) in Northern California. There and only then, she said could we decide our future's path, together or no. There was nothing I could do or say to dissuade her, so, with defeated resignation and a sufficiently dried heart, I agreed to meet her in San Anselmo in three weeks. With that secured, "my wife" left for "Caracas" (more likely to a romantic bay somewhere in the West Indies) the following day to, as she put it, "pick strawberries and meditate."

Kees, Jasper and Sandberg wanted me to forget about my transient wife and stay in Amsterdam with them. To help clear my head, Jasper filled my lungs with copious amounts of binnenlander smoke, and took me by debris-raft to one of his "secret places" – the 'hallemzaal' – (The Room That Repeats Itself). Somewhere in the bowels of a former canal front factory, we entered an ink-black space, Jasper closed the steel door, encasing us in dense nothingness – and as if his way was fully lit, my shamanic friend led me deep into the recesses of what must have been an enormous cavity. When we stopped, perhaps near the center of the room, Jasper whispered in my ear and instructed me to ask out loud in a normal voice what I should do with my life. When I spoke, the room nearly detonated from the strength of my simple words, as they caromed against the unseen walls of Jasper's chamber like resonant sonic bats. It was a truly fascinating experience, but much like the Scream Tunnel on Prinzen Island, it failed as an oracle, leaving my confusion and heartbreak intact.

The next day, during a torrential downpour, I thought that perhaps God would advise me. I hadn't been inside a church with the intent to pray for many, many years, yet with a questionable faith in my belly, I waded half way across Amsterdam to a small Protestant church that I had often admired – but when I got there, God's doors of perception were air-locked tight. Harboring an unrealistic sense of ultimate rejection, I walked the pouring rain back to the empty smuggler's house – feeling so desperately alone and ultimately without choice – my significant tears adding a heathen's salt to the streams of precipitation falling around me. With little more in the way of prelude, I said my good-byes to Kees and Jasper, gave Specula to Ad Petersen (then curator of Painting and Sculpture at the Stedelijk Museum), and spent a final joyous evening dining and reminiscing with Sandberg.

Over the last of daze in Amsterdam, I cleared the slates as best I could, left my few studio materials with Sandberg for archival storage, tapped my remaining collectors (including the Stedelijk Museum) for every last-philanthropic guilder I could squeeze out of them and bought a one-way ticket to California via La Guardia, hesitantly on the road again, but to Where?

Aloneward Bound

Once I had landed into the alien country of San Anselmo, Bruce and Nancie were overjoyed to see me, though Nancie's close friendship with Wendy and her X-communion with Bob caused her some discomfiture when I told them with assured uncertainty where Wendy was supposedly "picking Venezuelan strawberries". My reluctant, though seemingly unavoidable return to America was a thoroughly confusing ordeal for me, filled as it was with an intense reverse culture shock, and way too much readable and vaguely familiar input. When I first went into the quaint village that was then San Anselmo, I found it so disorienting that I sequestered myself inside the cottage Mackey for the next week, waiting for Wendy and her anti-climactic arrival.

Cool with one another, we warmly reunited with our dear friends from Bolinas, Max and Ruth Crosley, and made a brief sojourn into the City before retreating to the North Shore of Lake Tahoe, where Wendy's father, Norm, now retired from the Civil Engineers, managed the local bowling alley. Wendy's parents were extremely relieved to have their wayward daughter home again but decidedly unwelcoming and indifferent toward me. Who could blame them? I wasn't exactly anyone's description of a good son-in-law, and they fully supported Wendy's increasing but as yet unspoken desire to go our separate ways. When she finally did speak of it, I could only nod silently in resignation. She would remain at the lake resort with her bowling lane-enthusiast parents, and I would go to Wherever to lick my marital wounds. Before I could leave, however, I slipped on a stretch of black ice and grossly dislocated my Military School knee. Rather than delay my much anticipated departure, I borrowed a pair of ill-fitting crutches from Wendy's teenage brother and caught the return ski bus to the City, where I had made arrangements to recuperate in the third floor walk-up of an old friend. Juniper's place was near Duboce Park, across the street from the printing office of Rip-Off Press (of Zap Comix fame), and I had the relatively uninterrupted use of her apartment for two weeks of meditative convalescence, while doggy-sitting Ivan, her friendly though leviathan Russian wolf hound.

My bottom of the line reality was that I had returned to San Francisco after years abroad with absolutely nothing to show for it. I was homeless, and my creative impulses were locked away in what would become a twenty-year stasis. I was beginning what would prove to be an irreconcilable separation from Wendy, and I was unquestionably alone for the first time in nearly ten years. I felt terminally estranged from my immediate family, asea and without compass in life. I couldn't even get around my borrowed third-story apartment without a set of sticks! With a blurred sense of optimism I attempted to regain some semblance of self-respect by considering a new occupation. The trouble was, I really wasn't interested in anything. I got out the San Francisco phone directory yellow pages and, page by yellow page, job category by useless job category, I unequivocally eliminated my prospects A to Zed.

By the time my knee had healed enough to stand on it, I was still without a clue, sick of my long-term memory retention, and quickly falling under the minute-to-minute 'deja vu' I was experiencing in the City. So I gathered my recently acquired prayer beads, bit the bullet, and decided to pay an unexpected visit to my father and his wife Arlene – still living aboard the EPOCA, permanently docked on Terminal Island. Unfortunately, I was relatively certain they would not be particularly glad to see me. Dressed like an out-of-work square, in a freshly-purchased brown turtle neck with a haircut to match, I boarded the Southern Pacific at the Oakland train station, and sat staring blankly out the window, wondering what on earth I was going to say to my consistently unforgiving father.

I was brought out of my quandry-induced trance by a burly young man about my age. He sported an ash-blonde ponytail down to his belt loops, rucksack under one arm, holding an acoustic guitar in the other. His deep blue eyes sparkled with infinite humor, and he rather proudly wore an impressive Tibetan-style mala (108 prayer beads with silver-dorje and human bone enhanced mantra counters) around his sturdy neck. He sat down in the seat next to me, and as he politely introduced himself, "Hi my name's Rusty!" and without apparent hesitation, he reached over to gently rub his fingertips over what I thought were my well-hidden prayer beads. He smiled broadly at this, and with the assured voice of an itinerant sadhu asked, "Where'd you get your rosary, buddy?" Oddly (or perhaps intentionally), Rusty's family were originally Freislanders (the indigenous people of northern Holland), and like myself, he too was on his way to visit his father following a lengthy estrangement.

We shared tales of past adventures (he too was an Acid Test graduate) and even swapped prayer beads for awhile, exchanging our personal mantras written on small scraps of paper. My companion and I sat there for some time, contentedly staring out the window, silently chanting each other's call to God, when the train passed an open field. In the center of the field sat an immobilized church school bus whose destination plaque read: "Trust In Thyself!" We looked deeply, one into the other, and with spontaneous bliss in our hearts we broke into great roars of belly-laughter and intuitively discovered spiritual brotherhood. Over the next several hours of travel I confessed to Rusty my current state of disengagement from self-identity and society at large. He in turn spoke of his less than exemplary childhood and brief convict past (marijuana related), with time served in Terminal Island Prison! – and his great hope that his father would again welcome him into his home.

As the train pulled in to the privately coastal town of Santa Barbara, Rusty asked if I had ever been there before. I had not. He looked me straight in the third eye.

"Why don't you get off the train?" He suggested. "I'll be coming back through here in a few days. Your family doesn't even know you're in back the country – so why not spend some time on the sand, listening to the waves – chanting and thinking about all this stuff?"

I glanced out the window, and directly across the tracks was the aging Hotel California.

"I'll be in that hotel," I said.

As the train pulled out of the unfamiliar station, I waved goodbye to my new friend, and from the car's open window, Rusty called out to me with a jubilant, beatific smile on his face, "I'll see you next week, buddy!"

Walking toward the fading hotel's once-proud facade, I absorbed the extremely liberating concept of entering deja-new, a town and space where quite literally no-one on earth, beyond the hospitable psyche of an almost stranger, knew where I was. And though I would live well, and at times poorly through adventurous highs and lows over the next twenty years, my widely fluctuating profit and loss columns would only bring me to bear, thirty-three miles to the south, to the end-game desperation of Motel Room 101, with little more than a syringe full of death clutched in my right hand.

To be continued.......

Index

219

220

222

SAF, HELTER SKELTER and FIREFLY Books

Mail Order

All SAF, Helter Skelter and Firefly titles are available by mail order from the world-famous Helter Skelter bookshop.

Telephone: +44 (0)20 7836 1151
or Fax: +44 (0)20 7240 9880

Office hours: Mon-Fri 10:00am – 7:00pm,
Sat: 10:00am – 6:00pm, Sun: closed.

**Helter Skelter Bookshop, 4 Denmark Street, London,
WC2H 8LL, United Kingdom.**

If you are in London come and visit us and browse the titles in person.

Order Online

For the latest on SAF, Helter Skelter and Firefly titles, or to order books online, check the SAF or Helter Skelter websites.

You can also browse the full range of rock, pop, jazz and experimental music books we have available, as well as keeping up with our latest releases and special offers.

You can also contact us via email, and request a catalogue.

info@safpublishing.com
www.safpublishing.com

saf publishing

www.safpublishing.com